the mystery of unity

the mystery of unity: Theme and technique
in the novels of Patrick White

by Patricia A. Morley

McGill–Queen's University Press MONTREAL AND LONDON 1972

© McGill–Queen's University Press 1972
International Standard Book Number 0-7735-0112-6
Library of Congress Catalog Card Number 77-188136
Legal Deposit 2nd quarter 1972

Designed by Mary Cserepy

Printed in Canada by The Bryant Press Limited, Toronto

It requires moral courage to grieve;
it requires religious courage to rejoice.

Søren Kierkegaard

T. S. Eliot has reminded us that immature artists borrow, mature artists steal. Similarly, Northrop Frye has shown that both critic and artist exist within the context of a tradition and not in isolation. I would like to acknowledge my debt to *Anatomy of Criticism: Four Essays* (1957), in which Professor Frye demonstrates that literary criticism is a discipline in its own right, one which takes its techniques from within literature rather than from any of the allied disciplines which enrich the understanding of the literary critic.

The originality of the artist lies not in creating some new theme but in his way of handling great traditional themes. Patrick White's novels are in the mainstream of European literature. They evoke the works of such writers as Dostoyevsky and Tolstoy, Blake, Johnson, Schreiner, Bunyan and, far more basically, the older traditions upon which these artists draw, the Judaeo-Christian-Classical heritage. Through the use of archetypes and images common to Western literature, White's novels obtain a richness of association, a cumulative power and an impersonal dignity.

While believing in the validity of a variety of critical techniques and approaches, I have, like Professor Frye, given a prominent place to archetypal criticism. A definition of terms and an explanation of critical method will be found in my second chapter. The first chapter places White's novels in a religious tradition which is found throughout Western literature, while the last emphasizes the unity of vision which underlies all White's fiction. With the exception of Chapter Six, "God's Fool," Chapters Three to Eleven examine the novels in chronological order. One chapter is devoted to each work.

I would like to thank Dr. George H. Thomson for reading and criticizing the manuscript; Dr. Robert McDougall, for first introducing me to White's novels, and for discussions over the last three years; the Canada Council, for the financial assistance they have given to the research and writing of the work; and Mrs. Olga Whenham, Mrs. Isobel Perazzo, and Mrs. Betty Thomas, for typing the manuscript.

This book has been published with the help of a grant from the Humanities Research Council of Canada, using funds provided by the Canada Council.

P.A.M.

**Editions of Patrick White's fiction
cited in the text**

Happy Valley. London: Harrap, 1939.
The Living and the Dead (1941). London: Eyre, Spottiswoode, 1962.
The Aunt's Story. New York: Viking Press, 1948.
The Tree of Man. New York: Viking Press, 1955.
Voss. New York: Viking Press, 1957.
Riders in the Chariot. New York: Viking Press, 1961.
The Solid Mandala. New York: Viking Press, 1966.
The Vivisector. New York: Viking Press, 1970.
All page references are from these editions. Viking editions have been used throughout, except in the case of the first two novels, where the Viking was not concurrent with the original London edition, or is not easily available at this date. For a bibliography of White's work and of White criticism, see Janette Finch, *Bibliography of Patrick White*, Bibliographies of Australian Writers (Adelaide: Libraries Board of South Australia, 1966).

contents

*This thing we call existence; is it not a something which has
its roots far down below in the dark, and its branches stretching
out into the immensity above, which we among the branches
cannot see? Not a chance jumble; a living thing, a* One.

OLIVE SCHREINER, THE STORY OF AN AFRICAN FARM

chapter 1 The living tradition

The view of man and his world which underlies White's novels is
religious in its basic orientation. His heroes are seeking the true
permanence or unchanging structure beneath the illusory flux,
the true freedom which is valid even beyond physical death. All
his novels testify to the reality of another world, not outside
this one but inside, "wholly within," as stated in the first two epigraphs to *The Solid Mandala*. And essential to White's vision is
the affirmation that this other or spiritual world is immanent in
our natural one, *as well as* transcendent to it. William Blake
found God in a grain of sand; White finds him in a gobbet of
spit, or a table.[1] Like Pierre Teilhard de Chardin, White views
matter as something good, something inherently spiritual, not
opposed to spirit as the ancient Greeks conceived it to be. In his

---

[1] See *The Aunt's Story*: "There is perhaps no more complete a reality than a
chair and a table" (p. 129); " 'Only chairs and tables,' she said, 'are sane' "
(p. 162); and *Riders in the Chariot*: " 'Oh, Mordecai,' she whispered, 'I am
afraid. Tables and chairs will not stand up and save us.' 'God will,' he an-
swered, 'God is in this table' " (p. 149).

"Hymn to Matter," Teilhard blesses matter as he finds it revealed *in its totality and true nature:*

> 'I acclaim you as the melodious fountain of water whence spring the souls of men and as the limpid crystal whereof is fashioned the new Jerusalem.
> 'I acclaim you as the divine *milieu,* charged with creative power, as the ocean stirred by the Spirit, as the clay moulded and infused with life by the incarnate Word.'[2]

This passage could well be placed as the epigraph to all White's work.

His novels examine such problems as the meaning of suffering and the possibilities of salvation and atonement for evil. His basic concerns, that is, are theological, but existential rather than dogmatic in approach. Like Dostoyevsky, White believes that suffering is a necessary route to spiritual progress, beneficial both to the individual who suffers and to those involved in the suffering. The idea of the movement into the world and back to faith which we find in White's novels also underlies much of Dostoyevsky's writing. Indeed, much of White's work shows the influence of both Dostoyevsky and Tolstoy; and, like the works of these writers, it has received more recognition outside his own country than within. His vision is not original but traditional, an expression of the Judaeo-Christian cultural heritage from which it flowers. We find this tradition, or vision, expressed in centuries of our literature, from William Langland's fourteenth-century poem, through Bunyan, Blake, Hopkins, Browning, and Schreiner, to twentieth-century authors such as Eliot, Christopher Fry, Cary, and David Jones.

Although his novels *are* novels, not mystical essays as one critic suggests, the vision from which they spring belongs to the tradition of mysticism, which seeks direct experience or immediate awareness of God, and sees the soul as something wholly distinct from the reasoning mind with its powers.[3] The religious

---

[2] *Hymn of the Universe* (London: Collins, 1966), pp. 69-70.
[3] See David Knowles, *The English Mystical Tradition* (New York: Harper Torchbooks, 1965), pp. 1-2, and Gershom G. Scholem, *Major Trends in Jew-*

character of his vision and its insistence on the inadequacy of reason to solve man's ultimate problems are in opposition to the modern *zeitgeist,* so that a basic antagonism to White's whole way of seeing man and his world may be discerned in some of the criticism of his work.

Mysticism is by no means limited to the state of ecstasy or ecstatic meditation, although this experience lies at its root. Writing of the general characteristics of Jewish mysticism, Gershom G. Scholem, Professor of Jewish Mysticism at the Hebrew University in Jerusalem, emphasizes that there is no such thing as mysticism in the abstract, but only the mysticism of a particular religious system, Christian, Jewish, and so on: "the prevailing conception of the mystic as a religious anarchist who owes no allegiance to his religion finds little support in fact. History rather shows that the great mystics were faithful adherents of the great religions."[4] If this is so, White's vision must appear as ultimately Christian, although his novels of the sixties show obvious effects of the profound influence of Jewish mysticism and faith. As Professor Scholem admits, it would be absurd to deny a common characteristic to the mysticism of various religious systems. Robert McDougall describes the work of Joseph Furphy and Patrick White as follows: "Neither of these writers has any use for what Furphy calls 'ecclesiastical Christianity'. Yet both are profoundly religious and I would even say Christian writers, Mr. White in this latter respect perhaps more so than Furphy."[5]

Mysticism appears as a late or third stage in the historical development of religion: after the childhood of mankind, its mythical epoch where man encounters gods at every step, and after the second stage of formal or institutional religions:

> Religion's supreme function is to destroy the dream-harmony of Man, Universe and God, to isolate man from

---

ish Mysticism (London: Thames and Hudson, 1955), pp. 3-4, for further discussion of the meaning of 'mystic' and 'mysticism.' Both writers note the prevailing confusion in the popular use of these terms.

[4] Scholem, *Major Trends in Jewish Mysticism,* p. 6.

[5] Robert L. McDougall, *Australia Felix: Joseph Furphy and Patrick White,* Commonwealth Literary Fund Lecture (Canberra: Australian National University Press, 1966), pp. 15-16.

the other elements of the dream stage of his mythical and primitive consciousness. For in its classical form, religion signified the creation of a vast abyss, conceived as absolute, between God, the infinite and transcendental Being and Man, the finite creature. . . . The great monotheistic religions live and unfold in the ever-present consciousness of this bipolarity, of the existence of an abyss which can never be bridged. . . . Mysticism does not deny or overlook the abyss; on the contrary, it begins by realizing its existence, but from there it proceeds to a quest for the secret that will close it in, the hidden path that will span it.[6]

This is the hidden path explored by White's protagonists. And in light of this description of the mystic's quest we may understand Mrs. Godbold's repudiation, in *Riders in the Chariot,* of the importance of institutional religions. Despite her evangelical fervour, she sees formal religion as only the coat that men are told to put on at birth, a superficial covering over a deeper reality, something worn for a time and discarded at death.

Like Herman Melville's *Moby Dick,* White's novels suggest that a vast Design or plan lies behind apparent acts of free will or chance. Melville's novel uses the image from classical mythology of the Fates weaving at the Loom of Time: "This warp seemed necessity . . . —aye, chance, free will and necessity—no wise incompatible—all interweavingly working together."[7] The idea of chance, free will, and necessity being "no wise incompatible" is accepted by Christian Scriptures, which assume that God's omnipotence does not preclude man's freedom and responsibility. References to fate or design, to a divine teleology or master plan, form a consistent motif in each of White's novels. In *Riders,* Mrs. Jolley has "just freedom enough to wrestle with the serpents of her conscience" (p. 73), and Mrs. Flack's brick villa is ironically named Karma. The narrator suggests that the guard who chose Himmelfarb at the Friedensdorf death camp

---

[6] Scholem, *Major Trends in Jewish Mysticism,* pp. 7-8.
[7] Herman Melville, *Moby Dick* (New York: Modern Library, 1926), p. 214. All references are to this edition.

could have been directed without knowing it. And Himmelfarb allows himself to be directed to Brighta Bicycle Lamps because he believes that to abandon self is to accept the course that offers. Palfreyman refers to the "will of God," and Laura and Voss share a "sense of inevitability" (*Voss,* p. 83). Judd's hand contains the hard whorls of skin and fate; the blackfellow who examines Palfreyman's hand just before his death perceives "the lines of fate" (p. 200); and Harry does not return with Judd's party simply because "it was not intended" (p. 342) by the Master Planner. Laura's letter to Voss describes moments of severest trial as "the obscure details of a design that will be made clear at last—if we can endure till then, and for that purpose are we given to one another" (p. 235). In *The Solid Mandala,* Runt and Scruffy "accepted the fatality of their arbitrary relationship" (p. 171); the description is intended to remind us of the dogs' owners, Waldo and Arthur, who have not asked to be born as brothers, or even to be born at all. On the allegorical level there is the further connotation of the mystery of the relation between man's body and soul, identified with Arthur, and his intellect and self-will, identified with Waldo. The relation between these elements, and between man's temporal and eternal selves, concerns most of White's major characters.

White's novels, like the Christian and Jewish Scriptures, represent a divine Being as exercising a universal Providence in and over the world. The idea that nothing is too great or too small for the scope of this Providence is suggested in the New Testament by images of the numbering of hairs or the fall of a sparrow. At the same time, human freedom and responsibility are everywhere insisted on. God's purpose is to establish the kingdom of God, in which his will is done on earth as it is in heaven. Since man's fall from grace this can only be attained through a redemption, and the covenant of the Old Testament leads to the new covenant in Christ. White is very aware of what Theodora Goodman calls "a core of evil" in man, even in the characters which his novels present to us as admirable. While the concept of fate or Providence is evident in all his novels, the last three are especially concerned with the problem of redemption. The four Riders, Arthur

Brown ("getter of pain"), and the afflicted Rhoda are co-workers with the divine Providence to this end. The idea that suffering advances the individual's own spiritual progress, as found in the experience of Oliver Halliday in *Happy Valley,* is supplemented in White's later novels by the idea of the suffering of the spiritual elect as instrumental in the redemption of all men.

The inadequacy of reason to provide the solution for man's ultimate problems is a constant theme in White's novels. Himmelfarb's explanation for his refusal to apply for a post equal to his intellectual gifts is simply: " 'The intellect has failed us' " (*Riders,* p. 211). This remark, however, needs to be taken in the total context of the novel, as does the rejection of the intellect implicit in *The Solid Mandala* through that novel's association of intellect with Waldo, the spiritually dead brother. White's attitude to the intellect, as evidenced in his novels, reflects a contrast between two sorts of knowledge—spiritual wisdom and purely abstract rationalism—a contrast which has a place in the traditional themes of English literature and which conforms to New Testament attitudes towards knowledge. *Gnosis,* "knowledge," refers in the New Testament to an essential element of Christianity, since it is associated with the knowledge of God in Christ, with the knowledge of Christ himself, and with the personal experience of what is involved in the Christian life. Similarly, *epignosis* denotes the "full knowledge" of the mature Christian. Knowledge, which enables man to perceive the truth, is never *opposed* to faith in the New Testament. But these terms always imply an experience which is both spiritual and intellectual, something deeper than mere intellectual understanding. When Paul describes "Christ crucified" as "unto the Greeks foolishness," and sets the "foolishness of God" against the wisdom of man (1 Cor. 1: 23-25), he is referring to the speculative rational knowledge which distinguished Greek philosophy at the time. The Greeks considered the speculative intellect as the highest power of man, and an intellectual vision of truth as the goal of man's endeavour. White's protagonists obviously do not. In *The Solid Mandala,* Arthur seeks to understand the passage concerning the Grand Inquisitor in Dostoyevsky's *The Brothers*

Karamazov, not out of intellectual curiosity but in order that he may be able to help people, especially his brother. White's version of the holy idiot or divine fool, which is found in each of his novels, is an expansion of this concept of the sterility of the intellect when it is divorced from the spirit and from love.[8]

White's attitude towards man's sexuality is currently no more popular than his deflation of the intellect. While many of his characters experience fulfilled sexual love, the perspective afforded by his novels shows sexuality within a supra-temporal framework. The view that physical love is not the ultimate expression of love is more evident in *The Aunt's Story,* in which the leading character is a maiden aunt, than in his first two novels. His novels depict sex as only one way by which love and hate, good and evil may be expressed, and emphasize that spiritual fertility or creativity is not limited to physical reproduction. Latent in *The Aunt's Story* and the novels which follow, the Tiresias/hermaphroditic Adam motif becomes explicit in *The Solid Mandala.* Arthur reads: "As the shadow continually follows the body of one who walks in the sun, so our hermaphroditic Adam, though he appears in the form of a male, nevertheless always carries about with him Eve, or his wife, hidden in his body" (pp. 271-272). Tiresias, the blind bisexual prophet of classical mythology, is used in Eliot's *The Waste Land* as an image of spiritual wisdom and fertility despite physical blindness and sterility. Arthur's conversation with Waldo points to a change in White's use of the Tiresias myth. Whereas in *The Aunt's Story* he seems to be using the myth as it is used in *The Waste Land,* in *The Solid Mandala* it is the sterile Waldo who is associated with Tiresias, whose connotations now become purely those of sterility. The hermaphroditic Adam, by contrast, represents the truly bisexual New Adam or perfect man, whose "wives" or loves are within him, without loss of their own identity. The idea forms a mystic human version of the Chris-

---

[8] See Patrick White, "The Prodigal Son," *Australian Letters* I, 3 (1958), 38: "Demobilisation in England left me with the alternative of remaining in what I then felt to be an actual and spiritual graveyard, with the prospect of ceasing to be an artist and turning instead into that most sterile of beings, a London intellectual, or of returning home."

tian trinitarian concept of different persons in one divine substance. Indeed the myth which gives us the word *hermaphroditic*
itself suggests the union of intellectual powers and love denoted
by New Testament usage of *epignosis*. As Arthur notes, the
brevity of Tiresias' experience of life as a woman is different
"from the hermaphroditic Adam who carries his wife about with
him inside" (p. 273). To Waldo the idea is both mad and
obscene.

In *Riders in the Chariot,* White introduces a similar concept
into the dream of the dying Himmelfarb: "Again, he was the
Man Kadmon, descending from the Tree of Light to take the
Bride. . . . This, explained the cousins and aunts, is at last the
Shekinah whom you have carried all these years under your left
breast" (p. 462). The references are to the kabbalah (literally
"tradition"), the body of Jewish mysticism concerned with
things divine. Kabbalistic speculation centres in the realm of the
divine emanations, or *sefiroth,* the divine attributes in which
God's creative power unfolds: "But to the mystics it was divine
life itself, insofar as it moves toward Creation."[9] The kabbalah
identifies the God of the *sefiroth* with man in his purest form,
Adam Kadmon, Primordial Man: "Here the God who can be
apprehended by man is himself the First Man."[10] The kabbalah
depicts the masculine and feminine, begetting and receiving,
potencies of God in the conception of the union of two *sefiroth,*
the king and his royal consort or bride, the *Shekinah.* This becomes an apocalyptic image or metaphor for the sacred marriage
between God and his people, which was for the kabbalist merely
the outward aspect of a process that takes place within the secret
inwardness of God himself.

Similarly, human love or charity is shown in White's novels to
belong to this context of the divine love between God and his
people, which is, to the mystic, another form of God's love for
himself. In *Happy Valley* the consummation of love between
Oliver Halliday and Alys Browne is shown to be spiritually fruit-

---

[9] Gershom G. Scholem, *On the Kabbalah and Its Symbolism,* trans. Ralph Man-
heim (London: Routledge and Kegan Paul, 1965), p. 35.
[10] Ibid., p. 104.

ful. It becomes necessary to sacrifice it only when it becomes destructive through the complex interrelationships which are involved. White's second novel shows that Eden's early experiences of sex are abortive, spiritually sterile, reflecting the sterility of her life before her encounter with Joe Barnett. Even the physical consummation of Eden's and Joe's love, however, seems escapist, solving nothing, and overruled by their unhappiness at the misery of the sick and dying world which surrounds them. Theodora Goodman is the first of White's protagonists to represent the spiritual fertility embodied in the concept of the sacred marriage or *conjunctio* of masculine and feminine principles in the Godhead. In this novel and in those which follow, White's major figures illustrate both fulfilled sexual love and spiritual love. Sometimes the protagonists arrive at a state described in *Riders in the Chariot* as "equanimity" after passing through sexual experience as a temporary stage in which *caritas* co-exists with erotic love. Sometimes they are physically barren throughout life, in order that we may come to understand that the seed can be sown in many ways, as the printer says of the childless dyer from Holunderthal. The Jewish Adam Kadmon parallels images of Christ, as the New Adam or "last Adam" (1 Cor. 15: 45), the whole perfect man in whom the faults of the first Adam are redeemed, and as the bridegroom whose bride is the Church or body of his followers.[11] Christians await the coming of the bridegroom, and the marriage feast becomes a symbol of final joy.[12]

Jewish mysticism concerning the sexual wholeness of the Godhead, and Christian mysticism concerning Christ and his bride, afford a fascinating parallel with the theory of the *anima* and *animus* found in the analytical psychology of Carl Jung. White's novels indicate that he is familiar with Jung's theories of the bisexual nature of the human personality, and the archetypes of the collective unconscious. While it is not our task to attempt to determine whether Jung's work is a *source* for White's use of the mandala and quaternary, he is obviously familiar with Jung's

[11] Mark 2: 19; John 3: 29.
[12] Matt. 25: 1-13; 22: 2; Rev. 19: 9; 22: 17.

concepts. Jung emphasizes racial foundations of personality, viewing the individual personality as the product or container of its ancestral history. The foundations of man's personality are primitive, unconscious, and universal. Inherited predispositions affect personal reactions, and a racially pre-formed collective personality both acts upon and is modified by individual experience. This unconscious life, common to all men, is expressed in dreams, myths, and archetypal images or symbols. Jung sees the total personality or psyche as composed of a number of interacting systems—ego, conscious mind, personal unconscious with its complexes, and collective unconscious.

The transpersonal or collective unconscious is one of the most original and controversial features of his theory of personality, and is the system of the psyche which Jung considered to be the most influential and powerful. It is the storehouse of latent memory traces or predispositions inherited from man's ancestral past, the psychic residue of man's evolutionary development, accumulated in consequence of repeated experiences over many generations. These latent fears and desires may become actualized through individual experience. Jung believed that the collective unconscious, as the inherited racial foundation of the whole structure of personality, holds vast possibilities beyond those of the conscious mind and could be of immense benefit to man. An archetype is a universal thought form or idea which contains a large element of emotion. These primordial or mythological images are the structural components of the collective unconscious and result from a similar type of experience having been constantly encountered by many generations. Archetypes are not isolated but may interpenetrate one another. Jung considers the *persona* or public mask, and the *anima* and *animus,* to be special archetypes so far evolved that they should be treated as separate systems in the personality. Jung ascribes the feminine side of man's personality and the masculine side of woman's personality to archetypes. The feminine archetype in man is called the *anima,* the masculine archetype in woman is called the *animus*; these archetypes result from the sexual experiences of many generations and races. Physiologically, both males and females have both male and female sex hormones; psychologically, each individual has masculine and feminine characteristics. In his portrait of Molly Bloom in *Ulysses,* Joyce makes use of the Jungian theory of the *anima,* along with the Gaea-Tellus myth of the original bisexual nature of the divinity.[13] In general it is no exaggeration to say that many of Jung's ideas are now widely accepted, and occupy an important place in twentieth-century literature. Nor are they foreign to the tradition of European literature, which has frequently depicted divine grace as feminine, as in the literature of the troubadours, of Petrarch, and of Dante. In *The Solid Mandala* Arthur Brown is frequently associated with the feminine principle, and both he and Mrs. Poulter are linked with the *Magna Mater.*

Voss's two disciples, the intellectual Frank and the devoted Harry, are frequently identified with masculine and feminine principles, respectively. Throughout his novels White associates human characteristics with masculinity and femininity. The intellect, controller and initiator of action, is masculine; the spirit, which includes qualities such as humility, mercy, and "loving-kindness," a recurring word in White's novels, is feminine. These are associated with action and passion, as the two poles of being. God's nature includes both, as does man's (i.e. every human being's). Waldo Brown's *maleness,* a motif in *The Solid Mandala,* is a parody of true masculinity, since he remains virgin and creates neither children nor intellectual work nor fruits of the spirit. The mere thought of sexual acts gives Waldo "the gooseflesh, whether from disgust or envy, he couldn't have told" (p. 181). He finally burns his abortive literary efforts, entitled *Tiresias a Youngish Man.*[14] Similarly, his intellectual pretensions are a parody of *gnosis,* the intellectual powers working in co-

[13] In Greek mythology, Gaea (Latin, *tellus*) is born of Ge (earth) and Uranus (sky) and is the mother of Zeus and the other Olympians; originally a bisexual divinity, she was made a female by the gods. Gaea was widely worshipped under many names, and identified with the Great Earth Mother or *Magna Deum Mater.*

[14] The title of Waldo's novel is a parody of Joyce's *Portrait of the Artist as a Young Man.* Waldo is himself the sterile Tiresias and the eternally "youngish man." Unlike Oliver Halliday in White's first novel, he stoutly resists the love and suffering which might make him mature or progress.

operation with spirit. In *Riders in the Chariot* and *The Aunt's Story,* spiritual strength is identified with masculinity; the four Riders are *hard* in this sense, whereas Mrs. Jolley and Mrs. Flack are soft and flabby. Many of White's heroes are bisexual in a psychic sense, a pattern which begins in Theodora Goodman and culminates in Arthur Brown.

I have described the vision expressed in White's novels as essentially religious, and belonging to the tradition of Christian mysticism. Denis de Rougemont describes the two great streams into which all mysticism divides as *unitive* and *epithalamian*:

> The first stream is that of *unitive mysticism,* which aims at a complete *fusion* of the soul with the divine. The second stream may be called *epithalamian mysticism,* which aims at the *marriage* of a soul to God, and which therefore implicitly maintains an essential distinction between creature and Creator. . . . Otto distinguishes East and West by calling these two forms of mysticism respectively eros and agape. . . . [The Eastern concept of nirvana] cannot accept *sansara,* which is life in its diversity and infinite flux. Eckhart, on the contrary, discerns the presence of God in every creature, so that through the soul of a believer all creatures 'pass from their existence into their being.'[15]

Orthodox Christian mysticism brings about a "spiritual marriage" between God and the individual soul in this life as well as the next. De Rougemont stresses that the essence of Christian mysticism is a *communion* rather than a *union.* He quotes from a sermon by Meister Eckhart, the German philosopher and mystic from whom White takes one of the epigraphs of *The Solid Mandala,* where Eckhart says that the divinity is still God and the soul is still a soul. At the heart of what de Rougemont calls orthodox Christian mysticism is the doctrine of the truly incarnated Christ, of the transcendent God becoming immanent in our natural world and in the human body in order that this

---

[15] Denis de Rougemont, *Passion and Society,* trans. Montgomery Belgion (London: Faber, 1956), pp. 153-154.

nature may be suffused with divine grace. The Christian mystic returns from communion with God to accept human life.[16] This acceptance of the human or creaturely limitations, but with a renewed spirit and regained life, is the essence of Holstius' advice to Theodora Goodman in *The Aunt's Story*. And this same spirit operates throughout White's novels, which reveal the other world lying within this one, "wholly within."

White's basic theme, man's eternal quest for meaning and value, is universal and timeless. His expression of this universal theme, however, is through his own particular land and time, twentieth-century Australia, the setting of seven of his eight novels. From the little community of Happy Valley to Sarsaparilla and Barranugli, the special territory staked out in his novels of the sixties, the reader ranges through a mystic land, as peculiarly White's own as Yoknapatawpha County is Faulkner's. White has done for twentieth-century Australia what Shakespeare has done for seventeenth-century England, and Dostoyevsky and Tolstoy, for nineteenth-century Russia. He presents a wide range of social classes and character types, sometimes on an epic scale, sometimes on a smaller and more intimate canvas, but always with the sure touch of mastery. His comic sense does not conceal his compassion, and his simplicity reveals the depth of his vision, like water in a deep pool of exceptional clarity. White's novels present time in its conjunction with eternity, the eternal *now* of T. S. Eliot's *Four Quartets*. As the Jew tells the madwoman of Xanadu, in *Riders in the Chariot,* "a moment can become eternity, depending on what it contains" (pp. 161-162).

---

[16] See de Rougemont, *Passion and Society*, p. 149: "But by Christian mystics, on the contrary, the reality of the mystical state is subjected to the test of the deeds and works that issue from it"; and p. 168: "St. Teresa deemed good only those visions that impelled her to act better and love more."

The novelist's aesthetic always sends us back to his metaphysic. The critic's task is to bring out the author's metaphysic before evaluating his technique.

JEAN-PAUL SARTRE, "TIME IN FAULKNER: THE SOUND AND THE FURY"

My task . . . is, before all, to make you see.

JOSEPH CONRAD, PREFACE (1897), THE NIGGER OF THE 'NARCISSUS'

chapter 2 Technique and vision

Art is both expression and communication. As communication, the artist's task is to convey the essence of his poetic vision, " 'to make you *see*' " (*The Solid Mandala,* p. 51). Ruth Godbold, in *Riders in the Chariot,* has struggled with the same difficulty: " 'If I was to tell,' the creature attempted, 'it doesn't follow that you would see. Everybody sees different. You must only see it for yourself,' she cried, tearing it out helplessly at last" (p. 284). To this end, literature relies heavily on communicable symbols such as archetypes, typical images which *recur* in literature often enough to be recognizable as an element of literary experience as a whole. Archetypes belonged to art for centuries before the word was popularized by Jung. The archetypal is the conventional element in literature, and reminds us of Eliot's contention, in "Tradition and the Individual Talent" (1919), that literature forms a continuing body or ideal form, and appreciation of it requires a sense not only of the past but also of its presence. While the literary artist may consciously draw upon literary conventions and the works of other writers, his use of archetypes may be to some extent unconscious. They are part of his vision, his way of seeing the world and of conveying what he sees through his art. Unlike much of the literature of past centuries, contemporary literature tends to ignore or conceal its conventional basis and to use archetypes only implicitly, while the secular spirit of the age and the dwindling number of classical scholars have made the interpretation of archetypes seem factitious to some literary critics.

The archetypal is the *social* as well as the conventional or cyclically recurring aspect of literature. It deals with man in society rather than with the isolated individual. Narrative, from the archetypal point of view, is *ritual,* the generic, recurring actions analogous to weddings and funerals, seed-time and harvest, and so on. Similarly, theme, from the archetypal point of view, is the desire or dream of *social* rather than personal goals: the perfect city, the tended garden instead of a wilderness, domesticated animals rather than wild beasts. The archetypal metaphor usually identifies a natural object with the social goals of human desire. And the individual natural object is identified with its class—all roses, all trees (poetic not botanical), and so on. Both ritual and dream contain a dialectic of desire and repugnance, so that archetypal criticism deals with two organizing rhythms or patterns: one cyclical, one dialectical. The narrative is the theme in motion, while the theme is the narrative in stasis.

The anagogic metaphor moves beyond this social frame of reference towards a centre of imaginative experience. Northrop Frye describes the anagogic perspective as follows:

> In the anagogic phase, literature imitates the total dream of man, and so imitates the thought of a human mind which is at the circumference and not at the center of its reality. . . . Nature becomes, not the container, but the thing contained, and the archetypal universal symbols, the city, the garden, the quest, the marriage, are no longer the desirable forms that man constructs inside nature, but are themselves the forms of nature. . . . This is not reality, but it

is the conceivable or imaginative limit of desire, which is infinite, eternal, and hence apocalyptic. By an apocalypse I mean primarily the imaginative conception of the whole of nature as the content of an infinite and eternal living body which, if not human, is closer to being human than to being inanimate.[1]

White's fiction demonstrates this anagogic approach in some degree from his very first novel, but far more confidently in *The Aunt's Story* and the novels which follow. He uses the mandala, which reaches its full development in the seventh novel, as an anagogic metaphor throughout his work to suggest the infinite and eternal living body in which man has his being, the symbol which unites all other symbols, the Word that contains all poetry.

In the analysis of White's technique, the terms "archetypal metaphor" and "anagogic metaphor" are used, rather than the more common terms "symbol" and "symbolism," to denote hypothetical identity between two or more objects. The term "apocalyptic image" is used as a synonym for "archetypal metaphor." In current criticism, "symbol" suffers from widely varying and even contradictory meanings. C. S. Lewis, in *The Allegory of Love,* equates symbolism with sacramentalism, defining it as the attempt to "read" or see the immaterial, spiritual world in its "copy," the material world. The thought stems from Plato's dialogues, where the Sun is the copy of the Good, and continues through the diffused Platonism of the Middle Ages and the Renaissance to emerge in the Romantic distinction between symbolism and allegory: "Symbolism is a mode of thought, but allegory is a mode of expression."[2] Since literature contains a variety of meanings and types of literary symbolism, the romantic terminology is at best inadequate, and at worst misleading. Northrop Frye defines symbol as "any unit of any literary structure that can be isolated for critical attention"; and

---

[1] Northrop Frye, *Anatomy of Criticism: Four Essays* (Princeton: Princeton University Press, 1957; reprint ed., New York: Atheneum, 1965. References to reprint ed.), p. 119. See also pp. 117-122, on the anagogic aspect of literature.
[2] C. S. Lewis, *The Allegory of Love: A Study in Medieval Tradition* (New York: Oxford University Press, 1958), p. 48.

defines literary criticism itself as basically "the systematizing of literary symbolism."[3]

White has described his writing as being "on two planes, the immediate detailed one and the universal."[4] Metaphor provides the relation between the symbols or isolated units of a literary structure. The radical metaphor is a statement of hypothetical identity: let x be y. Two things are identified, while each retains its own form: "Identity is not uniformity, still less monotony, but a unity of various things."[5] White uses simile only infrequently, and more in his first two novels than in his later ones. The radical metaphor provides a natural vehicle for the expression of his vision of the interpenetration of the natural and spiritual worlds. This is *not* to suggest, as one critic does, that a work such as *Riders in the Chariot* is a "fictional essay" on mysticism rather than a novel, a work of art. Literary meaning is hypothetical and autonomous. It exists for its own sake, as a detached pattern whose meaning is primarily inward or self-contained. The truth of art is not dependent upon conformity with fact or external reality. The *poetic sense* is the total statement made by the novel as a work of art, the *form* in which its *vision*[6] is conveyed. Form and vision cannot be separated without distortion. Critical commentary, however, is allegorical, insofar as it attaches ideas to the structure of poetic imagery and divides the unity of the work of art, whose form and vision as art are indivisible.

Apocalyptic imagery presents objects and experiences in the forms of human desire. The biblical Apocalypse with its organizing metaphors of city, garden, and sheepfold provides what

---

[3] Frye, *Anatomy of Criticism*, p. 71. In my text, the terminology is a simplified form of Frye's usage in *Anatomy of Criticism*.

[4] Ian Moffitt, "Talk with Patrick White," *New York Times Book Review*, 18 August 1957.

[5] Frye, *Anatomy of Criticism*, p. 125. See pp. 123-125.

[6] See Jacques Maritain, *Creative Intuition in Art and Poetry* (Cleveland and New York: Meridian, World Publishing, 1955), p. 97: "this word 'vision' is probably for them [artists] a very close equivalent of what in a philosophical perspective we call poetic intuition." Cf. Jacques and Raissa Maritain, *The Situation of Poetry: Four Essays on the Relations between Poetry, Mysticism, Magic and Knowledge,* trans. Marshall Suther (New York: Kraus reprint, 1968), p. 1: "in the poetic work, the poetic sense is inseparable from the formal structure of the work."

Northrop Frye calls a grammar of apocalyptic imagery for literature as a whole. Demonic imagery presents the inverse of apocalyptic imagery; it presents that which is naturally repulsive to us,
a world of horror and pain, waste and confusion. In White's
fiction the demonic scene is frequently presented in terms of
a parody of the desirable or apocalyptic state. This nightmarish,
perverted or demonic world is seen in the relationship between
Hagan and Sidney and between Elyot and Muriel Raphael, in
White's first two novels; in Boyle's station at Jildra; in the witch
imagery associated with Mrs. Flack and her fellow conspirators
in *Riders in the Chariot*; and in the perverted desires of Waldo
Brown. The striking contrast formed by the apocalyptic and
demonic, and the ironic or seeming contradiction of the paradox,
are basic to White's style.

As in the biblical Apocalypse, however, this dualism is contained within a comprehensive unity. In the anagogic perspective,
everything in the universe is potentially identical with everything
else. Just as the biblical images tend to converge into one vast
anagogic metaphor, in which the conception "Christ" unites all
the various images of Lamb of God, tree of life, water of life,
and vine of which we are the branches, so White's images of rose,
lotus, golden ladder, rope, chain, fire, tree, quest, quaternary,
and mandala tend to become identified with one another. Within
one novel, an image may be used repeatedly so as to form a continuous motif such as we find in the ship image associated with
both Dulcie and Mrs. Poulter in *The Solid Mandala*. The image
serves not only to make us see essential qualities in each woman
but also to relate the two, Arthur's two "wives," to each other,
and thus to supply a link between them which is not found on the
narrative level. Other images, such as the mandala and quaternary, may be traced not only within any one novel but throughout White's fiction.

Within the synoptic framework of literary criticism found in
Northrop Frye's *Anatomy of Criticism,* the structural classifica-
tion of fiction is based, firstly, upon the hero's power of action in
relation to his audience or reader. In terms of the five generic
modes so defined: myth, romance, the high mimetic mode, the

low mimetic mode, and the ironic mode, White's novels may be classified as belonging principally to the fourth or low mimetic mode, that of comedy, melodrama, and "realistic" fiction, where the hero is superior neither to other men nor to his environment. Unlike the superior protagonist of the high mimetic mode, the comic hero is on a level with ourselves, someone with whose common humanity we can identify. In the ironic mode, the hero is inferior in power and intelligence to ourselves, lying in the gutter, so to speak, so that the mood is one of absurdity or frustration. This is the mode of Samuel Beckett's drama and fiction; his tramps, that is, are heroes of the ironic mode. Although White's characters may descend to the gutter in times of crisis, like Stan Parker following the discovery of his wife's infidelity, and Arthur Brown, after his brother's death, they generally return to a level with ourselves. White's fondness for dumps and tramps is displayed in some of his shorter fiction, such as "Down at the Dump," where the mode is more ironic than in his longer fiction. In the latter the tramp or outcast figure is ennobled, dignified, brought towards our own level and often, in his personal and spiritual qualities, far beyond. White's basic mode, that is, is the low mimetic rather than the ironic, but his comedy encompasses both romantic and ironic phases.

Comedy's grand theme is the integration of society, the incorporation of the hero into a desirable society or the society to which he naturally belongs. Its action moves primarily towards the formation of an ideal or redeemed society. Tragedy's theme is the inverse of this, the exclusion and isolation of the tragic hero. The two poles of comic emotion are sympathy and ridicule, corresponding to pity and fear in tragedy. "Comic" and "tragic" may refer to these two main tendencies of the narrative, not simply to comedy and tragedy as forms of drama. Twentieth-century criticism and aesthetic taste retain a lurking suspicion that tragedy is the superior form, a residual prejudice descending from Aristotle's admiration for that genre and the Victorian preference for what Arnold calls "high seriousness."

The characters in a comedy may be grouped so as to suggest two different societies, one false or usurping and one true. The action reveals the undesirable qualities of the first group, and allows a new society to crystallize around the hero. The *inclusive* tendency of comedy, however, drives towards the conversion rather than the repudiation of the undesirable characters, and their integration into the desirable society. In White's comedies we may illustrate this principle by the change effected in the characters of Hilda Halliday in *Happy Valley,* and Mr. and Mrs. Bonner in *Voss,* so that these characters are sympathetically aligned with the hero and/or heroine instead of being in opposition as at the beginning of the action. The ending of *The Living and the Dead* attempts to bring Elyot into the company of the living and to remove him from his deathly isolation, but the endeavour seems half-hearted, as if the author hesitates between the comic and the tragic modes in his conception of this novel. The comedy of manners, which forms one aspect of each of White's novels, displays the undesirable society as "a chattering-monkey society devoted to snobbery and slander."[7] Frye uses the monkey image to describe the undesirable society, just as White does, in *Riders in the Chariot,* in the luncheon party scene with Mrs. Chalmers-Robinson and her society friends. The undesirable or disagreeable societies, in the White canon, include the Furlows of *Happy Valley,* the Parrotts of *The Aunt's Story,* the Armstrongs of *The Tree of Man* and the Pringle society of *Voss.*

In ironic comedy the characters who are opposed to or excluded from the monkey-society have the reader's sympathy. The conclusion may be an ironic deadlock, in which the hero continues to be regarded as a fool or madman by this society while the reader has been led to see his superior worth. We find a deadlock such as this in Dostoyevsky's *The Idiot,* White's *The Aunt's Story* and *The Solid Mandala,* and, in a more qualified sense, in *The Tree of Man* and *Riders in the Chariot.* Ironic comedy, that is, exhibits the desirable society in its infancy, suppressed by the society it should replace. Ironic comedy may also provide an intellectualized parody of melodramatic formulas, as we find in the parts of *The Tree of Man* which deal with the

[7]Frye, *Anatomy of Criticism,* p. 48.

Armstrongs and with Madeleine, heroine of Amy Parker's "novelette." Irony, a sophisticated mode, merely states, suppressing explicit moral judgments and leaving the reader to interpret the ironic tone himself. The author's objective stance, however, is only apparent, an assumed mask behind which the author-narrator remains in charge of the reader's reactions. Without resource to overt comment, the point of view may be controlled in numerous ways, through selected detail and incident, image and symbol, pacing, juxtaposition and so on.[8]

The incongruous and the inevitable are the opposite poles of irony: "The archetype of the inevitably ironic is Adam, human nature under sentence of death. . . . The archetype of the incongruously ironic is Christ, the perfectly innocent victim excluded from human society."[9] Reading *man* for *Adam*, the former archetype applies to all White's characters, for his vision clearly recognizes that death is the destiny of the natural man. It is from within this framework that men must seek reality and permanence. The latter archetype appears in extreme form in characters such as Palfreyman and Himmelfarb. The "crucifixion" scenes of *Voss* and *Riders in the Chariot* are perfect examples of the incongruously ironic.

One of the structural bases of White's novels is the spiritual quest of the hero or heroine. Unlike the quest of the romance mode itself, which involves external movement and marvellous adventures as well as inner significance, the journey of White's protagonists is primarily *inward* into the depths of their own natures, there to discover undesirable qualities repellent to themselves, and there to seek a happier state. This spiritual quest for redemption is depicted in terms of four archetypal stages: the Edenic state of innocence, the adult recognition of guilt, the assumption of suffering, and a fourth state which lies beyond death and outside temporal limitations. White's versions of the Edenic state include the Meroë and New Abyssinia of *The Aunt's Story,* and the childhood of his protagonists. Adult ex-

---

[8] See Wayne C. Booth, *The Rhetoric of Fiction* (Chicago and London: University of Chicago Press, 1965).
[9] Frye, *Anatomy of Criticism*, p. 42.

perience eventually leads his characters to an understanding of the destructive qualities of their nature, as Theodora Goodman discovers "a core of evil" in herself that is hateful to her, and Himmelfarb's sensual excesses force him to recognize the "intolerable" nature of both his father's behaviour and his own.

From the epigraph of his first novel, which describes moral progress as being dependent upon "the law of suffering," White's writing demonstrates the necessity of suffering in human life. His vision encompasses not merely the inevitability of suffering in man's experience but the possibility that suffering may be both exemplary and redemptive, for the individual who suffers and for all those involved. And from his first novel he uses the Passion of Christ as the basic archetype of redemptive suffering. In the suffering and death of the third archetypal stage, death may be physical or psychic. Each of the four protagonists of *Riders in the Chariot* passes through a psychic death before arriving at a state of blessedness which the little dyer of purple hands describes as "equanimity." The state following upon such a death is one of a passionate love for others; it is at once personal and *impartial,* unlike the *preferential* concern and love of our normal experience. This fourth state within human life anticipates a blessed condition after life, the "heaven" of formal religions. White's fictional versions of the heavenly state include the life led by the Sandersons in *Voss,* the state of "equanimity" reached by the four Riders, and Theodora's encounter with Holstius in *The Aunt's Story.* This near-heavenly state corresponds to the land of Beulah in the works of Blake and Bunyan, and the term itself is taken from Isaiah 62: 4.

Hell and purgatory are also aspects of the fourth state, hell being shown by White as a demonic parody of the blessed state, as in Boyle's station at Jildra, and Waldo Brown's dream of an island "paradise" of disease and luxurious hotels where his vanity will be satiated. Purgatory is demonstrated in the luncheon scene of the Crab-Shell, the Bon-bon and the Volcano, in the last chapter of *Riders in the Chariot,* where the society ladies have foundered on "the rock of love," and are "craning in hopes that saving grace might just become visible in the depths of the obscure purgatory in which they sat" (p. 525). In the same chapter, Mrs. Jolley and Mrs. Flack are shown "in hell," tormenting each other and themselves: "Night thoughts were cruelest, and often the two women . . . would lead each other gently back to the origins of darkness. They were desperately necessary to each other in threading the labyrinth. Without proper guidance, a soul in hell might lose itself" (p. 516).

The quest of White's protagonists is shaped, in part, by the quest-myths found in the Bible, and in medieval romance literature with its dragon-killing theme. Romance focusses upon the conflict between the hero and his enemy, making the hero analogous to the mythical Messiah or deliverer who comes from an upper world; White uses the St. George myth, but his hero finds his chief enemy *within himself*. Moses is the archetypal leader who guides the Jewish people out of bondage under Pharaoh, to begin the long and arduous quest for the Promised Land. Northrop Frye describes the Bible's two concentric quest-myths, a Genesis-apocalypse myth and an Exodus-millennium myth, as follows:

> In the former Adam is cast out of Eden, loses the river of life and the tree of life, and wanders in the labyrinth of human history until he is restored to his original state by the Messiah. In the latter Israel is cast out of his inheritance and wanders in the labyrinths of Egyptian and Babylonian captivity until he is restored to his original state in the Promised Land. Eden and the Promised Land, therefore, are typologically identical, as are the tyrannies of Egypt and Babylon and the wilderness of the law.[10]

Despite the tremendous influence of the Bible upon Western literature, biblical typology is now almost a dead language. The difficulty experienced by the contemporary critic in "reading" biblical typology points to the difference between this tradition and our own rationalistic *zeitgeist*.

In White's modern comedies, where the idealized and super-

[10] Ibid., p. 191.

natural forms proper to romance and myth are displaced by a narrative of verisimilitude or apparent "realism," myth is used as archetypal and anagogic metaphor. *Riders in the Chariot,* for example, uses both the Exodus-millennium myth and the Genesis-apocalypse myth; the two converge in Part Six with the identification of Passover and Easter. At the end of Part Two, as Himmelfarb reaches Australia, a pillar of fire appears to rise up before him on the tarmac, recalling that which preceded the Jews on their forty-year desert journey to the Promised Land. His choice of Australia as the farthest, perhaps also the "bitterest," of lands relates his suffering to the bitterness of the Egyptian bondage and the desert hardships. In *The Tree of Man,* both the great flood and the colour *yellow* are identified with the wilderness of the law or the Old Covenant by which death is the reward of transgressions. In their four-stage quest, White's protagonists move towards the apocalypse/millennium, the New Eden and the Promised Land. Patrick White's fiction belongs to the great iconological tradition which comes down through classical and religious scholarship into Dante and Spenser and which was written in stone during the Middle Ages.

White frequently draws upon music, drama, painting, and poetry in order to illumine his own art, the novel. At least one of the other arts is important to each novel and helps to fuse the immediate and the universal. *The Vivisector* introduces two new arts to the traditional canon: cooking and making love. Nance Lightfoot's art of love provides a hilarious balance to Hurtle Duffield's love of art. Duffield, the artist-protagonist of *The Vivisector,* comments on the closeness of music and painting. White himself has said that music seems to help him with the structure of a novel: " 'It helps me to shape a book.' "[11]

In *Happy Valley* the sentimental music of Chopin and Schumann and the waltz music at the ball is associated with the early stages of the love which develops between Oliver Halliday and Alys Browne, before this love is matured by suffering. *The Aunt's Story* uses the music of Moraïtis, the Greek 'cellist, as an image of the fourth archetypal stage in man's spiritual progress,

[11] Quoted in Moffitt, "Talk with Patrick White."

the New Abyssinia sought by Theodora herself and by those who are her "compatriots in the country of the bones" (p. 102). Like Theodora, the musician accepts isolation and distance; his music expresses pain and suffering, the dark and the tragic, but its last movement rises "above the flesh" to express a state where sun and sky pass between living bones. Kathy Volkov's ordeal by music, like Duffield's painting, is depicted as a kind of spiritual justification and as belonging to this same quest. In *Riders in the Chariot,* the Bach organ music heard in the cathedral by Ruth Joyner becomes for her a lasting image of heavenly bliss.

Folk songs and nursery rhymes are all grist to White's mill. They support the general mood and, more frequently, serve as archetypal metaphor, as in the song "No more love," which Elyot Standish feels is both meaningless and pointed. In the children's joyous clowning, at the end of *Riders,* White uses song much as we find it used in Bernard Kops's drama, such as *The Hamlet of Stepney Green.* Alf Dubbo's drunken songs, at Khalils', are full of thematic images; the Friday night of the "big shivoo" is also the beginning of the Jewish sabbath, and "Nail the difference till it bleeds" is both a general comment on one of the less desirable aspects of human nature and a specific prophecy of the novel's Part Six. Songs are even more frequent in *The Solid Mandala.* Arthur composes one on love for the celebrations which mark the end of the war (p. 243). Some of his other songs range from the pure clowning of " 'Como, Lugarno,/Have a banarno' " which makes the prim and pedantic Waldo fear that his brother may become dangerous, to " 'I am the bottom of the bottom' " (p. 126), which is both funny and darkly enigmatic.

The art of dance is used in *The Solid Mandala* to permit a concentrated poetic statement of the novel's theme. Arthur's mandala-dance comes far closer than direct commentary could to telling us what the entire novel is about, to making us *see,* in the Conradian terms which Arthur uses more than once. His dance expresses the nature and the interrelationships of all the main characters in the novel, draws its two main images of quaternary and mandala into one all-inclusive anagogic metaphor, and reaches a climax in a re-enactment of the crucifixion: "Till in the centre of their mandala he danced the passion of all their lives, the blood running out of the backs of his hands, water out of the hole in his ribs. His mouth was a silent hole, because no sound was needed to explain" (p. 257). This arche-type of redemptive suffering recurs in most of White's novels, most strikingly in the death of Palfreyman in *Voss* and in the treatment of the Jew in *Riders in the Chariot*. Norm Fussell's ritual-dance of the primordial bird, on queans' night at Han-nah's, permits the author to remind us indirectly that realism, so-called, is no more than the convention to which we are most commonly accustomed: "Just as the chorus girl was smuggled into Norm at birth, her elderly but professional soul had now invaded the body of this pink bird, making it *real by the conven-tions which those present recognized*" (*Riders in the Chariot,* p. 379, italics mine). Mrs. Pask, Alf's guardian, had been sadly in need of the reminder, and the same critical spirit has been applied to White's own conventions at times when, as in parts of *Voss,* he seems to offend the canons of verisimilitude.

The art of painting is important in *The Vivisector, The Tree of Man,* and *Riders in the Chariot,* where the artist is one of the four protagonists, the four "living creatures" of Ezekiel's chariot of redemption. Indeed, *Riders* gives us a Chinese-box effect of art within art within art,[12] as White's own art incorporates Dubbo's depiction of the poetry or poetic word-pictures of the prophets, primarily Daniel and Ezekiel. The poetic meaning of each art is identified with that of the others to produce a feeling of converging significance. The ignorant and insensitive react to Dubbo's paintings, and to those of Mr. Gage in *The Tree of Man,* either with laughter or with horror. After Dubbo's death, his paintings fetch a few shillings and cause "a certain ribaldry," reminding us of Mrs. Pask's dislike of his early paintings as "most unnatural." Mr. Gage's art meets with a similar fate. After his suicide, his wife arranges his paintings "in lines of shame" for the local audience, and the fearful silence of the first shock is

---

[12] Cf. modern experimental novels such as Flann O'Brien's *At Swim-two-birds* where the novelist is writing about a novelist who is writing about a novelist.

soon replaced by the oppressive "smell of their mirth" (p. 290).
Both Dubbo and Mr. Gage have one fictional admirer, one con-
noisseur who appreciates what the paintings truly are. Humphrey
Mortimer and Mrs. Schreiber are used by White to guide the
point of view of his own audience or reader. And, as in the comment on the conventions of Norm's dance, we feel White's own
comment in Mrs. Schreiber's " 'But, of course, works of art
really prove nothing. They must be judged for themselves' "
(p. 288). The paintings have a traumatic effect on Amy Parker:
she sees herself in Mr. Gage's ant-woman, and her goal in his
painted flame which is the same *within* the ant's body as in his
universal sun. In *The Living and the Dead,* the "conviction"
expressed in the Poussin painting demonstrates to Elyot that
"certainty exists" (p. 202).

To maintain the two planes which White has called the immediate and the universal, he makes use of dramatic situations
where the characters may be drunk, delirious with fever, or
dreaming. These states permit the characters to speak more truly
than they know, or than their conscious minds might permit. The
extreme simplicity of the divine fool, the relative simplicity of
the uneducated, and the conscious irony of an intellectual may
all be used for double entendre in this way. Popular clichés and
aphorisms such as we find in the conversations between Mrs.
Jolley and Mrs. Flack, Mrs. Poulter and Mrs. Dun or the
O'Dowds also serve as vehicles for apocalyptic or demonic
utterance, and frequently have the added advantage of being
extremely funny. As with nursery rhymes and popular songs,
this folk material permits the use of myth and archetype in a displaced technique of apparent verisimilitude. Remarks such as
Mrs. Jolley's " 'Young people are the devil' " with reference to
Blue, or her warning that herring in tomato sauce is " 'asking
for resurrections' " with a sour stomach, contribute to the theme
while being, at the same time, perfectly suited to the character
and the situation. A prophetic comment on the way in which the
narrative will develop is concealed in the drunken salesman's
warning to Stan Parker that " 'the Almighty 'asn't yet shown 'Is
'and' " (*The Tree of Man,* p. 36), or Turner's quoting of Le
Mesurier: " 'Contracted with a practisin' madman, you was,

accordin' to your own admission, for a journey to hell an' back' "
(*Voss,* p. 39).

White's technique of using drunkenness, madness, and simplicity may be compared to the sermon to the sharks in Melville's
Moby Dick. At Stubb's command, the old Negro cook addresses
the sharks as if they were human. Melville is using the dramatic
situation and old Fleece's extreme simplicity as an apocalyptic
image of man's situation. The problem, as the old cook sees it,
is " 'to gobern dat wicked natur, dat is de pint . . . for all angel
is not'ing more dan de shark well goberned.' "[13] The mate com-
mends his discourse as "Christianity," but old Fleece thinks it is
little use preaching to " 'such dam g'uttons.' " The sharks, like
man without God, can fill their bellies and die. Stubb tells the
cook he must " 'go home and be born again,' " reinforcing the
point with an analogy from sea life as to the futility of trying to
get to heaven " 'through the lubber's hole, cook . . . you don't
get there, except you go the regular way round by the rigging' "
(p. 297). The reference to spiritual rebirth, under pretext of
cooking advice, is analogous to the oil and water imagery associated with the two "parties" in *Voss.* Old Fleece reinforces the
identification of man and shark as he limps away, muttering that
Stubb is " 'more of shark dan Massa Shark hisself' " (p. 298).

While his fictional techniques vary, they recur from one novel
to another, and together make up a style which is as uniquely
White's own as any of those commonly called experimental.
Capital letters, for example, are used from time to time for an
emphasis which is usually ironic; the reader takes another meaning from the one intended by the character within the fictional
situation. In *The Solid Mandala,* Waldo tells his acquaintance
leaving for "that hypothetical Front" that he might not be very
good at war: " 'Who knows who'll be good at what', Wally said;
it was an evening of truths, and he had written poems in his day.
(Wally, in fact, was so good at war he got killed for it, and they
sent a medal to Cis)" (p. 120). Reason rejects death as absurd
or unreal, just as Waldo finds it hypothetical, but the absurdity of
death is not negated by this suspension of belief.

The stream of consciousness technique popularized by Joyce

[13] Herman Melville, *Moby Dick* (New York: Modern Library, 1926), p. 295.

and Woolf is used occasionally for specific purposes. We find it in Waldo Brown's thoughts on what he would do if Arthur died, in Mrs. Poulter's reveries of her early married life, Vic Moriarty's day-dreams in *Happy Valley,* and Elyot Standish's night-thoughts or literal dreaming of a "personal Spain" (*The Living and the Dead,* p. 284). White more often uses the "objective" technique developed by Henry James whereby indirect narration is given from the point of view of the fictional character and not from that of the author. White's own viewpoint is fused with those of the fictional characters, often through irony. He uses a multiplicity of reflectors in this technique of limited consciousness, so that the unity comes primarily from theme and vision rather than from the use of a single central intelligence such as James favoured. Most striking is the degree of concentration found in these novels. The prestige which has traditionally been accorded to poetry among literary genres may have come, in part, from the concentration and purity of that genre. In the hands of masters such as Joyce and White, the twentieth-century novel has reached the same degree of artistic purity, where hardly a word can be altered or deleted without injury to the whole.

White's novels contain superb comic scenes, and characters who rank with the immortal clowns of literature. They are also comic in a structural sense, moving towards the "happy ending" of the redemption and the integration of the hero and his society. Like Dante in *The Divine Comedy,* White sees a happy issue to man's pain and suffering. He sees, that is, the possibility that pain may be accepted and transformed into something good even within this life, and that decay, as Miss Hare tells the Jew, "even the putrid human kind," does not necessarily mean an end. Stan Parker's mother is pained by many incidents "in a world that is not nice," and Alf Dubbo seeks in vain to convince Mrs. Pask that what she sees as ugly or horrible is "all, really, beautiful" and will so appear when he has perfected his techniques of expression. White's mature technique should enable us to see that to which Mrs. Pask remains blind. His novels contain a unified vision of the extraordinary behind and within the ordinary, the "mystery and poetry" which makes our lives bearable; this vision is expressed not through the dreary techniques of "journalistic realism,"[14] but through artistic techniques which are *one* with his vision.[15]

---

[14] See Patrick White, "The Prodigal Son," *Australian Letters* I, 3 (1958), 39: "Above all I was determined to prove that the Australian novel is not necessarily the dreary, dun-coloured offspring of journalistic realism."

[15] Cf. *The Journals of Kierkegaard 1834-1854,* a selection, ed. and trans. Alexander Dru (London and Glasgow: Collins, Fontana, 1958), p. 168: "And providence, which is infinite love, has also bequeathed me this marvellous fund of profundities which I have understood, a present which I can dispose of poetically, and can also put to good use by communicating it in the proper way: *poetically.*" All further citations from Kierkegaard's *Journals* are from this edition.
Cf. J. F. Burrows, "Archetypes and Stereotypes: 'Riders in the Chariot,'" *Southerly* XXV (1965), 47: "the mythic element is ultimately neither factitious nor esoteric but something essentially related to contemporary issues as explored by White."

Joys impregnate. Sorrows bring forth.

WILLIAM BLAKE, THE MARRIAGE OF HEAVEN AND HELL

chapter 3 Embryonic forms

The main theme of *Happy Valley* is stated in the epigraph[1] from
Mahatma Gandhi, which describes suffering as "the one indis-
pensable condition of our being" and speaks of measuring progress by the amount of suffering undergone. *Suffering* and *progress*
are the key words.[2] Oliver Halliday's story provides an illustration
of Gandhi's law: by his suffering—firstly through alienation from
his family and secondly through separation from Alys—Oliver
achieves a new inner life, or moral "progress," to use Gandhi's
term. Progress, however, is a word which White later becomes
chary of, and which he mocks in *The Solid Mandala*. It is a redemptive process, rather, through which Oliver moves; and,

---

[1] The epigraphs to six of White's novels (*Tree of Man* and *Voss* have no epigraphs) are not only highly significant thematically but also progressive in
technique, moving from the didactic statements of Gandhi and Helvétius, in
the first two novels, to the imaginative and poetic epigraphs taken from novelists and mystics such as Olive Schreiner, William Blake, Dostoyevsky, Paul
Eluard, and Meister Eckhart, in the later novels.

[2] One of Dostoyevsky's major themes, the beneficial effects of suffering, is developed in his novel *The Insulted and the Injured*. Dostoyevsky's influence is
evident in several of White's novels.

although the term "suffering servant" is perhaps unjustifiably grandiloquent in the case of Oliver Halliday, nevertheless his experience prefigures, in minor key, the experience of Himmelfarb in *Riders in the Chariot*.

Considered in terms of archetypal ritual, the narrative has two movements: one cyclical, the other dialectical. Cyclically, Oliver moves from innocence (his early sympathetic but sentimental identification with his patients) through experience and suffering to a new state which includes his earlier experience but transforms it. "Maturity" may be the psychological term for his new state. Whatever we call this state of reconciliation, it allows Oliver to experience happiness—a happiness from which personal suffering and the knowledge of pain and evil are not excluded but accepted and transformed. This is the cyclical movement which underlies the experience not only of Oliver but also of Alys and, less prominently, of Rodney Halliday and Margaret Quong. The dialectical movement lies in a tension between desire and repugnance. Suffering is repugnant, happiness is desirable; the attempt to avoid suffering leads most of the characters to long for escape from Happy Valley. Alys, Margaret Quong, and Oliver all dream of escaping to California (an archetype of Eden in American literature) and Rodney longs for Sydney, a golden city pealing with bells. Sidney Furlow's dream, consistent with the inverse pattern of demonic imagery which is associated with this character, is of self-destruction.

In the first chapter the doctor's attendance at a difficult labour, which ends in a stillbirth, makes him aware that "perhaps he had become callous" (p. 12). His spiritual state, suggested by the dead child and the deep cold of Happy Valley in winter, is deathly in its cold isolation. Lacking compassion, he sees people as animals (the labouring woman as a cow; her husband, an unwanted dog) and although he is conscious of his own brutality, he seems unable to change. He is aware that, intellectually and emotionally, he is still only sixteen, and that without faith "pain only made you bitter, or made you ashamed because you were bitter and afraid" (p. 18). The petty intellectual aspirations of his earlier life are condemned by Oliver himself, and satirized by the author. The

Miracle of Thought extolled by the Sunday newspaper is shown
as the abortive attempt to write "a play with some kind of metaphysical theme, only the trouble was to find the theme" (p. 16)
or the feverish effort to copy Great Thoughts into a notebook.
Oliver (in Part One) prefigures Waldo Brown as well as Himmelfarb, but, unlike Waldo, Oliver senses both the futility of the
theories which refused to be jostled (p. 74) and their comical
aspect ("that damn pretentious book").

As the relationship with Alys develops, Oliver becomes more
aware of his isolation and his inability to make contact, and his
awareness of some *core* in Alys (pp. 103-105) beneath her frailty
and silliness begins to break down his coldness. His simultaneous
awareness of Alys and Rodney as *persons* to be treated with respect is prophetic of the dilemma he faces in Part Two, where he
must choose between family and lover. Chapter 11 marks a major
step forward in Oliver's realization that he has become "a kind of
machine for doing" (p. 123). His state of inhuman objectivity,
which had developed as a reaction to his youthful romanticized
pity for his patients, has been shattered by Alys; now he sees
Ernest Moriarty for the first time, and feels that Alys has made
this possible. As he identifies with Moriarty's problems, he begins
to recover his earlier attitude of sympathy, but with a new maturity, recognizing himself as an *instrument* rather than a machine,
a hypodermic needle:

> It was different. As if you suddenly saw yourself at one ex-
> treme and Happy Valley at the other on a kind of balance,
> and now you had begun to tip it down, standing in the scales,
> touching with your hands Moriarty's arm, as the scale swung
> with the weight, and you began to feel you had made some
> considerable onslaught on the battalions of energy cased up
> in rock and earth with which Happy Valley bludgeoned a
> hitherto feeble human opposition. (P. 123.)

Oliver's recognition of himself as an instrument picks up an
earlier reference to "instrument of mercy," and, when reinforced
by the weight-in-the-balance image, suggests that the human in-

strument is used to convey some supernatural mercy to suffering humanity. Oliver's awareness of himself as an instrument, or servant to the suffering, grows slowly throughout Part Two. At this stage, however, his relationship with Alys is escapist, the lovers existing for a time on an idyllic island "apart from the reality of Happy Valley" (p. 122). On his return to Australia from Europe, Oliver had found the people very young, "almost embryonic" (p. 19). Similarly all the characters in this novel are young: Oliver, still sixteen by his own admission; Alys, young, romantic, virginal; and Sidney, a spoiled child. Some, however, are growing or progressing, in Gandhian terms, through suffering.

By Chapter 18, Oliver has realized that he can no longer hope to escape through Alys but rather that their relationship forces him to recognize his affinity with his family and the people of Happy Valley. Hilda is increasingly identified with a weak, sick, and suffering world which cannot be ignored. In his new state of awareness Oliver begins to pity Hilda, but he fears that pity is suicide, the death of the new person Alys has helped him to become. Voluntary renunciation of his new self is the answer to the dilemma: "because Hilda is the world, poor, sick, and there is no forsaking it" (p. 201). Oliver understands this, but does not yet *will* it, despite his written commitment to the other doctor to leave in August. He vacillates, and fears he is undergoing some kind of moral disintegration. His conviction that it is wrong to love Alys, "rotten and disintegrating" (p. 202), is altered soon after to the belief that is right morally, if not conventionally. At the same time he realizes that fear is followed by hate, and that compassion overcomes fear.

The relation between Hilda and the world, which is first established at the allegorical level ("Hilda is the world, poor, sick"), is translated into the full metaphorical statement of identity by the archetypal handling of narrative. The metaphor is strikingly reminiscent of Hosea's relation with Gomer. Although White has reversed, on the superficial level, the roles played by husband and wife in the Old Testament narrative, since it is Oliver who is unfaithful rather than Hilda, he has retained the basic orientation of this archetypal story. In both cases the movement is towards reconciliation,[3] with the wife symbolizing suffering humanity and the husband-prophet bearing a commission to help the sufferer. Hilda and Oliver are reconciled after Moriarty's death, and a genuine affection is established between them.

At the Grand Race Week Ball, under the deceptive spell of waltz music, Oliver decides to leave Hilda and to go to America with Alys. As the lovers attempt to leave together the following night, Fate intervenes in the form of Ernest Moriarty's dead body lying on the road out of Happy Valley. The turn taken, the path chosen at the dance is reversed. As Oliver goes to investigate what is lying in the dark Alys feels that they have returned from another world and she knows that now they will never go away together. Similarly, Oliver realizes that they have returned to the inevitable starting-point, that Happy Valley permits of no escape and that Hilda and Moriarty were joined "by a link of frustration and pain" (p. 275). His bitter feeling of impotence has changed to a state of acceptance by the time he has discovered that Vic Moriarty is also dead and that Alys has gone from the car.

Chapter 29 underlines the interrelations between theme, narrative, and character. The Moriartys, like Oliver and Alys, were "two people running away from themselves" (p. 291), "two people trying to escape from the inevitable" (p. 294). Oliver, in facing the murdered Vic Moriarty, has faced the meaning of destruction, in all its futility and pain. After this confrontation, he refuses to assist the destructive forces, knowing that he must oppose them in order to keep his self-respect. This chapter closes with a triumphant vindication of Alys' and Oliver's love, which will continue despite their physical separation and which is *one* with their existence. Alys thinks: "There is no fear attached to going away by oneself, there is nothing that can destroy, no pain that is final" (p. 298). There is the same mood of peace and confidence in Chapter 33, at the novel's end, where Oliver's emotions have been swept as clean and bare as the boards of the house they are preparing to leave. He has a new relationship, a new intimacy

[3] The names of the children of Hosea and Gomer (*Lo-ruhamah* 'Unpitied,' and *Lo-ammi* 'Not my people') are changed to their opposites to symbolize the movement towards reconciliation and inclusion: Hosea 1: 4, 6, 9; 2: 22, 23.

with his wife, who has also been changed by suffering and who gropes towards confidence. Earlier, Hilda has identified herself with the suffering of the publican's wife. As she leaves Happy Valley she feels that she is joined to Alys by a link of pain.

After the publication of *The Tree of Man*, Marjorie Barnard described White as being "obsessed with pain and loneliness," and his novels as failing to portray any "satisfactory and satisfying human relationship."[4] This judgment acknowledges only *part* of White's theme and one which, taken in isolation, badly distorts the whole. It is true that White is very concerned with pain and loneliness; it is not true that White's novels portray love as an illusion, or fail to portray satisfying human relationships. As Oliver leaves Happy Valley with Hilda, he feels that Alys is part of him for all time: "this is not altogether lost, it is still an intimate relationship that no violence can mortify" (p. 327). His strength to *withstand* flows jointly from Hilda and Alys; through love he is immune from all but the physical death of his body.

The structure of the narrative in *Happy Valley* is based primarily upon an intricate system of contrasts and parallels which centre in two contrasting and triangular love affairs. Much of the effect in the early part of the novel comes simply from the juxtaposition of dissimilars. Alys, Oliver, and Oliver's family (especially Hilda and Rodney) form the first triangle; Alys feels herself to be "the negative coefficient in Oliver's equation, Oliver, Hilda and Alys Browne" (p. 297). Sidney, Hagan, and the Moriarty family form the second triangle. The fruitful relationship between Alys and Oliver is contrasted with the destructive one between Sidney and Hagan. The latter relationship is a demonic parody of love. Roger Kemble supplies one variant in the basic Sidney-Hagan-Moriarty triangle, and there are others. Sidney despises Roger as a "gelding," since this polite young man offers little or no resistance to her ferocious will. The geometry is complicated

---

[4] Marjorie Barnard, "The Four Novels of Patrick White," *Meanjin* XV (1956), 170. She continues: "In Patrick White's philosophy of pain and loneliness it would seem that none were possible. . . . Love is an illusion, pain a certainty. . . . And pain is its own reward." The one-sidedness of this interpretation is revealed by phrases such as "the frustrated and the inarticulate . . . the mad and the lost," unlike the balance and contrast suggested by the title of White's second novel, *The Living and the Dead*.

by the numerous interconnections established between the characters, as juxtaposition gives place to interdependence.

Parallels also abound. As Oliver's family is being harmed by his relationship with Alys (or would be if the relationship continued), so the Moriarty family is destroyed by Hagan after the pathetically weak Vic has deluded herself into thinking that Hagan's lust is really love. As the young Margaret Quong is hurt by Alys' neglect, so Rodney is hurt by his father's. The children's behaviour, in general, parallels that of the adults, revealing its twofold aspect of love and hate. In the sadism of the schoolboys, the "reluctantly relinquished pleasure" (p. 57) taken by bullies Andy Everett and Arthur Ball in Rodney's pain and fear, lies the seed of those forces of destruction which are shown in the novel to bear such dark fruit.

There are other structural patterns auxiliary to the basic love triangles. Part One is based, like Joyce's *Ulysses*, on the slow passing of one day, from early morning until late at night. Its last chapter weaves together the night-thoughts of the characters in a dream-like fantasy, until Happy Valley achieves "the pathetically compulsory unity of purpose that informs a town asleep" (p. 112). In Part Two, the seasons rather than the hours of a day serve as an organizing principle as well as a symbol of the spiritual forces involved. While the single day of Part One takes place in mid-winter, Part Two progresses through a brief spring and hot summer to an early autumn. Winter is identified with a deathly spiritual isolation, and autumn with peaceful anticipation, fruition, and hope. Thirdly, White uses the Passion story, archetype of redemptive suffering, as an auxiliary structural principle in a cluster of chapters in Part Two, those concerned with the Autumn Race Week, its Ball, and the Race itself. There is no suggestion of the crucifixion, as there is in *Voss, Riders*, and *The Solid Mandala*, or of the resurrection; nevertheless, many references and images suggest events of the Passion week from the Thursday to the Saturday when Christ lay in the tomb. This is quite possibly the weakest of the novel's structural principles, since it is used only in this block of chapters, not consistently throughout the novel. There is a unity of imagery, however, centering on blood and roses, which links this mythic framework with the rest. It was blood, through the cut in Alys' hand, which originally brought Alys and Oliver together. All the structural principles in the novel are thus closely related to the theme of progress through suffering.

Several references to *Anna Karenina* are woven into White's narrative. Alys Browne has read a chapter of this novel and finds Tolstoy "interesting" (p. 43). Later, when the doctor has dressed the cut on her hand, she asks herself if either Vronsky or Karenin "was parallel" (p. 104). Structurally, there are many similarities between the two novels. Both work with a large cast of characters interrelated by a fairly complicated plot. Both are based upon an intricate system of parallels and contrasts centred in two triangular love affairs. Both novelists arrange the narratives in blocks (White's unit is usually a chapter, Tolstoy's is several chapters) which deal alternately with the two main groups. When we define "comedy" and "tragedy" by generic definitions based upon narrative structure, we may call *Happy Valley* a comedy with an ironic and tragic sub-plot, the Sidney-Hagan affair; and *Anna Karenina* is a tragedy with a comic sub-plot, for it is Anna's story, not Levin's, which dominates the book.

Happy Valley is more unified than Tolstoy's novel. The interrelationship of White's characters becomes more and more obvious in Part Two, as groups which have been seen first in relative isolation are shown to be intimately related with one another. In Tolstoy's novel there is a superficial relation established on the level of plot, since the characters know one another and share family ties; there is, however, no thematic relation *except contrast* between Anna's and Levin's love affairs. In *Happy Valley*, on the other hand, it is the realization of the destruction and the suffering caused by the Sidney-Hagan-Moriarty triangle, as well as the understanding that Hilda *is* all the unhappy inhabitants of Happy Valley, that brings about the change in Oliver and Alys and ends their plan to escape.

Both *Happy Valley* and *Anna Karenina* represent humanity as besieged by opposing spiritual forces. In *Anna Karenina* the beatific visions belong to Levin, whose goodness is luminous and whose simplicity suggests the childlike characteristics which are

praised in the Gospels. His marriage ceremony, described at
length in Part V, is symbolic of Christ and the Church, with the
love between Levin and Kitty symbolizing the relationship
between man and God. Tolstoy uses the ritual of the marriage
ceremony to convey archetypal meaning, drawing attention continually to the spiritual significance both of homely details such
as new candles and of the words of the marriage ceremony:
" 'Eternal God, that joinest together in love them that were separate.' "[5] Levin's conversation with the peasant Fyodor, who
speaks of the righteous peasant Fokanitch as living "for his soul,
in truth, in God's way," releases a flood of significant ideas from
Levin's mind in a rush of light. He finds it mysterious and marvellous; and while the vision is one that cannot be explained by
reason, it clearly involves the happiness which follows from
obedience to God's will, and a recognition of *the whole world as
miracle*, " 'the sole miracle possible, continually existing, surrounding me on all sides, and I never noticed it!' " (p. 925).
Levin's attitude here is very similar to the vision which underlies
all White's novels.

The desolation seen by Anna is depicted with searing power.
While her misery is augmented merely by the *mores* of fashionable society, this same society is frequently treated as an agent
of a spiritual force far stronger than itself. Alexey Alexandro-
vitch acknowledges the two forces which compete for possession
of his soul and his life, and feels that the Princess Tverskoy is
"the incarnation of that brute force" which hinders his attempt
to love and to forgive Anna (pp. 495-499). The efforts of both
Anna and Vronsky to separate are countermanded by the Princess and by Stepan, who are linked to the "brute force" both by
direct statements and by images. The sense of evil as an active
spiritual force, effecting its purposes through human agents,
operates as a continuous undertone in the chapters related to
Anna and Vronsky, becoming more marked as the tragic con-
sequences of their passion begin to torment her, and dominating

[5] Leo Tolstoy, *Anna Karenina*, trans. Constance Garnett (New York: Modern
Library, n.d.), p. 532. All quotations from *Anna Karenina* are from Garnett's
translation as cited.

Part VII, which ends with her death. In the chapters which follow the physical consummation of their love, this tone of spiritual warfare is strongly marked. Just before the consummation, Anna and Vronsky are described as being possessed by "the spirit of evil and deceit" (p. 175); after it Vronsky feels "the murderer's horror before the body of his victim," while Anna feels horror and loathing, and both suffer shame at their *spiritual* nakedness.

As Anna and Vronsky become alienated in Part VII, Anna's misery is described as the strife waged by the "evil spirit" which is in possession of her heart. In her poisoned state, all naturally good things are turned to their opposites, as Tolstoy—like Blake, White, and the Hebrew prophets—images evil as the inverse of good. Anna realizes that she has lost all, and gained nothing; that she despises everyone and everything; and that nothing matters to her now. Kitty's pity is unable to help Anna, but only adds to her sense of mortification and of being an outcast. Anna decides that Kitty hates her, that everything is hateful, that every human being hates every other human—and that she herself hates Vronsky before all. In the "glaring light" of this desolation, Anna sees that men are held together only by hatred and by the struggle for existence, and that her relationship with Vronsky has really been "hell." In the last minute of her life, this glaring light makes a child appear hideous, a happily married couple repulsive. Hence, Anna desires only to "put out the light" which reveals such horrors. Tolstoy emphasizes the subjective nature of Anna's vision at this time. Another light is implicit, where all that is seen in this glaring light is shown to be a distortion of the truth. Anna's suicide is an attempt to punish Vronsky and to escape from herself, or from "the power that made her suffer." For an instant before death, this darkness that had covered everything for her was torn apart, and she sees life and joy; in the next instant, her life is "quenched forever." All that Anna suffers may in one sense be summed up in Levin's thought of the evil jest of some devil against which Levin, unlike Anna, has struggled successfully.

In *Happy Valley* the relationship between Sidney Furlow and

Clement Hagan, the new overseer at the Furlow ranch, provides a demonic parody or destructive inversion of the creative relationship between Oliver and Alys. This parallels the structure of relationships in Tolstoy's *Anna Karenina,* including the contrast set up between Anna's and Levin's love affairs. Notice that the relationship of Alys and Oliver does not correspond to that of Anna and Vronsky. Stated algebraically, Sidney is to Hagan as Anna is to Vronsky; and Oliver is to Alys, as Levin to Kitty. Once again, as with the Hosea-Gomer parallel noted above, there is an inversion of the archetype at the superficial level, combined with a close parallel with the archetype's significance regarding the two contrasting types of love. In White's novel it is the adulterous couple whose love is creative or spiritually fruitful, the cause of "progress," in Gandhian terms, whereas adultery leads Tolstoy's Anna to destruction. The spirit or force which Tolstoy repeatedly calls "brutal," White centres in Sidney and Hagan, through a related cluster of images: snake, whip (or stick), glass (diamond), and metal.

Hagan's name, which is "rough" (p. 266) against Chuffy Chambers' tongue, is sufficiently hard and unpleasant in itself to suggest the nature of Hagan's character even to the reader unacquainted with Scandinavian and Germanic legends, or Wagner's *Ring des Nibelungen.* In the legends, Hagan (or Hagen) is the murderer of Siegfried and the son of Alberich, the dwarf who guards the Nibelung treasure and whose curse follows the ring wherever it goes. In Wagner's first opera, *Das Rheingold* (1869), Alberich forswears love to gain gold and the boundless power it bestows; similarly Hagan, in his first appearance in White's novel, thinks of the power of money and of its invaluable assistance to one's sense of self-importance (p. 24). Hagan is unconscious of natural phenomena "except as a source of economic advancement" (p. 149), and his motto is "you always got back your money's worth" (p. 156). White's Hagan is as wily as his Germanic namesake, who knew the one spot where Siegfried was vulnerable, and as cowardly: Siegfried is stabbed in the back. White seems to have combined the characteristics of both Alberich and Hagen in his Hagan, whose first name

Clement (merciful, humane, mild), is not primarily ironic in its intention but, rather, an indication of man's piebald or dual nature,[6] which is one of White's continuing themes. Martin Buber has emphasized the essential evil of treating people as *things*.[7] It is this evil which is associated with Hagan. Just before the reaction of Chuffy Chambers to Hagan's name, noted above, Hagan thinks of Chuffy, that harmless, simple soul, as "it" (p. 265) and resents his being "loose." This follows hard upon his treatment of Vic Moriarty as *object*, not person.

Hagan notes the hardness, the harsh masculinity of Sidney's name, and although he sees that she is "hard as a nail" (p. 151) he continues, against his better judgment, to desire her. A network of imagery, centering on snake,[8] whip, glass, and metal, helps to reveal her character and the nature of their relationship. The images work both forwards, prophetically, and backwards, illuminating what has occurred. The red cock who treads the hen on the day Hagan arrives at the Furlow ranch presages Hagan's eventual marriage to Sidney, but Hagan is also the whipped and broken snake of Chapter 17, which has been foreshadowed in his thoughts at the bar before reaching the ranch: "you couldn't argue with a snake, you broke its back" (p. 52). Marriage to Roger Kemble ("so handsome, so English in boots," p. 137) would be, Sidney knows, only an exchange of labels, a too-easy way out; Sidney is a "sterile spur," and Roger, the gelding who finds "no contact at all" in her smile. Although destructive towards herself and others, Sidney is less naive than Roger. Her dream of escape centres not in a change of environment but in suicide—"it'd be rather fun to blow out one's

---

[6] In *Happy Valley*, Oliver's son looks at the piebald horse who was "born like that" (p. 198); in this novel and in *The Solid Mandala*, piebald is used as an image of man's dual nature and capacity for both creative and destructive behaviour.

[7] See Manfred Mackenzie, "Yes, Let's Return to Abyssinia," *Essays in Criticism* XIV (1964), 433. White has read several of Buber's books and found him a great help.

[8] The snake imagery may be traced through pp. 49, 52, 86, 181-186, 216, 227, 231, 248, 266, 288-290 of *Happy Valley*. This does not include all its extensions through *coldness, whip,* and *stick.* The power of the poet's words are established not only by definition but also by variety of context. Tolstoy develops a similar pattern of imagery around the worldly Stepan Arkadyevitch.

brains" (p. 142)—or in submission to sex, envisaged as a kind of suicide. Hagan, she hopes, would be to her the untamed horse through which she seeks destruction, whose hoofs would trample blood upon her mouth. The Sidney-Hagan relationship is symbolized by the movie, full of violent and sadistic scenes of sex, which Vic and Hagan see: "no answers to questions, only a statement of energy" (p. 156). (The *outcome* of Vic Moriarty's relations with Hagan is also prefigured here, although not the nature of their affair, which is one of simple lust rather than violence, and sadistic only in a limited sense, with respect to Hagan's total insensitivity to Vic as a whole person.)

Sidney engages Hagan in a struggle for power, something fierce and irrational like the brush fire in which Sidney exults. Their relationship, like that between Hagan and the colt, is "a conflict for superiority between two brutes" (p. 179). But although Hagan is successful in breaking the colt and killing the snake, Sidney is the stronger of the two. In the strange snake-killing episode, strongly reminiscent of ritual scenes in the novels of D. H. Lawrence, Sidney adds her will to Hagan's so that both seem to be killing the snake: "she was directing his arm, it was her arm" (p. 182). Their mingled attraction and repulsion is expressed in Sidney's caressing of the dead body of the snake, sensual yet cold. Both Sidney and Hagan desire to treat each other as they have treated the snake, and do so—mouths and bodies, whip and spur replacing snake and stick. Sidney's thoughts reveal that full sexual relations are to her the annihilation she both fears and desires. After fleeing the scene and overcoming her hysteria, she knows that she is the stronger of the two, that she has "killed him who had killed the snake" (p. 186). When her father has returned to the ranch the cold "whipped snake" (p. 216) is both Hagan, whose job would be lost should Sidney inform her father of what has happened, and also Sidney, annihilated through Hagan's body. The connection between sex and coldness (sex without love, or lust) is related to the cool fire of diamonds, a material even harder than metal, another substance frequently associated with Sidney. In Chapter 24 this snaky coldness becomes the coldness of a dead body, sug-

gesting the emotional death which accompanies lust and antici-
pating both Sidney's spiritual state and Vic's physical one.

Chapter 28 is handled ritualistically, like Chapter 17. Hagan
is the snake killed by a Sidney who exults in power and in her
ability to induce fear in her victim. The relation to the theme,
presented *inversely* through Sidney and Hagan, is emphasized
in this chapter. Marjorie Barnard considers that "Hagan is
saved from possible implication in the murder" by Sidney's offer
to give perjured evidence and to marry him.[9] "Saved," however,
can only be used ironically with reference to the novel as a whole.
Earlier, Sidney has killed her pity for her parents (like the
anemones squashed at the beach) by deciding that "she must
free herself, she must get away, discard pity to live" (p. 287),
which is Oliver's final decision in reverse. The novel shows that
the "life" gained by discarding compassion and love is not life,
but death. Hagan's relation to Sidney means his annihilation, as
Sidney knows: "I is me is he but me" (p. 290). This psychological version of cannibalism provides an excellent illustration
of Northrop Frye's discussion of demonic imagery. He writes:

> The demonic human world is a society held together by a
> kind of molecular tension of egos. . . . Such a society is an
> endless source of tragic dilemmas like those of Hamlet and
> Antigone. In the apocalyptic conception of human life we
> found three kinds of fulfillment: individual, sexual and
> social. In the sinister human world one individual pole is
> the tyrant-leader, inscrutable, ruthless, melancholy, and
> with an insatiable will. . . . The other pole is represented by
> the *pharmakos* or sacrificed victim, who has to be killed to
> strengthen the others. In the most concentrated form of the
> demonic parody, the two become the same.[10]

Thus Sidney is the tyrant-leader, and Hagan, the sacrificed victim whose spirit and will are devoured by Sidney in order to
strengthen her own. Such a relationship is a demonic parody of
the relationship between the soul and God.

[9] Barnard, "The Four Novels of Patrick White," p. 158.
[10] Frye, *Anatomy of Criticism,* pp. 147-148.

Happy Valley is remarkable as a first novel, with its great theme of progress through suffering supported by a firm structure and strong characterization. The handling of archetype and apocalyptic image is already masterly, despite occasional lapses such as the somewhat naive cyclamen-image associated with Vic Moriarty's passion. Pink, plump Vic, who intends that Hagan will "accidentally" find her at the piano singing of the mating of bluebirds, is the first of White's memorable comic characters.

The solution to Alys' and Oliver's liaison is not the sentimental one of escape to California, nor the tragic death of one of the lovers as in *Anna Karenina,* but the *acceptance* of pain and suffering, and its transformation and sublimation into love for all men. Oliver's discovery that this is possible prefigures Holstius' advice to Theodora Goodman in *The Aunt's Story* that she should accept the two irreconcilable halves of joy and suffering, life and death. Oliver Halliday's confident belief, that there is "a mystery of unity about the world" (p. 166) which underlies its temporal expression in cleavage and pain, reflects White's own conviction.

*There is a great chasm fixed between us; no one from our
side who wants to reach you can cross it, and none may pass
from your side to us.*

LUKE 16: 26

chapter **4** Things fall apart

The title of White's second novel, *The Living and the Dead,*
embodies not only the theme—which is, in a very limited sense,
White's constant theme—but also a conception of that theme
which is reflected in the weaker technique of this novel. It is perhaps the only one of White's novels which misses greatness. The
novel deals with two groups of people, the spiritually living and
the living dead, but it leaves the two groups unrelated to each
other, as Tolstoy leaves Anna and Vronsky's story almost unrelated to Kitty and Levin's. This seems to follow of necessity
from the conception of the dead as totally isolated, unable to
make contact with other human beings. In his first novel, however, and in all the novels which follow, White shows the gulf
between the "living" and the "dead" being bridged by love and
redemptive suffering. In both *Anna Karenina* and *The Living
and the Dead* the relation between the two groups is simply one
of contrast, as if Tolstoy and White envisaged a great gulf stand-
ing between the two groups. The horror of Elyot's state of living
death is related to the horror of pain and suffering in Spain, and

to the destination of physical death for man and beast alike, identified with the dead dog staked in the marsh. But this also points up the feeling of distance, the conception of the problem as remote—in Spain, rather than in London. The attempt by the "living" Joe and Eden to come to grips with death and suffering simply results in their leaving the stage.

Elyot's tragedy dominates this book, as Anna's dominates Tolstoy's. The first page describes Elyot in terms of a skull, a traditional emblem of death: "The sockets of his eyes were dark. Two empty saucers in the bone" (p. 11). And the first chapter presents the archetypal situation embodied in the parable of the good Samaritan, the opportunity to help a fellow man in need. Like Hugh and the consul in Chapter 8 of Malcolm Lowry's *Under the Volcano,* Elyot fails to take this opportunity and thereby to identify with the clown-like drunk: "The night dissolved without bringing you closer. Either to Eden, in spite of a chance moment of illumination, or to the excess humanity spewed out of pub doors. It was a remoteness once alarming, then inevitably accepted" (p. 13). Elyot feels as sick at this failure to prevent the traffic accident and to make contact with other human beings as if he had been guilty of murder. He suspects that he is substituting death for life within a self-built cocoon, and his *devotion* to scholarship is "a devotion to the dust" (p. 20). The word "devotion" is italicized by White and repeated three times in two short sentences, drawing attention to the irony of its use in connection with dust (another traditional emblem of death) instead of with the deity or with human persons. Frequent references to death sound like a drumbeat, muffled but ominous, through the first chapter and throughout the novel.

The pattern of Elyot's deathly isolation is consistent from his childhood days, when he is frightened because he had no part in anything, to his early middle age. (Ten years elapse between Chapters 7 and 8.) By the time he has come down from Cambridge, he is "happiest behind a closed door" (p. 111) and finds himself beginning to hate. His relationship with Eden is a source of constant frustration. During and after their adolescence he is forced to acknowledge that "he didn't know her any more . . . he hated her . . . because in this intimate relationship he failed to understand the paradox of distance" (p. 113). Here, as in the portrayal of the school children in *Happy Valley,* hate thrives on fear and ignorance. In Elyot's "relationless existence" (p. 123) this hate for Eden looms as the one reality, without which he would cease to exist.

Part One ends by returning to the deathly quality of Elyot's chief occupation, his scholarship, something safe "even if smug" (p. 163), which he holds between himself and doubt. In making Büchner the object of Elyot's study, White creates an ironic pattern similar to that of James Joyce's short story, "A Painful Case." Mr. James Duffy, Joyce's protagonist, strongly resembles the Michael Kramer of Hauptmann's play by that name. It is ironical that Duffy, engaged in translating this play, fails to heed its warning and suffers a fate similar to Kramer's own.[1] Georg Büchner was an early nineteenth-century dramatist, a political radical and militant socialist—strong fare for the conservative Elyot Standish. In his play, *Dantons Tod* (*Danton's Death,* 1835), Danton first appears as apathetic and conservative, but his idealistic commitment leads to his defiance of Robespierre and to his death. Elyot's very lack of commitment results in his present and continuing spiritual death, alone in a room with his notes on Büchner. The pattern of imagery connected with Elyot's studies is continued in Part Two, where he is "a raker of dust, a rattler of bones" (p. 170) and has begun "to arrange his life in numbered pages" (p. 190).

Each of the secondary characters in the novel is associated with either Eden or Elyot Standish, the two chief representatives of the living and the dead in the novel. In choosing to associate with the cold and calculating Muriel Raphael, Elyot is choosing to continue his isolation, for he remains in isolation when they are together. Mrs. Standish, noticing his attraction to Muriel,

---

[1] A full discussion of Joyce's use of Hauptmann may be found in Marvin Magalaner, *Time of Apprenticeship: The Fiction of Young James Joyce* (London, 1959). Magalaner notes that the orderliness of Duffy's room closely resembles Hauptmann's stage directions for Kramer's studio, and that the climactic scenes of Hauptmann's play and Joyce's story are very similar.

thinks that Elyot had chosen distance, even as a child, and that he is still the same sullen child. From Muriel's assurance and self-satisfaction in the supper club with Elyot (pp. 244-245) White creates an amusing scene which prefigures the luncheon party of the Crab-Shell, the Bon-bon and the Volcano in the last chapter of *Riders in the Chariot.* Muriel, preening, is like a great gawdy parrot with mauve lids and scarlet claws. The amusing *cachet* provided by Schiaparelli suggests the scarlet woman or Whore of Babylon of the Apocalypse.

The general pattern of imagery associated with Muriel, as with Sidney in *Happy Valley,* is based upon metal and glass. Elyot actually finds Muriel repulsive, with a voice that cuts and a body that is one with her dress, steely textured, "metal-plated" (p. 199). On another occasion she appears to be "lacquered all over like her hat, altogether brittle. Her face set in a lacquer smile" (p. 211). Both Sidney and Muriel are cold and hard, but whereas Sidney is shown within a demonic context based on her actively malignant will, Muriel is merely one of the living dead, harmful chiefly to herself. Looking at Muriel, Elyot sees that their intimacy is only "the last flicker of boredom experienced by two people that habit kept united" (p. 277), nothing but a "glassy tension" (p. 280). And this, Elyot realizes, is what he has chosen and encouraged. Their non-relationship is a relationship between the dead.

In the first chapter, White uses the image of a cocoon to indicate withdrawal from life, and connects this to the plain descriptive meaning that Elyot likes to remain shut in his room. Although "like" and "as" are omitted, the verbal construction is that of a simile rather than metaphorical identity. Near the end of the novel the cocoon image begins to expand and move towards archetypal and anagogic metaphor, a statement of hypothetical identity. The white cocoon of Elyot's lit room at night begins to assume the aspects of tomb or grave cloths. Within this receptacle Elyot is contained, and into it washes "no intrusion from the outer darkness" (p. 283) such as that which affects the pathetically ingenuous but sympathetic Connie Tiarks. There is a curious inversion here, reminiscent of D. H. Lawrence, of the traditional associations of light and darkness, with Elyot being "suspended, isolated" in light (compare the "glaring light" of the demonic vision of Anna Karenina) and the living world being part of the darkness beyond. In Chapter 19 the cocoon becomes a "private shell" (p. 307), but the type of image has returned to the level of the descriptive metaphor. Elyot refuses even to attempt to understand or accept his mother's fall from grace. He lacks the emotional energy to condemn and is content, like the dying Mrs. Standish, to abandon the incident to an attic-ful of sordid mistakes. The attic, repository of dead objects, seems to provide a suitable graveyard.

In the last few chapters we begin to see, as something crystallizes in Connie Tiarks' mind, that the novel's theme is based upon an *if only*—"If only the world had been made in a different way. If only the blind could see" (pp. 316-317)—a *cri de coeur* which is simultaneously perceived by the author to be false: the world has *not* been made in a different way. But whereas the statement made by literature (art), the "poetic knowledge"[2] conveyed by the whole poem or novel, is *hypothetical*, it cannot be *false,* by the very definition of a work of art. The literary hypothesis, "let us suppose that," is based upon faith, not falsity. On the inadequate basis of an "if only," compassion tends to degenerate into pity. After Mrs. Standish's death, Connie speaks the theme that has failed to materialize: "We're not meant to live in isolation. We're—I could love you" (p. 320). With Elyot's cold refusal, her passion is exorcized: "she couldn't give what Elyot wouldn't take" (p. 321). The telephone box in which Connie makes her decision to marry Harry recalls the box of Elyot's bedroom-study, which has become cocoon and tomb. Connie, unlike Elyot, is in touch with what lies outside her box.

The final chapter of this novel is imperfectly linked to the whole. It is almost an epilogue, in the sense of an appendix rather than a natural conclusion which is an integrated part of the whole. Indeed this short chapter suggests a mood of recantation

---

[2] Jacques and Raissa Maritain, *The Situation of Poetry: Four Essays on the Relations between Poetry, Mysticism, Magic and Knowledge,* trans. Marshall Suther (New York: Kraus reprint, 1968), *passim.*

which attempts the reversal of what the work has portrayed, like the palinode in medieval literature. Elyot now drifts in a state of Limbo, instead of the isolation of the tomb-like white cocoon. The queasy drunk (prototype of the man who fell among thieves, the fellow human being in need) whom Elyot had rejected in the first chapter is now "accepted" (p. 333) and is part of himself. The invisible but impassable walls which have divided Elyot from other people throughout the book are now dissolving. Limbo is suggested once more in the description of Elyot as "bound nowhere in particular" (p. 334). He feels distance unfurling; the bus journey attempts to suggest a spiritual journey or quest which is to reach safe harbour at last. Elyot yawns like someone who has been asleep and has only just wakened. White is reaching here for the archetypal and anagogic metaphor which he handles so superbly in his next six novels.

In *The Living and the Dead,* however, something has gone wrong. Not only is the last chapter unsupported by the rest of the novel, but even *within* the chapter itself the vision behind it seems to be continually undercut by a scepticism which is at odds with the attempted metaphor. The faces are only *potentially* communicative, the mouths *almost* spoke, the faces are *almost* sentient. It appears that "soberly, by daylight" Elyot *still* lives "a life of segregation" (p. 334), his defences against other people are still raised and his tomb-like isolation is still intact.

One of the main metaphors in this last chapter is that of the Chinese boxes, "one inside the other, leading to an infinity of other boxes, to an infinity of purpose" (p. 333). The first boxes, which suggest the image to Elyot's mind, follow from his recognition of his own house as two receptacles which contain the material possessions and the aspirations of those who have occupied the house. Elyot thinks, or hopes, that "alone, he was yet not alone, uniting as he did the themes of so many other lives" (p. 333). On the next page, the boxes become an infinity of boxes, whose unity has no end. But whereas the entire novel supports or validates the box image as Elyot's isolating cocoon or tomb, it repudiates and denies the Chinese-box metaphor of the last chapter.

We have noted that Connie's attempt to reach out to others has been linked with a telephone box, and the glass box which Elyot has associated with Muriel has actually been the gift of Connie. After Connie has left, for she cannot give what Elyot will not take, he notices the box, "so intimately connected with the two alternatives, Muriel Raphael or Connie Tiarks" (p. 322). But the alternatives seem to be between two forms of death rather than between life and death, with Muriel remaining "brittle glass" and Connie "the possessive eiderdown" (p. 322). Once again, the image is simply a descriptive metaphor or simile; it does not posit identity, as do archetypal and anagogic metaphors. Since death by suffocation seems no more desirable than death by shattering or by cold, Elyot seems to be correct in dismissing these two alternatives, but the "suggestion of growth" (p. 322) beyond them is left unsatisfactorily vague.

And is the author's conception of Connie consistent throughout this chapter? Is the Connie who gives us an epiphany—"We're not meant to live in isolation"—the same Connie who is only a possessive eiderdown? The Chinese boxes which reach to infinity seem intended to relate to Connie's boxes so as to form a pattern of box imagery of life and love which will contrast with the box and cocoon pattern of deathly isolation. In his later novels, White uses such opposing patterns of imagery to great effect, as with the rope/chain imagery of *Riders in the Chariot*. But this is not so in *The Living and the Dead,* where the pattern is undercut by rejecting Connie and by detaching the image from theme and narrative. Imagery must support theme rather than attempt to work against it. While the novel's theme remains "If only the blind could see," the situation cannot be remedied by Chinese boxes.

The dust-jacket of the 1962 reissue of this novel informs us that it is Eden who represents the living. Certainly Eden is intended to be one of the chief representatives of this select group. Her unhappy experiences in youth, her abortive efforts at living which culminate in an actual abortion in Mrs. Angelotti's room, have given her some understanding of life and love: "a knowledge of the sterile years, made her compassionate" (p. 258).

Mixed, however, with the conception of Eden as *growing* in goodness or vitality[3] are two other conceptions of her character which undercut the effect of the first.

On the one hand there is a suggestion that Eden is "right from the start," to paraphrase Pound's Mauberley. In the first chapter she is linked with "the positive people" (p. 16), the word positive being repeated three times in three consecutive sentences. This too-static concept of her goodness is expressed in her conversation with her love, Joe Barnett, on the superficiality of party politics: "I can believe in right as passionately as I have it in me to live. This is what I have to express, with you, anyone, *with everyone who has the same conviction*" (p. 239, italics mine). The last phrase suggests the rigid conception implied in the title and developed in the theme, a conception of two groups of people (one vital, one petrified) and a great gulf fixed between. It is part of Elyot's tragedy that Eden cannot relate to him except in opposition. This is one way in which Eden's goodness and vitality differs from Arthur's in *The Solid Mandala*. Whereas Arthur is passionately concerned for Waldo's fate, Eden's passion is directed solely towards "the right" as an impersonal ideal; for those who do not share this passion she feels nothing but scorn: "The arch-enemies were the stultifying, the living dead. The living chose to oppose these" (p. 331). Even as a child, her "life" is contrasted with Elyot's "death." There is, then, something too isolated and rigid about Eden's goodness.

On the other hand, however, Eden is portrayed as naively idealistic, sentimental and lacking in compassion. At times she is as isolated as Elyot ("less communicative than furniture") and at no point does she attempt to disturb Elyot's isolation. As a child she hates him with a passion equal to his own, and as adults they are related only by external circumstances, as by the crowd which jostles them against each other, making a relationship which otherwise "didn't exist" (p. 292). If this conception of Eden as naive and sentimental were confined to the first part of

---

[3] Cf. D. H. Lawrence's *natural aristocrat* who belongs to a higher order because he is *more alive*: "Aristocracy," *Reflections on the Death of a Porcupine and Other Essays* (Bloomington: Indiana University Press, 1963).

the novel, it could be harmonized with a conception of her as growing in understanding. But Elyot finds her, at the novel's end, "as stubborn in an attitude, as unchanging as a picture on the wall, the surprised child or the sulky flapper, was the same Eden in a different frame" (p. 331).

There seems to be something unresolved in White's conception of Eden's character which is underlined in the choice of alternatives seen at the end; the living dead are to be opposed by "the protest of self-destruction or by what, by what, if not an intenser form of living" (p. 331). The latter alternative is left vague, and something of Eden's and Elyot's confusion as to the *nature* of this intenser form of life seems to belong to White's own youthful vision. The former alternative, the protest of self-destruction (which had attracted Sidney Furlow, and was associated in *Happy Valley* with a pattern of demonic imagery), is the choice made, in one sense, by both Eden and Joe. Eden sees her relation to the spiritual dead strictly as one of *opposition*, a concept used repeatedly in the novel in the words or thoughts of Eden and Joe. They wish to oppose the living to "the destroyers" (p. 240), the diseased, the indifferent. In White's later novels, on the other hand, the spiritually alive are concerned with helping, not merely opposing, the "dead."

After Joe's death, Julia remembers his conviction that the world is full of promise and significance, that it will be "a world to live in" (p. 325). Nevertheless, the chapter which marks Joe and Eden's consummation of their love emphasizes the helplessness of human love to alter the sickness and horror of the world, "a sick world mewing at the windowpane, lying with its guts frozen on the sea wall" (p. 261). Their love is an escapist interlude, a personal warmth incapable of touching the vast cold beyond themselves. In *Happy Valley*, Hilda is the world, sick, suffering. In *The Living and the Dead*, the world is imaged as already dead and hence past hope: "I love Eden, he said, but what can this do for the world, the sick, stinking world that sits in the stomach like a conscience? He was helpless" (p. 262). Despite his personal conviction that "a state of rightness" (p. 186) must exist and must ultimately prevail, Joe seems to be as helpless as Connie Tiarks in the face of Elyot's refusal to accept love.

Many of the minor characters and events in this novel reveal White's comic genius and the wide range of mood or emotional tone, from pathos to rollicking laughter or wry satire, encompassed by his novels. Wally Collins, Mrs. Standish's lover after she has reached middle age, prefigures the Parkers' Irish neighbours, the irrepressible O'Dowds of *The Tree of Man.* The saxophonist's vulgarity, cockiness, and touching stupidity do not hide his goodness and kindness. The scenes with Wally—in his residence at the Godiva Mansions, at Brighton one weekend, in the supper club where he plays the saxophone—are comic triumphs. There is more than a touch of vaudeville as well as the bravura of melodrama in their affair.

The Sunday night party in Maida Vale, "the archetype of parties" (p. 297), is comedy with all the stops out. It prefigures the "perv" party in *Riders,* where Norman struts out the ritual dance of the primordial bird. At the Maida Vale party, people and objects seem to *flow,* except for the two china elephants on the mantelpiece, which are anchored by means of their shocking ugliness. The point of view shifts constantly from character to character. Wally thinks: "Just when the party began to go, it made him mad, and nice and warm and matey, with a girl in hand, so many girls in so many hands, not that the Old Girl, gee, and a big blue bump on the side of her face" (p. 305). White uses stream-of-consciousness technique to indicate the increasing confusion of Mrs. Standish's mind, with her drunkenness increasing until she vomits the last fragments of her dignity onto the carpet:

> It goes rrrrr. Bbpp! Take it from me. I know. Spinning and spinning and spin—
> That the voice broke the thick gelatinous effort to talk or think it was the last shred the red put on for a purpose you looked to find on the carpet the big booming rose bury your face and hide bury the sick tick.
> Take it easy, she heard.

It was not so far to the carpet, kneeward, to lay down a head, and the roaring funnel of a mouth. (P. 306.)

The epigraphs of *The Solid Mandala* speak of "another world" *inside* this one. In *The Living and the Dead,* there are "two countries" (p. 236), two languages of intuition and reason. The glass box, connected at this point only with Muriel, represents the *opacity* of reason or "finite knowledge." White has Elyot use the word "symbol" here in its first or literal sense, as the communicable unit of knowledge. While these two countries may *suggest* the two worlds as revealed in *The Solid Mandala,* they are by no means synonymous with them. Both reason and instinct (which is frequently the meaning of "intuition" in *The Living and the Dead*) belong to the physical or outer world, as Northrop Frye notes in connection with the romantic symbolism of the early Yeats and the French Symbolists: "The world as will is, of course, an essential part of the order of nature, hence it is really a hyper-physical world, and in no sense a spiritual one."[4]

The epigraph from Helvétius for White's second novel is relevant to this conception of the living and the dead which contrasts those who live by intuition with those who live by reason. Helvétius puts his reader under the guardianship of pleasure and grief; these two are to watch over thoughts and actions, engender passions, excite aversions, loves and hates; to reveal truth and to plunge one in error; and to lead, eventually, to "*les principes simples*" whose development is attached to the order and goodness of the moral world. The dualism in Helvétius' first phrase (pleasure and anguish) suggests the experience of the novel's characters. The simple resolution of Helvétius' conclusion, however, finds no adequate expression in the novel, despite a small but significant pattern suggestive of some universal design in the universe. One wonders about the adequacy of Helvétius' vision: what if the world is not *simply* orderly, moral, and good? Where do "the blind" of Connie's anguished cry fit into Helvétius' scheme? Kitty's father, Mr. Goose the blacksmith, seems to

[4] Northrop Frye, "Yeats and the Language of Symbolism," *University of Toronto Quarterly* XVII (1947), 9.

speak for Helvétius, eighteenth-century materialist philosopher and encyclopedist, when he tells Kitty that man is fundamentally good, rotted by circumstances but "born for the expression of positive good" (p. 44). Joe has a similar faith in faith and a conviction that "even if something had gone wrong, man in himself was right enough" (p. 84). Helvétius believed that morality and law should be defined by the public interest, with the good being that which is best for the greatest number. We hear an echo of this in Eden's conception of "the futility of Joe, as Joe. Just another drop. But the many Joe Barnetts, Elyot. It's the drops that fill the bucket. . . . It's the bucket that'll make the splash" (p. 331). None of White's later novels present this additive or mechanical view of the human being as merely a unit in a sum.

It is Julia Fallon, Joe's cousin and the Standish family servant, who shares with Eden a prominent place in the world of intuition and the land of the living. Julia, in youth, is like a Flemish primitive, and in maturity, a comfortable Vermeer. The first chapter connects her with bread and cheese, bones and flesh. Integrity and humility form the basis of her character. It is Julia, living largely by intuition, who comes closest to Elyot, through her senses rather than her mind. In Julia's relation to *things* we find the closest link between this and White's other novels. Julia's honesty somehow corresponds to the honesty of substances. "Honesty" is a word we find frequently used throughout White's novels. The novel posits "a correspondence between Julia and the form of the yellow table" (p. 16). The imagery frequently remains on the level of descriptive metaphor or simile: "Her words, her hands were as stolid as yellow cheese" (p. 16). It seems to be moving, however, with Julia, towards the radical metaphor of the later novels, the full metaphorical statement of identity of the archetypal and anagogic imagery. Julia's whole existence is real and tangible; she and the objects that she touches are "united by this strain of absorption" (p. 58). To the mystery of the world at large, Julia can only oppose "her own too solid flesh" (p. 325). Eden and Joe, in their search for "a substance for which the symbols stood" (p. 204), are linked with Julia and contrasted with Elyot and Muriel Raphael. After the death of Joe Barnett,[5] Eden tries to reject the body, since it must die, and to deny "the kindness of the body, the many articulate ways it can have. It was easy to over-value these, and to set up the physical image as Julia did" (p. 328). This partial rejection of Julia by Eden—and by White?—seems to be part of the general failure in the conception or vision behind this novel which results in the final palinode.

In *The Solid Mandala,* the theme of the spiritually living and the living dead is embodied in the relation between the twin brothers. Waldo's narcissistic self-absorption and total inability to love make him dead throughout his long life; as Mrs. Poulter reassures Arthur at the novel's end, he was "ready to die. He only took such a time dying" (p. 303). Waldo is like Elyot Standish in his intellectual pretensions, his smugness, his suppressed fear at his inability to relate to others, and his refusal to take or accept love. Arthur, like Connie Tiarks, comes to the agonizing realization that he can't give what Waldo refuses to take. But Arthur blames himself for not loving sufficiently, and feels at times that he and Waldo are equally lost. He has none of Eden's self-satisfaction, nor her lack of compassion for those whose attitudes differ from her own. In his second novel, White seems to be wavering between comedy and tragedy. If the story is to be Elyot's tragedy, why the final palinode? It seems rather to be intended as comedy, but "the paradox of distance" (p. 113) and the mystery of failure are left unresolved.

Unlike White's other novels, *The Living and the Dead* is marked by the particular period of its birth, the late 1930s. The politico-social conscience of the times and a strong proletarian sympathy are reflected in much of the literature of this period, and White's second novel is no exception. Eden might even be taken as a forerunner of the "angry young man" of the fifties. A split in White's sympathies may be detected in the contrast between the politically activist attitude of Joe and Eden, and Julia's peculiar insight which issues in scorn for things political: " 'If

---

[5] The 1941 Viking edition of the novel is dedicated "To Joe Rankin, for his selflessness and patience," a dedication dropped from the 1962 London edition.

you're working up political, Joe Barnett, you'll hear me sick out loud' " (p. 185). Earlier, Eden's activist orientation has been contrasted with Connie's concern for the Spanish people, a concern which the narrator implies is worse than useless in its quietism. Yet Joe is a cabinetmaker by trade and, like Julia and the protagonists in most of the novels which follow, an initiate of the pleasure in familiar things, the clean grain of wood or sweet smell of pine shavings. The ambivalence in White's sympathies at this period has been fully resolved before *The Aunt's Story,* seven years later. Henceforth, his common man or woman (Stan Parker, Mrs. Poulter) is simply *man,* and words such as *proletarian* or *bourgeois,* with their political connotations, do not apply. His later protagonists combine Joe and Eden's love and concern with Julia's peculiar insight and sensitivity to the mystery in familiar substances. And their way is *inward.*

*And so, it comes to pass in time, that the earth ceases for us
to be a weltering chaos. . . . Nothing is despicable—all is
meaningful; nothing is small—all is part of a whole, whose
beginning and end we know not.*

OLIVE SCHREINER, THE STORY OF AN AFRICAN FARM

chapter 5 A modern odyssey

The epigraphs to the three parts of *The Aunt's Story* suggest a
state of tension between a set of apparent opposites which the
characters in the novel seek to reconcile. The first epigraph, from
Olive Schreiner, opposes distance or isolation, "that solitary land
of the individual experience," to nearness or communication with
others. The second, from Henry Miller, opposes fragmentation or
division to unity. The third, again from Olive Schreiner, contrasts
madness and sanity, appearance and reality. And in Part Three
White, like Schreiner, inverts the normal perspective: as Theodora Goodman's life becomes most real, the established community pronounces her mad. She is advised to defer, however, to
the wishes of the reasonable ones, who are described as admirable though limited. Ultimately, the novel shows that the opposites suggested in the epigraphs (freedom/necessity, distance/
nearness, fragmentation/unity, appearance/reality) are to one
another as Theodora/Ludmilla is to Alyosha Sergei, "that complementary curse and blessing, a relationship" (p. 193).

The first chapter suggests what Holstius later terms the "two irreconcilable halves," establishing a tension between the pairs: freedom and entrapment, life and death, love and hate. Meroë, evoked in Theodora's thoughts by Lou's questioning, is the Goodman family house in which "the human body had disguised its actual mission of love and hate" (p. 11) beneath the surface of the commonplace. Mrs. Goodman's death has set Theodora free, but this freedom is seen in the perspective of the final containment of the coffin towards which Theodora herself moves; or, as Theodora later thinks, sitting in a public house with Pearl Brawne, "Life is full of alternatives, but no choice" (p. 120). The wooden box which holds Mrs. Goodman's body lies upstairs, but in one sense it occupies the centre of the stage throughout the chapter.[1] The box "endeavoured" to contain a mystery; the narrator implies that the endeavour fails, not because there is no mystery but because the mystery will not be contained in the box or revealed in the corpse, but involves some freedom which is not negated or cancelled by death. An emphasis upon freedom is found once again at the beginning of Part Two. Theodora, with her newfound freedom to travel, is now in the Hôtel du Midi on the Mediterranean, yet she feels that something is needed to "justify her large talk of independence to Henriette" (p. 132). The novel builds steadily from the problems and paradoxes posed in the first chapter towards Holstius' revelation, in the last chapter, of the unity and continuity (or true permanence) in which these halves are contained.

Theodora's conversation with Moraïtis, the Greek 'cellist, is thematically important. Theodora likens the Greece of Moraïtis' description, a bare country of bones, to Meroë, her childhood home. She too comes from a country of bones. This is re-emphasized as Moraïtis takes his leave of Theodora; they are "compatriots in the country of the bones" (p. 102), a country from which Huntly Clarkson is excluded. Earlier, Theodora's headmistress had prophesied that the girl would "see clearly, beyond the bone" (p. 56). Her conversation with the 'cellist points to the paradoxes in the first chapter and to some continuity of life, as

---

[1] "The child shivered for the forgotten box, which she had not seen but knew" (p. 125).

Moraïtis terms it, which contains these paradoxes within a larger unity. Theodora, however, perceives that Moraïtis has reached some further phase or stage than she has herself achieved to date. Moraïtis accepts the distances, the isolation, and his own inadequacies. And something flowing, or overflowing, within him cannot be contained by either his body or the room.

The last chapter provides an orchestral finale to the whole work. The musical analogy is made within the novel itself at this point, and is justified not only by bravura passages such as the following but also by the entire structure of the chapter:

> Sometimes against the full golden theme of corn and the whiter pizzicato of the telephone wires there was a counterpoint of houses . . . a smooth passage of ponds and trees . . . a big bass barn. . . . It was a frill of flutes twisted round a higher theme, to grace, but only grace, the solemnity of living and of days. There were now the two coiled themes. There was the flowing corn song, and the deliberate accompaniment of houses, which did not impede, however structural, because it was part of the same integrity of purpose and of being. (P. 253.)

This passage should be correlated with the opening paragraph of the chapter. The first and fullest golden theme of corn is also the flowing corn song which trumpets "as if for a judgment" (p. 249).

Comparing the images in these passages with some of the images in White's first two novels, we note a curious inversion of technique. In the earlier novels, the image often remains on the descriptive level of simile. Contextually, that is, it is simile, even when "like" and "as" are omitted. In *The Aunt's Story*, on the other hand, the image may be technically a simile (the corn trumpets *as if* for a judgment) yet in the total context it is apocalyptic imagery which posits identity between the blaring, trumpeting corn and some judgment bearing on "the frail human reed" (p. 249). Time and eternity, those two coiled themes, are in the process of becoming one. Meanwhile, the passage of days (the counterpoint of houses) shares the "integrity of purpose and of being" with the golden trumpet-call to some final revelation. The mood and tone of this last chapter in *The Aunt's Story* is plainly apocalyptic.

Mrs. Johnson, who shelters Theodora briefly, is part of that integrity of being. She is described as having, even as a girl, an unconscious confidence in "the logic of growth and continuity" (p. 266). Mrs. Johnson, however, like Theodora's friend Violet Adams, belongs to the sandy shallows of life. It is natural that she should call the reasonable world to her aid when she is faced, in the mountain shack, by a situation beyond her comprehension. Disintegration and solidity, appearance and reality, madness and sanity are constantly reshaping themselves so that, as Holstius tells Theodora, "there is sometimes little to choose between the reality of illusion and the illusion of reality" (p. 272). At the foot of the mountain, below Holstius' hut, a *disintegrating* light falls upon man's illusions of solidity. Illusory permanence can be as deathly as congealed blood and stagnant water. The Johnsons' marble clock may remind the reader of Vic Moriarty's clock, which is associated with her life in time and which is smashed at the time of her death.

Theodora, in the hut above the disintegrating world where light and silence hint at some ultimate revelation of truth, doubts her capacity for humility. Into this situation comes Holstius, the owner-apparent of the mountain shack. His approach is heralded by fire (Theodora's little fire is soon to consume her doubt, p. 270) and fire imagery continues to surround the man: his skin is "ruddy fire" and the bowl of his pipe flowers with rosy fire.[2] Holstius invites Theodora to "accept the two irreconcilable halves" (p. 272) of joy and sorrow, life and death, and to recognize that "true permanence is a state of multiplication and division" (p. 278). Subsequently, Theodora watches for Holstius' return through the trees; she watches "for the tree walking" (p. 273), the living tree of man which will become the basic symbol of White's next novel.[3] While waiting, she scrubs the wooden floor

---

[2] Holstius' name is a near-anagram of "holiest"; in Matt. 3: 11, the baptism of fire is associated with the Holy Ghost.

[3] See Frye, *Anatomy of Criticism,* p. 146: "The tree of life may also be a burning tree, the unconsumed bush of Moses, the candlestick of Jewish ritual, or the 'rosy cross' of later occultism."

of the hut, mindful of "its ingrained humility and painful knots" (p. 273) and feeling herself to be as simple as a scrubbed board. The image recalls the end of *Happy Valley* and the relation that is suggested between Oliver's emotional state and the condition of his house, which has been swept clean and bare for the next occupant. And, indeed, the mood at the ending of these novels is very similar. In both, it is one of calm and happy anticipation. Both Oliver and Theodora are victors, with their triumph unrecognized by the world at large.

Structurally, *The Aunt's Story* is a comedy, according to the generic definition of the archetypal narrative structures given in Chapter 2 above. The novel ranges through all the different phases of comedy, from the first or most ironic phase, to romantic phases of comedy which approach the romance proper. In a romance, the central movement is dialectical: "everything is focussed on a conflict between the hero and his enemy, and all the reader's values are bound up with the hero. Hence the hero of romance is analogous to the mythical Messiah or deliverer who comes from an upper world and his enemy is analogous to the demonic powers of the lower world."[4] In *The Aunt's Story* it is Holstius, not the heroine Theodora, who is analogous to the mythical Messiah. Generically, *The Aunt's Story* is not a romance, since the protagonist is fallible and human, not idealized, and since at the end of her quest she defers to the ordinary world, whose values are opposed to hers.

The novel moves, in its ending, into the most ironic phase of comedy, in which a humorous society triumphs, at least to outward appearances. This is the ironic triumph of the reasonable ones who come to offer Theodora simple, nourishing food and to encourage her to relax in a hospital room, where she may tell the story of her life. The opening of the last chapter is as ironic as its close. Theodora faces the nervous man in the train, a man who lives only on the surface of life and who talks of his home, his mother, and his cocktail cabinet.[5] The majority of Part Three,

---

[4] Ibid., p. 187.

[5] Contemporary dramatists have frequently identified the cocktail cabinet with modern society. John Osborne makes use of it in *Epitaph for George Dillon*. Harold Pinter, in one of his rare comments on his own plays, described his dramatic theme as follows: " 'I write about the weasel under the cocktail

however, before the Johnsons return with the doctor, is comedy which verges on romance rather than irony. Northrop Frye describes the romantic phase of comedy as presenting a society which is moving towards redemption, taking on an increasingly religious cast so that it seems to be drawing away from human experience altogether. If it were to move further in this direction, that is, it would pass beyond literature into an apocalyptic or abstractly mythical world. *The Aunt's Story* does not follow the path to this end; it remains firmly within the world and within human experience, while extending, as great art always does, the former limits of that experience.

The Aunt's Story uses Homer's *Odyssey* as a mythic framework for Theodora's quest, just as Joyce used it in *Ulysses,* but with a far looser parallelism of event and character than we find in Joyce's novel. *The Odyssey,* as archetypal quest, is one of the two structural pillars in *The Aunt's Story*. In this novel, as in his others, White uses another archetype common in Western literature, that of the four levels of experience or states of the human soul—from the innocence of childhood, through experience, suffering and death, to redemption (variously described as Paradise Regained, the New Jerusalem, the land of Beulah, and so on). The specific use of Meroë and Abyssinia to connote the first and the last of these four states, seems to have been suggested by Samuel Johnson's eighteenth-century philosophical romance, *Rasselas*.[6] But *Rasselas,* as it turns out, is not *The Aunt's Story*'s only myth, as the numerous references to Homer's *Odyssey* (surely a more powerful version of the quest than Johnson's story) make clear. The successful quest has three main stages: conflict, death-struggle, and discovery or exaltation of the hero. While these three parts are found in *The Aunt's Story,* there is no simple correspondence, in this order, to the three stages of romance narrative structure. The three stages, however, sometimes incomplete, may be found within each of *The Aunt's Story*'s three parts.

cabinet' ": Ralph Hicklin, "Pinter's Sitting Pretty (Ugly)," *Globe Magazine,* 22 April 1967, p. 10.

[6] See Manfred Mackenzie, "Patrick White's Later Novels: A Generic Reading," *Southern Review* I, 3 (1965), 8: "*Rasselas,* it turns out, is *The Aunt's Story*'s myth."

There are two legendary countries within the novel which correspond to Homer's Ithaca: Moraïtis' Greece, and Theodora's Meroë. The "country of bones" is associated with all three. The Meroë outside Sydney in which Theodora spends her childhood and experiences the state of innocence corresponds to the Ithaca of Odysseus' youth, before the Trojan war and his many years of wandering, while the legendary Meroë in Abyssinia, to which she hopes to return at last, is Ithaca as the Promised Land, the goal of the quest, the state of reconciliation after conflict and suffering. Theodora reaches her goal with Holstius on a mountain in the American West, above a trumpeting of yellow corn. Since the American autumn corresponds to the Australian spring, the imagery surrounding Theodora's "return to Abyssinia" (p. 251) suggests that she is embracing all continents, all seasons.

Chapter 2 depicts Theodora's childhood innocence in Meroë, the Goodmans' family home. Roselight pervades the *morning* of Theodora's life, "in which she curled safe still, but smiling for them to wake her" (p. 14). A feeling of tension, which reminds us of the paradoxes established in the first chapter, relates the northern side of the house, where pines reflect a dark green light, to the southern side, with roselight of morning. Theodora's parents are part of this pattern of tension; Father ("not unlike a tree," p. 15) is consistently associated with the pines (through the placing of his room, his door, and a dense network of images throughout the chapter) and Mother, with the roses. Whereas Mother and Fanny, the frivolous ones, do not accept the grub at the heart of the rose, the serpent in Eden, Theodora is unwilling to condemn something belonging to "the sum total of the garden" (p. 14). There is even the subtle implication that Theodora has something in common with the grub, for the foetal imagery quoted above, which at first appears to suggest innocence, follows hard upon the description of the curled grub. This suggestion (of a self-destructive element within Theodora as the grub is within the rose) is reinforced by later parts of the novel, as she matures and discovers within herself the ability to hate.

Theodora's father, the scholar who reads Herodotus and Homer, tells Theodora of "another Meroë . . . a dead place, in the black country of Ethiopia" (p. 15). The novel systematically develops this second Meroë as an analogue of a superior state or level of being ("New Abyssinia," as Manfred Mackenzie has termed it[7]) as in the after-life of the Christian myth. For the time being, however, the reader is simply aware that it is natural for a child to fear death, and that the child Theodora fears this other Meroë, where roses are brown, curtains ashy, and "the eyes of the house had closed" (p. 16).[8] All the images of this second Meroë are identified with man's physical death. Mrs. Goodman also fears death, but her solution, which is not to be Theodora's, is "let us be reckless. . . . And die" (p. 18). Father is grimly aware that death lasts for a long time.

As for the first Meroë, Theodora feels free to love its golden stone and to take possession of its peaceful mystery. Her childish composition describes the first Meroë as "big enough for peace of mind" (p. 16), but she finds this Eden circumscribed: "Our Place was not beginning and end" (p. 17). It is the same detached viewpoint which first suggests to Theodora some inadequacy in Father, "who was thick and mysterious as a tree, but also hollow" (p. 18). Holstius, the father-surrogate in Part Three who appears as the living tree, ultimately replaces George Goodman, grazier, the *hollow* man whose quest is unsuccessful. In *The Solid Mandala,* the twins' father is a very similar figure; both George Brown and George Goodman suggest "The Hollow Men" of Eliot's poem, type of the secular modern man. Theodora's own quest is not simply the desire to "know everything" (p. 32) but also the need to be rid of an intolerable burden of sadness which she carries unbeknown to the world (p. 18). Her quest thus suggests two archetypes: the insatiable thirst for knowledge typified by Goethe's Faust, and the great burden of guilt and despair carried by Bunyan's Pilgrim and imaged by Kierkegaard as an abyss of despair. Twentieth-century literature abounds in versions of this archetype, from Saul Bellow's *Dangling Man* to Camus' *L'Étranger.* Since Theodora's efforts *to know* are not confined to the rational mind and to books, as

[7] "Yes, Let's Return to Abyssinia," *Essays in Criticism* XIV (1964), 435.

[8] Cf. Eccles. 12: 13: "and those that look out of the windows be darkened."

Father's tend to be, and since she retains the strengths of simplicity and humility, Theodora's way is that of Bunyan's pilgrim,
not of Faust.

Theodora's twelfth birthday is marked by two events—the
lightning, and the visit of the Man who was Given his Dinner.
Apocalyptic imagery surrounds this figure, tramp or prophet,
whose conversation "made the walls dissolve . . . as flat as water.
. . . But the man walked on the dissolved walls, and his beard
blew" (p. 34). While Theodora finds the Man unlike anyone she
knows, except possibly Father, the Man tells her that she is like
her father used to be. Although Mrs. Goodman's act, refusing to
eat dinner with her husband's old friend, is more terrible than
the lightning, it is Theodora and the Man who are more closely
identified with its power. Theodora shares his humiliation as he
eats outside the house ("his act covered their shame," p. 35) and
listens to his story of himself and her father, lost in the moun-
tains in a snowstorm. One man's need for another is illustrated
at its simplest, physical level, as shared body heat saves them
from freezing. The archetypal significance is reinforced as the
chapter ends, with their encircling arms revealed as a mandala,
a living circle of love. By her twelfth birthday the girl has replaced her father in this spiritual odyssey, for it is Theodora who
sits, in an eternal now, beneath the sheltering tree with the Man
who was Given his Dinner.

Chapter 2 has shown Theodora's first steps from innocence to
experience. At school (Chapter 3) she is beginning to accept isolation and contempt, to recognize the essential loneliness of the
quest which is so poignantly expressed in the epigraph from
Olive Schreiner. The stained glass window of the church near
her school which shows St. George's victory over the dragon suggests one more archetypal version of the quest; Theodora's
offers "subtler variations" (p. 48), for Theodora is herself both
dragon and saint, or saint and sinner, rather than the idealized
hero of romance proper. This becomes clear in the long fifth
chapter, where the parallels with Homer's *Odyssey* are most
marked. Here Theodora realizes that she has within herself "a
core of evil" (p. 115) which she finds altogether hateful, and

that "the great monster Self" (p. 122) is the dragon to be slain.

The headmistress's silent prophecy, that Theodora would be both honoured and despised, and would finally achieve a state in which the opaque world would become transparent, anticipates what the whole novel leads us to see is Theodora's experience; and, further, it suggests the other world *within* this one which we find in all White's novels from *The Aunt's Story* to *The Vivisector*.[9] The headmistress has added one more paradox, honour/contempt, to those we have already noted.

The fresh phase which follows Theodora's return from school covers the end of her adolescence, the end of her life at Meroë, and the end of her father's life. References to, and parallels with, Homer's *Odyssey* are frequent in Chapters 4 and 5, as Theodora begins to take upon herself "the perpetual odyssey on which George Goodman was embarked," a dream "more actual even than the dream of actuality" (p. 59). *The Aunt's Story,* like all White's novels, asks us to reconsider what *is* actuality and what is dream. The frequent association in the second chapter between Father and the pine trees now reinforces the archetypal quality of the Goodmans' spiritual journey. In Father's quest, Theodora is Nausicaa (p. 60), the young Phaeacian princess who conducts Odysseus to her father's court. Even as a child, Theodora had sensed that she was really "guiding Father" (p. 14), despite his show of leadership.[10] The burden of sadness which she bears is once more associated with Father through her dream of the faceless body struck by lightning and her fear that he would suffer some humiliating exclusion, "the fate of the Man who was Given his Dinner" (p. 71). Death is the ultimate exclusion to be suffered by George Goodman, "a decent cove, educated, but weak and lazy" (p. 77), according to his neighbours. The remark recalls their earlier judgment, for Theodora herself does not judge: "Her stomach was sick with the sense of responsibility that

---

9 Cf. Mackenzie, "Patrick White's Later Novels," p. 7: "For while Theodora is in one sense mad, and therefore inferior to society, she is immensely superior to 'real life' in her perception of it as a form of madness itself, in seeing 'real life' as Hell when it is cut off from the Meroë state."

10 In *The Solid Mandala* there is a similar play on apparent and actual leadership. And Arthur's sadness is rooted in his sense of his brother Waldo's exclusion from life, as Theodora's is for her father's.

Father, they said, did not have" (p. 17). In the end, as Father tells Theodora twice (pp. 77, 78), he never saw Greece.

She suffers at this time the second of her several deaths. Earlier, she has destroyed herself by shooting the little hawk with the red eye. In Chapter 2, Theodora has been identified through appearance and action with the hawk; later, she finds that shooting the hawk was like aiming at her own red eye: "I was wrong, she said, but I shall continue to destroy myself, right down to the last of my several lives" (p. 64). Now she feels dead with Father, and her childhood home is "grey water, grey ash" (p. 78). The first Meroë, as Manfred Mackenzie notes, is really a state, "a state of being associated with the country property"[11] and of being related to George Goodman as child to father. These states are now ended.

Up to this point Theodora has been, in the Homeric parallel, both Odysseus and Nausicaa. Now Theodora has set sail alone: "The sea of pines swelled, hinting at some odyssey from which there was no return. . . . But Mother had not embarked. Her world had always been enclosed by walls, her Ithaca, and here she would have kept the suitors at bay, not through love and patience, but with suitable conversation and a stick" (p. 82). Mrs. Goodman is thus an ironic version of Penelope. But Mrs. Goodman is also the sea-nymph Calypso, the tyrant Polyphemus (the one-eyed Cyclops), the cannibal Laestrygonians and the enchantress Circe. Joyce, I think, would have appreciated the joke. Theodora, living with her mother in Sydney, is discovering that any place is habitable. Just as Calypso kept Odysseus imprisoned for seven years, so Mrs. Goodman holds Theodora captive for several decades. She hopes that Theodora will not be "so heartless" as to reject filial duty, but a horrid suspicion that her daughter may yet escape "kept Mrs. Goodman breathless with anxiety" (p. 85). The possibilities of escape continue to present themselves, with Mrs. Goodman "like a one-eyed queen squinting for weaknesses. . . . It was the great tragedy of Mrs. Goodman's life that she had never done a murder. Her husband had escaped into the ground, and Theodora into silences" (p. 89).

[11] Mackenzie, "Yes, Let's Return to Abyssinia," p. 434.

Like Circe, Mrs. Goodman aspires to change Theodora into some other shape, something foreign to her daughter's own nature. And like the cannibal Laestrygonians, Mrs. Goodman aspires to consume Theodora's heart and soul, to lock them "in a little box" (p. 86) upon which Mrs. Goodman's words and will may beat as regularly as an African drum. This startling image of psychological and spiritual cannibalism is one of the few examples in *The Aunt's Story* of demonic imagery, a technique used frequently in *Happy Valley* to characterize Sidney Furlow. All the Homeric *personae* follow naturally from Mrs. Goodman's basic character as tyrant. Father had opposed her, over the Man who was Given his Dinner, and lost: "It was terrible, the strength of Mother" (p. 35). Huntly Clarkson sees Mrs. Goodman as "a small, neat, hateful woman" (p. 93), and beneath superficial friendliness he feels the strength of her tyranny. The Mrs. Goodman who has "never encouraged religion, as she herself was God" (p. 122) prefigures Voss, before his megalomania is changed by desert suffering and by his relationship with Laura. In comedy, however, the tyrant is unsuccessful. Mrs. Goodman is right in suspecting that her daughter will escape.

A more subtle danger to Theodora's odyssey presents itself in the person of Huntly Clarkson, her mother's solicitor. She finds him the more disturbing since his kindness seems to expect truth, and since both his kindness and his affluence threaten to engulf her. The pleasantness, the soft comfort of both his house and his existence relate the solicitor to Homer's Lotus-Eaters: "All the rich and sinuous sensations of silk and sables would not have been unlike the hours spent with Huntly Clarkson" (p. 98). His enjoyment is hampered by "a kind of puritan misgiving" (p. 96). The whole psychological complex of guilt feelings frequently associated with the word "puritan" in our century, often with a Manichean condemnation of the flesh and the natural world,[12] is foreign to White's novels. Hence it is interesting to find the word used by the solicitor, who seems to suspect himself of some misuse of the world's goods. Huntly collects unusual objects and hopes to add one more in the form of Theodora.

---

[12] See Patricia A. Morley, "Puritanism in the Novels of Hugh MacLennan," unpublished M.A. thesis (Carleton University, 1965), *passim*.

She is able to escape his lure when she finds him insensitive to the magnificent spectacle of an erupting volcano and "totally external" to the country of bones of which she and Moraïtis are compatriots. Listening to the music of the Greek 'cellist, Theodora perceives that the musician passes through hell and reaches paradise; and, to a certain extent, she shares in his journey. It is her first experience of the fourth state of being which in *The Aunt's Story* is associated with the "second Meroë." Moraïtis' music expresses the purity of primitive vision, and its simplicity and purity border on the dark and tragic: "But in the last movement Moraïtis rose again above the flesh. . . . There were moments of laceration . . . the savage lashes of violins. But Moraïtis walked slowly into the open. . . . The sun was in his eyes, the sky had passed between his bones" (p. 105). Moraïtis has experienced a spiritual rebirth which Theodora has temporarily shared. She holds close this shared experience, through which her existence has justified itself and her strength has been renewed. After the grotesque and somehow shameful incident at the shooting gallery, Theodora's relationship with Huntly is finished: "He was all acceptance, like a big grey emasculated cat" (p. 114). Theodora tells him that they have both survived a phase. Huntly's house provides no substitute for Ithaca.

Theodora's meeting with Pearl Brawne parallels Odysseus' encounter with the Sirens: "Theodora would have blocked her ears with wax, she could not bear to face the islands from which Pearl sang" (p. 121). On the level of "realism" or verisimilitude the purple colour which dominates the episode is suggested by the evening light of a restless sky and the neon lights of the city; and by the port wine which flows in a powerful purple stream and which Pearl consumes so enthusiastically (compare Homer's "wine-dark sea"). But *purple* is also, within this episode, the colour of blood: the veins of people on the city streets throb with "the same purple" (p. 118). It is within this pattern of imagery, then, that we find the meaning of the narrative. Pearl's "purple world" (p. 120), which Theodora finds so close yet ineluctably shut to "other hands" (that is, to Theodora herself), is the world of physical passion, Lawrence's world of blood-heat. This is the world which Theodora cannot bear and against which she blocks

her ears with wax: "Now her veins ebbed, which had flowed
before. . . . But Theodora had the strength of childhood" (p. 121).
This encounter has helped Theodora to see, more clearly
than before, that hers is not the ordinary woman's way of marriage and family. She is, as she informs Pearl, an aunt; she will
never be wife or mother: "Life is full of alternatives, but no
choice" (p. 120).

The shooting incident which terminates her relationship with
Huntly Clarkson involves a subtle parallel with the mythic
Tiresias. Theodora's character and experiences in the novel suggest an implicit identification of herself with the blind bisexual
prophet. Odysseus, after his various escapes from the Lotus-
Eaters, the Laestrygonians and Circe, descends into Hades to
learn from the ghost of Tiresias how he would reach Ithaca. The
chief characteristics of the mythic Tiresias are spiritual wisdom
and spiritual fertility or creativity, despite physical blindness and
sterility. White's Theodora is a mannish woman who endures the
humility of a moustache and who strides about like "some bloke
in skirts" (p. 60). Her *strength,* a masculine quality, is noted in
relation to Violet Adams, Pearl Brawne, her parents and the
Johnson family; and her final encounter with Mrs. Johnson reveals the reason behind the strength-motif: "Because she firmly
intended that this game for the soul of Theodora Goodman
should be finally hers" (p. 275).

There is a consistent pattern of stick imagery associated with
Theodora which provides an illustration of the symbol's dependence upon context. Thelma Herring notes that wooden images
are used to suggest Theodora's angular honesty. Lou's fluidity,
however, seems preferable to her brothers' rigidity; but when
Theodora's "oblong" dress and "carved" attitudes are contrasted
with the silky, insinuating bodies of fashionable women, "the
moral values implicit in the contrast are reversed."[13] Honesty is
depicted as a masculine quality in *Voss,* where Laura Trevelyan
offers "a frank hand, like a man" (p. 323). In *Happy Valley* the
imagery which associates Sidney with a stick or whip is used

[13] Thelma Herring, "Odyssey of a Spinster: A Study of 'The Aunt's Story,'"
Southerly XXV (1965), 19.

within a demonic context, whereas in *The Aunt's Story* the stick imagery supports the Tiresias motif. Mrs. Goodman remarks, somewhat caustically, that Theodora is "a stick with men" (p. 94), but the girl herself knows "it's good sometimes to be a stick" (p. 69). A Freudian interpretation, with the stick as a phallic symbol, would also support the Theodora/Tiresias motif. The context generally develops the stick imagery in relation to its straightness (as distinct from Pearl's generous curves) and its stiffness (the unswerving nature of Theodora's quest).

As Tiresias has experienced life as a woman,[14] so Theodora briefly experiences the feminine role on two occasions. The first is in her dance with Frank Parrott, where she is burnt by "his fire" and "they were pressed into a dependence on each other that was important" (p. 68); the second, with Frank beneath the apricot tree outside her house: "If she had touched him, touched his hand, the bones of her fingers would have wrestled with the bones in the palm of his hand" (p. 74). But Theodora finds herself unable to answer Frank's need, or her own, in this regard. She rejects Frank, as she is later to reject Huntly Clarkson. Her barrenness, which has been silently prophesied by the headmistress, is accepted and understood by Theodora herself as she journeys past Pearl's purple world of blood, wine, and passion.

The reader may still be puzzled as to why White uses the myth of Tiresias. In *The Aunt's Story,* the Tiresias motif points up at least three aspects of White's vision. The first is that sex, unlike love and hate, good and evil, is not of ultimate importance: "Life was divided, rather, into the kinder moments and the cruel, which on the whole are not conditioned by sex" (p. 24). Secondly, the bisexuality suggests a universal or unlimited quality of vision, which is not restricted to the experience of merely one half of mankind. This is one aspect of Tiresias that Eliot draws upon in *The Waste Land. The Aunt's Story* suggests that Theodora is limited neither by sex nor by age, as her face appears "ageless" (p. 95) by early middle age. Finally, fertility or creativity is not limited to physical reproduction; in *Riders in the*

[14] T. S. Eliot includes Ovid's description of this in his Notes to *The Waste Land* (1. 218).

Chariot the dyer's "seed" are the suffering people whom he loves. Theodora's reaction to the music of Moraïtis as something "more tactile than the hot words of lovers" (p. 106) expresses this spiritual sexuality. Theodora's fruit, as she is destined to be neither artist nor mother, is her soul (p. 275) or, more simply, her life and her life's goal, her quest: "Now existence justified itself" (p. 106).

Although Theodora may have the strength of childhood, she no longer has its innocence. Her life with her mother, a long stretch of years outwardly flat, is marked internally by her growing awareness of her own guilt. This guilt bears little or no relation to Huntly Clarkson's "puritan misgivings" but is her recognition of the insufficiency of her love and humility, and the terrible strength of her hate. She knows that it will not be by words ("frail slat bridges over chasms") nor by *conventional* religion that "the great monster Self will be destroyed, and that desirable state achieved" (p. 122).

In *Happy Valley* a newspaper account of a sensational murder is woven into the lives and deaths of Vic and Ernest Moriarty. Similarly, in *The Aunt's Story,* the Jack Frost incident is introduced, as Thelma Herring suggests, "proleptically, for its thematic value before the culminating appearance of the knife which Theodora picks up when tempted to kill her mother."[15] In Dostoyevsky's *The Brothers Karamazov,* Ivan is guilty, in intention and desire, of a murder he does not commit; Theodora, on the other hand, considers herself to be "guilty of a murder that has not been done" (p. 117). Dostoyevsky was fond of working into his novels actual criminal cases, as reported in the newspapers; whether or not White starts from actual cases, he transforms them, like Dostoyevsky, into archetypes and apocalyptic images of the human situation. The whimsical choice of name—Jack Frost—continues a pattern of imagery used in both *Happy Valley* and *The Living and the Dead,* where coldness is associated with death, and warmth with life. Following the newspaper account there is a repeated play on the word *frost,* as in the letter from Lou and the incident with Pearl Brawne. Both Frost and

15 Herring, "Odyssey of a Spinster," p. 19.

Theodora find it intolerable that the facade of life should be so readily accepted as the only reality. The ending of this novel reminds us of the epigraph from Olive Schreiner and the ironic description of Frost: "Always so decent and polite, under it all Frost was mad" (p. 90). The "reasonable" society, with its Frost-like facade of decency and politeness and its pretence that a smiling countenance denotes inner calm, is the 'reality' which is madness.

Mrs. Goodman's death leaves Theodora as empty as the filigree ball, hollowed out by the simplicity of what has happened and terribly aware of the "distances that separate, even in love" (p. 125). Chronologically, Chapter 6 takes us back to the point at which the novel opens, before we embark on the story of Meroë, that old house where "the human body had disguised its actual mission of love and hate" (p. 11). The basic images of the first chapter (coffin and filigree ball), which point towards Theodora's quest, recur in the sixth. The coffin is still a fact which must be taken into account in understanding the meaning and value of life; the filigree ball, still empty, waits to be filled with "sudden fire" (p. 124).

While the epigraph to Part Two does contain the paradoxes and apparent conflicts of Part One, as noted earlier, its basic affirmation is one of unity—a unity in multiplicity. In Part Three the myriad fragments of the Jardin Exotique are restructured within the definition of true permanence as "a state of multiplication and division." And the concluding statement of the epigraph to Part Two, "the great fragmentation of maturity," is clarified by the state of being which Theodora finally attains:

> In the peace that Holstius spread . . . there was no end to the lives of Theodora Goodman. These met and parted. . . . They entered into each other, so that the impulse for music in Katina Pavlou's hands, and the steamy exasperation of Sokolnikov, and Mrs. Rapallo's baroque and narcotized despair were the same and understandable. And in the same way that the created lives of Theodora Goodman were interchangeable, the lives into which she entered . . .

whether George or Julia Goodman, only apparently deceased, or Huntly Clarkson, or Moraïtis or Lou, or Zack, these were the lives of Theodora Goodman, these too. (P. 278.)

The fluctuating personalities of Part Two are really an expansion of this paragraph. In it, the movement is sideways, as it were, whereas in Part One it is forwards or sequential (the basic movement of the quest in romance structure). In Part Three the two directions of movement meet and coalesce.

The lateral movement of Part Two, like the universal quality which the Tiresias motif helps to give to her experience, suggests that the quest is not unique to Theodora. Sitting in the Jardin Exotique, Theodora knows that "this was not yet her crisis" (p. 162)—not, that is, insofar as she is an isolated individual. It is precisely this isolation, however, which begins to be broken down in the latter half of the novel. The experiences of the other guests at the Hôtel du Midi afford fresh reflections, "without mirrors," of Theodora's life, and her life mirrors and begins to merge with theirs. Soon after her arrival, she feels or senses the other people in the hotel, "and she waited to touch their hands" (p. 135). Just as Theodora suffers several deaths in Part One, so the number of her lives begins to multiply in Parts Two and Three. Once again we are reminded of Eliot's use, in *The Waste Land,* of Tiresias as brooding universal consciousness, one who has "foresuffered all/Enacted on this same divan or bed." This extension of individuality, this melting achieved in pity and fear, is defined by E. M. Forster, in *Aspects of the Novel,* as "prophecy."

J. F. Burrows suggests that White's technique in Part Two "asks no more of us than do those passages of Part One where, for example, Theodora identifies herself with the hawk."[16] The point is well taken. Basic to White's technique, in *The Aunt's Story* and his subsequent novels, is the full metaphorical identity of what is called apocalyptic imagery by Northrop Frye, and "the humanizing of the material world" by Robert McDougall

---

[16] J. F. Burrows, " 'Jardin Exotique': The Central Phase of 'The Aunt's Story,' " *Southerly* XXVI (1966), 156.

(in his Commonwealth Literary Fund Lecture of 1966).[17] The inclusion of Mrs. Rapallo, Julia Goodman, and Huntly Clarkson along with characters with whom Theodora has been sympathetically identified earlier in the narrative illustrates the *inclusive* tendency of comedy, with the "blocking characters"[18] being reconciled or converted rather than simply repudiated. This contrasts with the repudiation of Elyot and the other spiritually dead in *The Living and the Dead*.

Theodora's sympathetic identification with Sokolnikov, Katina, and the other guests at the hotel has exhausted her, but the exhaustion is one of plenitude, not frustration, "from receiving full measure, a measure of corn" (p. 249).[19] As she approaches the fourth stage of peace and reconciliation, her niece Lou, upset by her parents' attitude towards Theodora, stands at the end of innocence and the beginning of experience and suffering: "She was afraid and sad, because there was some great intolerable pressure from which it is not possible to escape" (p. 253). This parallels Theodora's experience when, as an older child, she was oppressed by a weight of sadness that nobody would lift, the state of *angst* in which her odyssey begins. As Theodora nears Ithaca, Lou is about to embark.[20]

This cyclic aspect of the theme reinforces the "fragmentation of maturity" of Part Two and corresponds to the seasonal imagery of the novel. The autumn-spring inversion of the two hemispheres suggested in Theodora's letter to Fanny ("your

---

[17] Robert L. McDougall, *Australia Felix: Joseph Furphy and Patrick White*, Commonwealth Literary Fund Lecture (Canberra: Australian National University Press, 1966), p. 8.

[18] Frye, *Anatomy of Criticism*, p. 165.

[19] Cf. Luke 6: 38.

[20] Herring, "Odyssey of a Spinster," notes the following Homeric parallels in Part Three: "Theodora stripping herself of all her possessions recalls Ulysses returning to Ithaca in the disguise of a beggarman, the greeting given her by the Johnsons' scruffy red dog suggests Odysseus' welcome from his old dog Argus; when Mrs. Johnson brings Theodora water to wash herself, just before she gives herself a false name, we may remember Odysseus' old nurse washing his feet and recognizing him. But what White is concerned with is pointing up his theme by a very free method of allusion: the significance often lies in the variations and reversals" (p. 16). While I agree with Miss Herring's emphasis on the greater degree of freedom in White's use of the mythic framework as compared with Joyce's, I feel that her suggestion that these parallels are only "occasional echoes" underestimates the strength and extent of White's use of *The Odyssey* in this novel.

Abyssinian spring") relates to the unending succession of quests typified in Theodora's experience. In America it is late summer, not quite fall; in Australia "the world had not yet thawed. Lou waited for the aching shapes of winter to dissolve" (p. 252). The movement from innocence, through experience, to death and rebirth, by means of a structure of imagery which suggests cyclic movement (the passage of seasons, the growth of an individual from childhood to old age), serves to adapt to nature the apocalyptic and demonic structures of imagery, since the worlds suggested by these myths are the eternally unchanging. While Theodora's movement is lateral, Katina takes up the sequential movement of the quest in Part Two.

The Aunt's Story is more ironic than romantic, although it embraces both these opposite phases of comedy. The structure of imagery related to the romance mode is the analogy of innocence, which presents the human counterpart of the apocalyptic world. The spiritual figures in this mode are usually parental; and children may be prominent among the human figures, with an emphasis upon chastity as the virtue most closely associated with childhood innocence.[21] Thus Holstius replaces George Goodman as Theodora's spiritual father. Katina, Lou, Zack, and to a certain extent Theodora herself belong to this romantic structure of imagery,[22] as does the fire which demolishes the Hôtel du Midi, a fire survived only by the pure in heart.

The St. George motif in *The Aunt's Story* links this novel to Spenser's epic romance, *The Faerie Queene,* whose first book is described by Northrop Frye as representing perhaps the closest following of the biblical quest-romance theme in English literature. White's images and archetypes, like those of so many English authors, including Spenser, Bunyan, Blake, may be traced to the Bible. Frye describes Spenser's account of the quest of St. George as follows:

the protagonist represents the Christian Church in England,

---

[21] See Frye, *Anatomy of Criticism,* p. 151.

[22] See Mackenzie, "Yes, Let's Return to Abyssinia," p. 435: "You can't return to a childhood state, only to the likeness of one, a generic or Adamic childhood."

and hence his quest is an imitation of that of Christ. . . . The dragon, who is the entire fallen world, is identified with the leviathan, the serpent of Eden, Satan, and the beast of Revelation. Thus St. George's mission, a repetition of that of Christ, is by killing the dragon to raise Eden in the wilderness and restore England to the status of Eden.[23]

In *The Aunt's Story,* however, the dragon to be slain is within the heroine. Spenser's dragon is part of the literal action of his narrative even though, like White's, it represents qualities within man which the hero must conquer. In White's technique of displaced myth there is a further internalizing of the dragon figure. This is another indication that White's novel is not a romance in basic structure, despite its many affinities with the romance mode.

There is a recurring pattern of apocalyptic imagery based on tree, rose, corn, water, fire, and bone. These are identified with both life and death, in two related patterns of imagery. The pine tree is first associated with Theodora's father, but George Goodman proves to be a hollow or dead tree, and is replaced by Holstius, the living tree. The vibrant glowing corn also appears in its opposite or deathly form as popcorn, "the white and pappy stuff that is a decadence of corn" (p. 250). Similarly the quest appears as successful and unsuccessful. The quest theme of the road or way identifies the goal, the journey's end, with a state of recovered innocence where experience is transformed, not rejected. This adapts apocalyptic imagery to inorganic matter, as does the symbolism of alchemy, where the alchemical aspiration to transmute dross to precious metal is used metaphorically as an analogue of the purifying of the human soul. In *Voss,* Laura and Voss are the base metal which is to be transmuted to a purer form. The imagery associated with the Syrian's silver shawl, in *The Aunt's Story,* suggests that the alchemical process is moving in the opposite direction; the splendid shawl, which streams at first like falling silver water, becomes "a poor ragged flapping thing that fell" (p. 22) as the hole in its corner is revealed.

Both the shawl with its hidden imperfection and the rose with

[23] Frye, *Anatomy of Criticism,* p. 194.

a grub at its heart belong to the pattern concerning the core of evil which Theodora discovers in herself. A rose garden is part of the first Meroë, and the innocence of Theodora's childhood is drenched in roselight; even so, there is the grub at the heart of the rose, and "many bitter days at Meroë when the roselight hardened and blackened" (p. 20). At the novel's end, the *black* rose on Theodora's hat, which "trembled and glittered, leading a life of its own" (p. 281), belongs to the pattern of blackness associated with the second Meroë and with death, which she no longer fears.

Water, as in Eliot's *The Waste Land,* is identified with both life and death. The water imagery of Part Two frequently suggests death, as in death by drowning, but in Part Three, after Holstius' words and touch, water belongs to the ritual of baptism: "She looked at the world with eyes blurred by water, but a world curiously pure, expectant, undistorted" (p. 273). The paradoxes of the novel are gathered together and contained within Holstius' advice to accept the two irreconcilable halves. The inversion of reality and illusion, so frequently effected in the novel, and the deception or impostor theme of Part Two are now seen to apply even to life and death, the "eternal complement of skeleton and spawn" (p. 279).[24] Theodora cannot be sure which is which and must, for the time being, be reconciled to both without fear. The novel ends in a mood of *nunc dimittis* which suggests that Theodora's life is an unending continuity.

---

[24] Cf. Samuel Beckett's treatment of eggs and excrement in *Whoroscope* (Paris: Hours Press, 1930).

So man's insanity is heaven's sense.

HERMAN MELVILLE, MOBY DICK

chapter 6 God's fool

Man's intellect has a place in White's fictional exploration of human nature and of reality, but a place subsidiary to compassion, faith, and lovingkindness. He shares with Kierkegaard the conviction that a complete human life is something far greater than merely one of rational understanding: "For otherwise how near man is to madness, in spite of all his knowledge."[1] Each of his novels contains one or more "fools" or simpletons, who combine rational deficiency with spiritual insight and lovingkindness. Most frequently, these fools are mystics, sensitive to the divine essence in common objects. Their sensitivity belongs to the extreme *simplicity* of their nature, which the world is quick to repudiate as stupidity or even madness. During the destruction of Xanadu at the end of *Riders,* Else Godbold discovers Mrs. Hare's journal, with its description of Mary as a child: " 'Her statements stop a person short. Will not deny that M.'s remarks usually contain the truth. But the world, I fear, will not tolerate

[1] *The Journals of Kierkegaard 1834-1854,* a selection, ed. and trans. Alexander Dru (London and Glasgow: Collins, Fontana, 1958), p. 45.

the truth, at least in concentrated form' " (p. 504). White's use of this type of character serves two purposes. Firstly they illustrate that intellectual powers are quite possibly not as important as our age is accustomed to believe; and secondly these figures permit White to express his own apocalyptic vision in poetic form.

The etymology of *fool* and *simple* reveals the growing rationalism in European culture from the late Middle Ages to our own age, despite the various romantic movements of the last two hundred years. *Fool,* in particular, has been given a pejorative connotation which indicates the high value that Western civilization has come to place on the intellect. In biblical usage *fool* applies to a vicious or impious person, as in the opening words of Psalm 14: "The fool hath said in his heart, There is no God." From the early sixteenth century, however, it came increasingly to connote someone foolish or ridiculous. White's inversion technique gives us the divine fool as a simple soul, nearer than the average man to God, while his true fool, as in biblical usage, is the man who says in his heart, "There is no God." Arthur's role in *The Solid Mandala* draws on the medieval tradition of fool as clown or jester. He often exaggerates his clowning out of a spirit of love, in order to put others at ease in a difficult situation. The medieval jester was recognized as a wise man or philosopher, a tradition which fits well with White's inversion of sanity and madness, truth and illusory appearance. The idea behind the etymological series connecting *fool* with *illusion,* as 'fool's paradise,' 'fool's errand,' 'fool's gold,' also underlies some of White's ambiguities and allusions.

White's divine fools are *simple,* in the original sense of the word as being honest or free from duplicity, harmlessly innocent. The characteristics of the fool belong in some sense to all of White's characters who are presented as admirable. *Honest,* for example, is one of the author's favourite words and one we come to associate with Theodora Goodman, Stan Parker, the four Riders, and so on. Medieval usage of *simple* as *humble,* or free from ostentation and pride, relates to the Whitean virtue of humility. A pejorative connotation of this word, similar to that which surrounds *fool,* begins in the late Middle Ages, with the connotations of humility and simplicity modulating into *weakness, feebleness.* What one age has conceived of as a strength is inverted by another age into a weakness. By 1604, *simple* is 'half-witted' (*Oxford Universal Dictionary*) and is used colloquially for a foolish, silly, and stupid person. From the mid-sixteenth century onwards, the idea is associated with ignorance and feebleness of intellect. With reference to the characters, incidents, and images associated with both *simple* and *fool,* White's usage reflects the thought-world of the ages of faith, medieval or biblical, rather than our own *zeitgeist.* Another medieval meaning for *simple* was 'pure,' 'bare,' 'unmixed.' This relates to the symbolic use of the number one, in biblical and mystical writings, as an apocalyptic image of uniqueness, self-sufficiency, indivisibility, especially in relation to the divine unity. White's simpletons are the pure in heart who shall see God.

White's first version of God's fool is Chuffy Chambers, in *Happy Valley.* This minor figure in the novel is shown first with Hagan, who reaches Furlow's ranch in the mail truck driven from Moorang to Happy Valley by Chuffy. Structurally, he is related to Hagan, both in this second chapter and through his place in the events surrounding the Moriarty murder and Hagan's trial, where Chuffy testifies that he has seen Hagan leave the Moriarty house on the night of the murder. Thematically, he stands in strong contrast with Hagan, whose character is partly revealed through his dislike of and disgust for the harmless boy who wears his religious medals out of sight next to his skin and plays the accordion. Like Arthur Brown in *The Solid Mandala,* Chuffy is sexually impotent, but kind: "girls . . . were a sort of unrealized ambition with him. . . . They said he was loopy. Though he treated his mother well, he was a good boy, Chuffy, but—well, he wasn't quite all there, and you couldn't treat him altogether serious because of that" (p. 25).

The Living and the Dead has no obvious fool figure to compare with Chuffy, Bub Quigley, Harry, Miss Hare, or Arthur Brown. It is perhaps significant that this novel, where White's vision seems at times to falter, almost to doubt itself, should lack this character, except for a passing reference to local opinion that Mr. Goose (Eden's grandfather) is "mad" (p. 23); the blacksmith, however, continues in his conviction that man is essentially good. Even more important, the fool's characteristics of extreme simplicity, humility, and sensitivity to the divinity in all aspects of the natural world—characteristics which are strong in major characters such as Theodora Goodman, Stan Parker, the four Riders, and Arthur Brown—are not dominant in Eden Standish. It is Julia Fallon, whom the narrator leads us to associate with bread and cheese and all common natural objects, and who knows the *goodness* in the world of substances, who is closest to this figure in White's second novel.

In *The Aunt's Story* the fool is the protagonist, Theodora Goodman. White's divine fools may be either mentally deficient or commonly regarded as mad—both these states being crimes, so to speak, in the eyes of the world. The subtle inversions of madness/sanity, appearance/reality which the novel effects are at the core of its total statement and have been discussed at length in Chapter 5. The world is ready neither for Theodora's painful honesty nor for Mary Hare's blunt truths. As Stan Parker progresses in spiritual understanding, his reputation for oddness increases, until there are those who are ready to call *him* mad, or at least "a bit queer" (p. 225). This, of course, puts him in good company in the context of White's novels, where it is the sanity of the world which requires strict scrutiny.

The Quigleys, Stan's neighbours, are the divine fools of White's fourth novel, *The Tree of Man*. Bub and Doll, brother and sister, between them embody all the characteristics of White's divine fool. Bub, the mentally retarded boy (in old age a boy still, like Arthur Brown) is a nature mystic who sees the natural world as the miracle that it is. The saintly Doll, filled with the light of goodness, is the essence of Christian *caritas* and long-suffering patience. After a lifetime of caring for her retarded brother, the strain of her decision to kill Bub in order to save him from an institution is too much for her own wits. Convinced that she *is* Bub, Doll ends in a mental hospital—as do Theodora Goodman and Arthur Brown. Despite the "blinding logic" of her act, it has cut her off from God. Amy sees that Doll is "in hell," but sees also that this is a purgatorial suffering, not a permanent state: "Sin then, Doll, Amy Parker would have said, and left her friend to enter heaven by that way" (p. 484).

The duplicity of Stan's son, Ray, is contrasted with Bub's innocence and simplicity. White uses juxtaposition to great effect in a variety of contexts, but the technique is especially useful with the fool: Chuffy Chambers against Hagan, Harry Robarts against Frank Le Mesurier, Arthur Brown and his brother Waldo. Bub's simplicity is described by the narrator as *terrible,* and he is frequently associated with mandala images. When Ray is a child, Bub's favourite possession is a skeleton leaf which he describes as being from a lace tree. Ray, coveting the leaf, tears and crumples it in a fit of spoiled petulance, causing "circles of mystery, beauty, and injustice" (p. 116) to expand inside Bub. Ray's own simplicity, as child and adult, is a demonic parody of Bub's, as with "his simple act" (p. 245) in giving Mum North- cott a present bought with money stolen from her. Strong in innocence, Bub confronts the smiles of the dead without blanch- ing, and confidently blesses the body of the old man who has been found drowned: " 'That old fellow is good,' he said, meet- ing the face of an old man with his own rapt smile. 'See it?' he said. 'He is good. Good. You can tell' " (p. 83). In terms of the archetypal situations and characters of Shakespeare's *Hamlet,* Bub is Ophelia; Amy Parker, in old age, can make the identifica- tion after she is no longer frightened by Bub (p. 420).

In *Voss,* the good simpleton is Harry Robarts, one of Voss's two "disciples" who remain with him to the end. These two fol- lowers, Harry and Frank Le Mesurier, flank Voss in death, form- ing a trinitarian grouping like that of the three crosses at Calvary. White's juxtaposition of these two dissimilars, cynical intellec- tual and simple innocent, throws into relief the qualities of each. Voss describes the boy to Mr. Bonner as "good, simple," and Harry's wide eyes reflect "the primary thoughts" (p. 28). Although weak in wit, he enjoys the advantages of muscular strength and *the strength of innocence,* so that Voss feels "weak with knowledge" (p. 28) beside the boy. Harry puts both these strengths, physical and spiritual, at Voss's service, becoming his faithful shadow. His unwavering devotion is likened to a dog's, but far from carrying a depreciatory connotation, the image is identified throughout the novel with love and faith, as well as humility. Turner recognizes that "in these here circumstances, we are all, every one of us, dogs" (p. 262); in the next paragraph, "Laura herself was dog-eyed love," and, a little later, the gentle devotion of both Palfreyman and Laura has "the soft, glossy coat of a dog" (p. 284). Hence, the dog image serves to connect Harry with those who are drawing Voss towards God.

In *Pilgrim's Progress,* Bunyan refers to the will of the Lord, that comfort should be given to the feeble-minded (1 Thess. 5: 14), the simple and the humble (Matt. 25: 40). When death calls Mr. Feeble-minded to the Celestial City, he enters the river with boldness, leaving behind his feeble mind of which he will have no further need, and desiring Mr. Valiant to bury it in a dunghill. Without even the dignity of burial, Harry Robarts' body is treated like a dog's,[2] kicked and thrown into a gully; in death it has become "a green woman" (p. 383). *Green,* the colour of putrescence, is also the colour of hope, of new life in natural vegetation, and hence an apocalyptic image of eternal spring and rebirth. From his first novel, White uses colours symbolically, an accumulated weight of meaning attaching to each colour as the novel progresses. Faith is depicted, throughout *Voss* and in all White's later novels, as a feminine characteristic, in both the Jungian sense of masculine and feminine characteristics belonging to each individual of either sex, and the mystical sense of sexual characteristics within the Godhead. Hence the significance of the feminine appearance of Harry's body in death.

Riders in the Chariot plays on the idea of madness as spiritual sanity, while those who are blind to spiritual realities are depicted as truly mad. Mrs. Jolley condemns Miss Hare as mad, in

---

[2] Cf. Malcolm Lowry, *Under the Volcano* (Harmondsworth, Middlesex: Penguin, 1963), p. 376. At the end of Lowry's novel the body of a dog is thrown into the abyss after the consul's body. The pariah dog has followed the consul throughout the novel, as Harry follows Voss, and the drunken consul has addressed to the dog Christ's words to the crucified thief, stopping before the word *paradise.* Other parallels between *Voss* and *Under the Volcano* are discussed in Chapter 8.

order to preserve her own illusion of sanity. Mary Hare terms it "a sad, bad word. . . . Because it leaves out half" (p. 316). Himmelfarb is reluctant to call Miss Hare mad, because of his involvement in the same madness—that is, the problem of redemption. Here, madness is seen as mission, a mission to rescue men "from the rubble of their own ideas" (p. 329). Miss Hare is called mad for trying to enter a burning house. Since she believes the Jew to be inside, her act is one of self-sacrificing love. Mrs. Pask reacts to Dubbo's painting in horror, and condemns his vision as madness. As an adult, Dubbo retains something of Mary Hare's antipathy towards human beings, suspecting that he will be treated "like an idiot, or a black" (p. 364). He connects logic, and words generally, with white European culture, and it is the general duplicity of this same culture that has convinced him, before he witnesses the "crucifixion," that Christianity cannot be true: "Where he could accept God because of the spirit that would work in him at times, the duplicity of the white men prevented him considering Christ, except as an ambitious abstraction, or realistically, as a man" (p. 397). It is against such duplicity that the "infinite simplicity" of the Riders stands out in sharp relief. In Mary Hare's confrontation with Constable McFaggott after the burning of the Jew's house, truth is implicitly depicted as *simple* or *one,* in contrast with the law, here identified with the forked tongue of a serpent, a creature traditionally associated with the Tempter in the Edenic myth.

William Hadkin, the Hares' old coachman, is the only unsympathetic fool in White's novels. He is described as "*rather simple. Which means that what one knows is of a different kind*" (p. 44). There is something crafty and unpleasant about the coachman, who kills the old cock for food and laughs as the headless body dances out the last steps of its life. He speaks the truth, albeit one that is unwelcome to Mary's ears, in telling her that she and her parents were " 'the race of pretenders' " (p. 49). This seems to be tied to Mary's pride and arrogance, which is here contrasted with Peg's humility and "blameless" character. He thus anticipates, on a very minor scale, the role played by Arthur Brown as "divine gadfly" whose function it is to drive

Waldo to tears. Nevertheless, it is Mary Hare who is the divine simpleton in this novel.

Arthur Brown, in *The Solid Mandala,* is the culmination of this pattern, which begins with Chuffy Chambers in White's first novel. Arthur, as Waldo suspects and fears, is "the thread of continuity, and might even be the core of truth" (p. 177). Arthur's psychic sense includes sensitivity and love, which more rational minds may lack: "Arthur's incomplete mind must have included compartments in which delicacy predominated" (p. 162). Those who are sympathetically linked with him, who appreciate rather than scorn his qualities, are also simple and good. Mrs. Poulter, although an "inalterably stupid creature" (p. 54), usually seems to find an answer for Arthur's important questions. Speaking of Leonard Saporta to Waldo, Arthur says that simple people are somehow *more transparent*: "you can see right into them, right into the part that matters" (p. 23). Arthur's physical impotence, as "One-Ball Brown" (p. 219), is used to emphasize his spiritual fertility, and to convey White's conviction that men and women are not "all that different" (pp. 215, 249). This "backward brother," this "dill" whom Johnny Haynes suspects is not as "loopy" as his family assumes, is identified, through the "hermaphroditic Adam" passage which he reads in the library, with the Primordial Man or Adam Kadmon of Jewish mysticism and the last Adam of the New Testament image of Christ. The figure in the old raincoat is both fool and saint.

The fool has a long tradition, both in cultural history and in literature. In Arthurian legend, Perceval is one of the most famous of the Knights of the Round Table, figuring especially in the quest for the Grail. Ignorant of courtly manners, he commits a series of gaucheries in his first appearances at court, but eventually becomes one of the foremost Knights of the Round Table, and is finally rewarded with the sight of the Grail. The twelfth-century French epic by Chrétien de Troyes was reworked by Wolfram von Eschenbach, early in the thirteenth century. In the German version, Parzival is the guileless fool, totally innocent of sin and guilt. His religious faith and motivation, his humility, innocence and purity are all features of White's fool. Late versions of the Perceval story usually present him as virgin; Chuffy Chambers, Bub Quigley, and Arthur Brown are sexually impotent, while Theodora Goodman, Miss Hare, and Rhoda Courtney are presented as asexual. The guild fools of medieval times played an important part in the spread of literature and education, and formed part of the troubadour organization that permeated Europe. Shakespeare's Lear is accompanied in the storm by a strangely wise jester who comments on the behaviour of mankind. He disappears when Cordelia returns to assume his role as Lear's Fool, and both daughter and fool seem to be identified with truth. Bunyan's brief sketch of Mr. Feeble-minded is both powerful and compassionate.

White's use of the fool has parallels with nineteenth-century Russian fiction. Dostoyevsky's *The Idiot,* written between 1867 and 1869, attempts to portray "a perfect man," as he noted in a letter to Maykov.[3] Feeling the falseness and immaturity of his first attempts at the difficult theme, Dostoyevsky wrote and rewrote, producing eight successive versions of *The Idiot:* " 'The character of the idiot must be depicted in a masterly fashion,' " we find in his notes, which fortunately have been preserved.[4] His first problem, and one which has obviously occupied White, was whether to make his hero truly retarded or mad, or merely declared to be so by others. Dostoyevsky's saintly Myshkin becomes the embodiment of Christian love, and is finally identified with Christ. The theme necessarily involves an examination of truth and reality. Like White's, Dostoyevsky's art is religious in its basic orientation, and both authors are aware of the irrationalism of the individual's psychological processes. Dostoyevsky's *The Double* and Gogol's *Diary of a Madman* deal with the mental disintegration of the hero; while less relevant to White's fiction than *The Idiot,* they cast some piercing lights on the duplicity of the "sane" world. Tolstoy's Levin, in *Anna Karenina,* contrasts strongly with Anna herself. Levin is an intelligent man, but his extreme simplicity and faith belong also to White's fools, and

---

[3] Fyodor Dostoyevsky, *The Idiot,* trans. David Magarshack (Harmondsworth, Middlesex: Penguin, 1955), translator's Introduction, p. 9.
[4] Ibid., p. 16.

Tolstoy's technique of juxtaposition and contrast is one that White has mastered. His first two novels both show the influence of *Anna Karenina,* whereas his latter novels are closer to Dostoyevsky's mood and vision.

In American literature which is roughly contemporary with Dostoyevsky's work, Herman Melville's *Moby Dick* (1851) gives us a fool very like those of White's novels. Little Pip, the Negro cabin boy on the *Pequod,* is the castaway from the boat as it hotly pursues a whale. He is eventually rescued, but the intolerable loneliness of swimming for some time in an open sea, with no sight of man or boat on his ringed horizon, has made Pip a "castaway" from his wits:

> The sea had jeeringly kept his finite body up, but drowned the infinite of his soul. Not drowned entirely, though. Rather carried down alive to wondrous depths, where . . . the miser-merman, Wisdom, revealed his hoarded heaps; and among the joyous, heartless, ever-juvenile eternities, Pip saw the multitudinous, God-omnipresent, coral insects. . . . He saw God's foot upon the treadle of the loom, and spoke it; and therefore his shipmates called him mad. So man's insanity is heaven's sense; and wandering from all mortal reason, man comes at last to that celestial thought, which, to reason, is absurd and frantic; and weal or woe, feels then uncompromised, indifferent as his God.[5]

It is interesting to note Melville's understanding of the unconscious or subconscious, so long before William James, Freud, and Jung. The reference to "ever-juvenile eternities," the technique of paradox and inversion, the conception of the universe as "God-omnipresent," and the distinction between "mortal reason" and spiritual wisdom all parallel White's thought and technique.

Melville's development of Pip, however, is more elegiac in tone than the mood which usually surrounds White's fools. The association of Bub Quigley with Shakespeare's Ophelia, com-

[5] Herman Melville, *Moby Dick* (New York: Modern Library, 1926), p. 413.

bined with the problems which follow on this character's increasing animality in old age, affords the closest analogy in White's novels to the slightly diffused melancholy of Melville's treatment of Pip. As *Moby Dick* nears its climax, mad Pip contrasts strongly with the figure of Captain Ahab, the doomed tragic hero. Pip's sin, as he judges it, of cowardice in the whale hunt has cost him his wits; Doll Quigley pays a similar price for the mercy killing of her brother. Like Harry, in *Voss*, Pip's devotion to his captain is all the stronger in his unfortunate state; and Ahab's love for the boy is like Voss's for Harry. " 'Hands off that holiness!' " Ahab commands a sailor who seizes Pip roughly. Compassion for Pip's state makes him exclaim "Oh God! that man should be a thing for immortal souls to sieve through!" while Pip holds his captain's hand, calling it "a man-rope; something that weak souls may hold by" (p. 513). The man-rope image may be compared with White's pattern of rope (ladder, chain) imagery in *Riders in the Chariot*.

Melville develops the skin colour of man and boy, white and black, and their opposing characteristics of ruthless indomitability and loving tenderness, into his pattern of polarities. In Melville's tragedy, *both* are necessary, the "one daft with strength, the other daft with weakness" (p. 514), as the old Manxman puts it. White's heroes, however, resemble rather than contrast with his divine fools, and share their strength of innocence. (Voss would appear to be the exception to this generalization, but it applies to him in his final state, after he has accepted love and been transformed by suffering.) Harry Robarts' simplicity, like Ruth Godbold's, is proverbial. As Voss writes to Laura: " 'His simplicity is such, he could well arrive at that place where great mysteries are revealed. Or else become an imbecile' " (p. 212). Like Doll, who is reduced to "the essence of goodness, which is what made people ashamed or afraid, because it is too rare" (*Tree,* p. 480), or Bub, with his curious round stone in hand, White's fools hold the mystery of the world concentrated in their innocence and simplicity.

'Fair and foul are near of kin,
And fair needs foul,' I cried. . . .
'But love has pitched his mansion in
The place of excrement;
For nothing can be sole or whole
That has not been rent.'

W. B. YEATS, CRAZY JANE TALKS WITH
THE BISHOP

chapter 7 The quest for permanence

Writing in 1958 for an Australian periodical, White described his frame of mind in the years which followed his return to Australia in 1948. After a few years of contentedly soaking in landscape, he began to grow discontented, almost bitter. He found himself fearful of the exaltation of the average and appalled by "the great Australian Emptiness, in which the mind is the least of possessions."[1] Working in the consciousness of a cultural void, he wanted *The Tree of Man* to suggest "every possible aspect of life, through the lives of an ordinary man and woman," and at the same time to reveal "the extraordinary behind the ordinary, the mystery and poetry which alone could make bearable the lives of such people, and incidentally, my own life since my return."[2] The entire novel has the simplicity of true grandeur, like the big stringybarks on Stan's land. Yet White's simplicities are also profundities for, as Mrs. Fisher informs Thelma, " 'There is no such thing as simplicity' " (p. 442). We may correlate this remark

[1] Patrick White, "The Prodigal Son," *Australian Letters* I, 3 (1958), 38.
[2] Ibid., p. 39.

with Stan's horrified realization at the production of *Hamlet* that
he and Amy are "simple people" (p. 417)—simple, and quite
unfathomable. Stan's goal, the transcendent, is discovered to be
immanent in the substances and creatures of the natural world.
And this knowledge is "wrung out," to borrow a phrase from
Voss, only at the cost of a lifetime of search and suffering.

In *The Tree of Man,* as in White's other novels, we find the full
comic spectrum of moods, from the romantic to the ironic. The
romantic pastoral idealizes man while humanizing the myth; the
ironic tone results from a keen and objective intellect surveying
aspects of the world that are "not nice" but determined, unlike
Stan Parker's mother, to come to grips with this reality rather
than to attempt to evade it. In pure or undisplaced myth, the
imagery is organized into two contrasting worlds, one desirable
or apocalyptic and the other undesirable or demonic. At the
other extreme to pure myth is "realism," the art of verisimilitude,
likelihood or imitation of outer appearance, the technique used
in naturalistic fiction: "And as realism is an art of implicit simile,
myth is an art of implicit metaphorical identity."[3] The preference on the part of some contemporary critics for the art of verisimilitude is indicated by a suspicion of myth as something artificial or unnecessary.[4] White uses myth in the form of metaphor
within an apparently realistic structure, and the radical metaphor
or statement of hypothetical identity is basic to the technique of
The Aunt's Story and the novels which follow it.

In *Tree,* the identifying of one object with another is so frequent that it creates a feeling of flux or flow which is associated
with Stan's search for true permanence. This is the anagogic perspective, where the archetypal symbols are not the forms man
constructs in nature but are themselves the forms of nature, with
all nature being seen as the content of an eternal living body. In
the opening paragraph of *Tree,* the horse takes root and the tree

[3] Frye, *Anatomy of Criticism: Four Essays* (reprint ed., New York: Atheneum,
1965) p. 136.
[4] See G. A. Wilkes, "Patrick White's 'The Tree of Man,'" *Southerly* XXV
(1965), 26: "The strength of the book lies in its human relationships which
are weakened by the attempt to extend them into a 'myth'. . . . The mythic
framework is sometimes relevant to this theme of fulfillment, but more often
a distraction."

has hair; the second page expands this unity of tree and horse to include horse, dog, man, and fire in "a unity of eyes and fire-light" (p. 4). And at the same time as the phenomenal world is being humanized, both man and nature are being filled with or identified with spirit. Robert McDougall describes White's technique as follows: "Spirit enters matter. . . . Human nature and phenomenal nature are no longer separated; they are one, welded together in a juncture that shows no cracks."[5]

The four parts of the novel, the orchestral movements of Stan's spiritual quest, are based on analogies with the four ages of life from childhood to old age, with the four seasons, and with the movement of one day from morning to evening. Narrative events are important in this long and epic novel, the narrative episodes serving as archetypal images of man's basic experiences in all ages. In *Tree,* as in White's novels generally, the spiritual quest, the inward journey in search of permanence or reality, is seen in terms of four archetypal stages: innocence, experience, hell, and heaven.[6] Innocence is associated with man's youth, with morning ("the clear morning of those early years," p. 26), springtime and the honeymoon of marriage; its archetypal ordeal is flood. Experience, the first years of adult maturity, is the summer of life; it includes the ordeals of fire and war and, for Amy, the expulsion of Fritz as society's scapegoat. Autumn is identified with the dry years of suffering, psychic death, and loss of faith—ordeal by drought. Winter is the continuation of death begun in late fall, but includes the quiet joys of " 'winter sunshine' " (p. 435) and passes into early spring. The latter, in *The Tree of Man,* is identi-fied with Stan's recovery of faith and spiritual rebirth. This four-

---

[5] Robert L. McDougall, *Australia Felix: Joseph Furphy and Patrick White,* Commonwealth Literary Fund Lecture (Canberra: Australian National University Press, 1966), p. 8.

[6] Manfred Mackenzie's criticism of White's novels emphasizes these four stages as typical in the experience of White's heroes. See "Abyssinia Lost and Re-gained," *Essays in Criticism* XIII (1963), 292-300; "Yes, Let's Return to Abyssinia," *Essays in Criticism* XIV (1964), 433-435; "Patrick White's Later Novel's: A Generic Reading," *Southern Review* I, 3 (1965), 5-18; "Apoca-lypse in Patrick White's 'The Tree of Man,' " *Meanjin* XXV (1966), 405-416. A. K. Thomson, "Patrick White's 'The Tree of Man,' " *Meanjin* XXV (1966), 22, refers to the typical Whitean quest ("In every novel there is a journey, and the journey is towards God"), without noting its four-stage structure.

fold structure is conventional in literature, and White's use of it illustrates the originality and power which is possible within a conventional and traditional literary framework. The various ordeals, such as the desert in *Voss,* are unavoidable trials or tests, as integral to life as the seasons themselves.

Each of the four parts contains various seasons, for each represents the passing of many years. One season, however, recurs most noticeably in each, and dominates the mood. When Stan and Amy are in the autumn of their lives and Amy is "drying up" (Part Three), she thinks of their youth and early married life, "the floodtime of their lives" (p. 285), full of lost possibilities. This is analogous to the Edenic myth of the springtime of mankind which culminates in lost innocence and a lost paradise. Chief among Amy's lost possibilities is the boy from the floods at Wullunya who she feels would have been more truly her child than Thelma and Ray. Springtime, then, is both beginnings and failures to begin. Stan and Amy's summer is their early maturity, including the growth of their own "common trunk . . . the goodness of their common life" (p. 97).[7] In this period of their lives, a "firmly founded architecture had risen at Parkers'. Even in the flesh" (p. 109). Mandala images place first Stan, then both Stan and Amy, at the *centre* of existence[8] in the near-perfection of

---

[7] Mackenzie, "Apocalypse in Patrick White's 'The Tree of Man,'" posits a major contrast, a "qualitative separation" (p. 407) between Stan and Amy. He sees the latter as a study in neurotic self-destruction. This ignores the parts of the novel which emphasize the goodness of their common life, and slights Stan's own complicity in human weakness and guilt. Their relationship is important, and each has been initially attracted by the other's simplicity and honesty. Amy is much the weaker of the two and lags considerably behind Stan, hence the necessity for her "further sentence" (p. 497) after Stan's death. Like Judd in *Voss,* Amy is *greedy* for bread and human love, and finds the mercy of God mediated to her in the sound of wheels at the end of market day, and "a kiss full in the mouth" (p. 28). She is initially intolerant of Bub Quigley, as the humbler Stan is not. At the first news of the floods, her instinctive reaction is one of relief and pleasure that their own house is safely set on a hill. Stan does not attempt to possess the child found in the flood, to imprison him by force of love, as Amy does. In brief, Amy continues to long for a permanence which Stan senses to be illusory. However, her closeness to her grandson, Elsie's boy, her sharing in the "mysticism of objects" (p. 398), her compassion for Mrs. O'Dowd at the time of her death and for Doll Quigley after Bub's death, all indicate that Amy is proceeding along the right route in the spiritual quest.

[8] "All was ranged round him, radiating out from him in the burning afternoon" (p. 109); "And she drew the wool together, sitting at the centre of the night. He watched, and they were indeed the centre, but precariously" (p. 111).

their early maturity: "All was good, almost, that could come to this pass" (p. 109).

The images towards the end of Part Two set a different tone, one of apocalypse, as Stan and Amy are both tried and judged by fire and war. Part Three is their season "of stubble and dead grass when doubts did press up" (p. 302), the "years of drought" (p. 304) in their life generally and in their marriage, when communication seems to have failed. Amy succumbs to the temptation presented by the commercial traveller, who arrives on a *dry* autumn afternoon, as Amy shivers in a changing wind. Leo comments on the dryness and, ironically, a drink is his pretext for entering the house. Stan's discovery of her infidelity precipitates his loss of faith in God as well as in man and his period of great suffering. Their peaceful old age is a time of winter sunshine, of lessened activity when Stan can smile ironically at the sight of young Peabody, whose youthful confidence reminds Stan of his own springtime, just as Amy was reminded of the floodtime of their lives. After a temporary psychic death, the spiritual analogy to winter hibernation in nature's cycle, the last half-dozen chapters of the novel show the gradual evolution of Stan's spiritual rebirth.

Stan's quest of permanence is also a quest for true knowledge, the spiritual wisdom or *gnosis* which enables man to perceive the truth and which is contrasted in White's novels with abstract rationalism. The word *knowledge* frequently recurs in this novel, as does *permanence,* always in the context of this fusion of intellect and spirit which gives knowledge of something absolute and imperishable. In the church at the christening of his second child, Stan becomes aware of receiving "a light of knowledge" (p. 124) which he is unable to analyze. Ossie Peabody, the Parkers' discontented and unhappy neighbour, is contrasted both with Stan himself and with the simplicity and goodness Stan senses in the natural world. Stan is aware of "little spasmodic waves of knowledge and contentment," so that his "knowledge of goodness" (p. 156) is impervious to Ossie's meanness. The next page refers again to Stan's knowledge, while the imagery connects him with the sun. At the end of Part Two, when Stan is confronted with the news that war has broken out in Europe, his progress is summed up once again in terms of knowledge, "moments of true knowledge," which tell him of the presence of God and relate that presence to his wife's face and to a trembling leaf whose "veins and vastness were related to all things, from burning sun to his own burned hand" (p. 190). This is the anagogic perspective which dominates the novel. In Part Three, as Stan travels home from his fruitless effort to find and help Ray, who has been involved in a racing scandal, the "perpetual mystery" in scrolls of fallen bark allow Stan to exchange his ignorance for "knowledge" (p. 284). Mr. Gage's painting of the ant-woman with whom Amy identifies depicts "a small kernel of knowledge" in the woman's almond eye, a growing eye, part of the tree of man. Elsie's son shares this same knowledge; he is aware of a knowledge of poetry without knowing any particular poems, and asks Stan, " 'Don't you ever know, Granpa, about things, because you just know?' " (p. 407).

Stan Parker's initial stance, as he begins his search for understanding, is one of wondering acceptance: "there seemed no question of interpretation. Anyway, not yet" (p. 7). Like Beckett's Estragon in the opening line of *Waiting for Godot,* Stan knows that there is "nothing to be done" (p. 7). He is *there,* and stubbornly determined to survive. His stubborn courage is referred to both at the beginning of his life and at its ending, when he tells the young evangelist, " 'I would not be here if I was not stubborn' " (p. 495). Although Stan, in his simplicity and humility, is strikingly different from Voss, he does share one characteristic with the German explorer, and with his own mother—an aspiration towards something transcendent which he cannot describe. Despite his love for his land and all it contains, his eyes regard it from a distance. This is the discontent which balances his wondering love of his scrubby land, a love which gives shape to his life for the first time. A struggle between two desires is being waged within Stan, as "the nostalgia of permanence and the fiend of motion fought inside the boy, right there at the moment when his life was ending and beginning" (p. 8). And so begins his search ("if he had known it," as the narrator quietly informs us) of permanence. His quest must also supply the meaning of the land that contains him, since the technique is continually identifying Stan with natural objects—tree, cabbage, rose, animals, and his own house. Thus the basic image for Stan's quest, as reflected in the novel's title, is not progress along a road or way but growth. And the way is inward, coil by coil, towards the central core. A continuous process of discovery keeps both Stan and the grandchild who is close to him in a state of "endless being" (p. 397).

Stan's future, and what is in one sense a description of the narrative sequence of *Tree,* is contained in the remarks of Stan and Amy's first visitor, the stranger who sells Bibles and magnetical water: " 'Because the Almighty 'asn't yet shown 'Is 'and. You 'ave not been 'it over the 'ead, kicked downstairs, spat at in the eye. See?' " (p. 36). Drunkenness is a favourite device of White's for justifying apocalyptic remarks on the "realistic" level, and the stranger's madness is the disturbing kind that lights up some facet of the truth only too clearly. The storm which follows this visit is the first blow designed to teach Stan the limits of his strength which still appears to him unlimited.

The images of gold and ebony in the stranger's talk of the African Gold Coast evoke in Stan a vision of, and longing for, *all* beauty. Amy's Gold Coast is her little silver nutmeg grater. Stan, whose nature is less possessive than Amy's, is described as being a lesser victim of the same deception. His Gold Coast is his own land, glittering with promise. But although this land is now almost enclosed, his longing will not be contained within its fences. His eyes have assumed a distance from youth, and still attempt to focus on "something wood will not disclose," just as his ears are tuned to "the one theme" (p. 38) which threatens to burst from the sounds around him. In old age, Stan ironically watches young Peabody wrestling with earth and rock while fencing his land. The young man moves in the same fury of confidence as had Stan, "back in the dream time" (p. 374), before the trials of life and the complications of love have tempered his confidence.

The Almighty begins to show his hand soon after this, as Stan's fear that he is perhaps about to be hit over the head reminds us of the stranger's words. Implicit in the imagery of the great wind storm is the contrast between Stan's human father, the blacksmith, and the mythic god of thunder and lightning; and between man's weakness and the power behind the storm. Stan is suddenly insignificant, a thing of gristle; the house provides only an illusion of safety, and the hammer is inferior iron to the thunderbolts. When the wind has passed, Stan and Amy are described in mythic terms which suggest rebirth after death; even the dog shares in this state.[9] Stan is exhausted but at peace. From what little progress he has made, he concludes that "he was a prisoner in his human mind, as in the mystery of the natural world. Only sometimes the touch of hands, the lifting of a silence, the sudden shape of a tree or presence of a first star, hinted at eventual release" (p. 46).

As Stan and Amy struggle to repair the damage wrought by the storm, they are as ants on a tortuous path. The ant-man identification is one of the novel's recurring patterns of imagery which prepare us to understand Stan's final epiphany. In the days which follow the storm, Stan and Amy discover their weakness anew, this time in the face of death. The death of the cow precipitates Amy's fear of death and of all that she has not experienced; this in turn leads to her stumbling on the stones, and to the loss of her unborn child. The atmosphere of terror and helplessness in this episode suggests the lines from Sophocles' *Antigone* which Malcolm Lowry uses as one of the epigraphs to *Under the Volcano*: "Wonders are many, and none is more wonderful than man; . . . without resource he meets nothing that must come; only against Death shall he call for aid in vain."

The most dramatic suffering of the autumn of Stan's life is brought on by his wife and son, although this time of drought and doubts has a wider base in life in general. After Ray's involvement in a racing scandal, Stan journeys to the city in search of his son, full of hope and the innocent conviction that if he could only find his son, all would be made clear. His trip parallels

---

[9] "his new young nakedness . . . the new young naked man . . . the shining teeth, the streaming skin, and the clean, beautiful skull . . . their present state of purity. . . . The dog shook what remained of himself, for he was now his own skeleton" (p. 45).

the pilgrimage of Kumalo, the black pastor in Alan Paton's *Cry, the Beloved Country,* to Johannesburg in search of his lost son; or Ruth Godbold's trip to Khalils' after Tom, whom she is willing to follow "to hell if need be." All these episodes are patterned on the archetypal search for the lost beloved or the prodigal son.

For Stan, the path to hell lies "over a rime of rotting vegetables, and old newspapers, and contraceptive aids," and the stranger of whom he asks the way wonders whether Stan "was mad to expose himself thus nakedly at a crossroads" (p. 280). This is the same "madness" which makes Mary Hare ready to enter the burning house in search of Himmelfarb. The sweetish smell of rotten fruit which issues from the fruit shop, now closed, above which Ray has lived is identified with Ray himself. In Ray's career we have a demonic parody of the fruitfulness of Durilgai and of the tree of man; the rotten fruit and the bag of runty plums which Stan sees a woman pitch into the gutter form a prophecy of Ray's end. Stan refuses to join, however, in Thelma's facile assessment of Ray as *no good*: " 'It is too early,' he said, 'to say who is good' " (p. 283). This unwillingness to judge becomes, in the latter half of the novel, a recurrent motif, suggestive of the parable of the wheat and the tares (Matt. 13: 24-30). The imagery surrounding Ray's death is again demonic or repugnant: his second wife is "bloody horrible," cigarettes substitute for food, "friends" are those who "drink you dry," and flies and the smell of rot prevail (pp. 453-456).

The counterpart of the lost son Ray is the grandson, Elsie's boy, the sound fruit of the tree of man. This child is associated with the lost boy of the floodtime, a boy of whom we know little save that he refuses to be possessed by force, even by force of love.[10] He has taken the coloured glass from a flooded church and through it sees the world drenched in crimson. The lost boy is identified by Amy with the lost possibilities of their springtime.

---

[10] Cf. A. A. Phillips, "Patrick White and the Algebraic Symbol," *Meanjin* XXIV (1965), 458: "When the child vanishes we are confronted by a startling absurdity—why isn't every man in the neighbourhood out searching for that lost child? Gradually it dawns on us—the child is not real, it is a Symbol." Phillips suggests that the "algebraic symbol" is something artificial, an intellectual manipulation which is opposed to his idea of reality.

To this mythic pattern, which suggests the New Adam or man's recovery of lost innocence, belongs the description of Stan's "state of purity" after the rainstorm, the "new young naked man . . . with the shining teeth, the streaming skin, and the clean, beautiful skull" (p. 45), who Amy thinks would be like the son she *could* have. Her two actual children are demonic parodies of this desirable child: one a criminal, the other a neurotic whose pseudo-spirituality is like that of Rosie Rosetree in *Riders*.

Amy gives the red glass belonging to the lost boy to Elsie's son, who is kept in "a state of endless being" by his interest in things themselves (p. 397). In the short last chapter after Stan's death, the boy looks through the glass at the crimson mystery of the world. The colours of red and green dominate these final two pages, the same colours of the scene where Amy gives the glass to the boy (p. 399). The colours, of course, are complementary, hence operative at the level of verisimilitude. White habitually, however, uses colours as apocalyptic images. Crimson, colour of blood, belongs to the pain, suffering, and death which is part of Stan's final epiphany; green, to the promise contained in the boy, whose thoughts and life are green shoots put out by the eternal tree of man: "So that, in the end, there was no end."

When suspicion of Amy's infidelity has given way to certainty, Stan drives off in his old car, which seems to find its own way into the city. In *Tree* the apocalyptic city or desirable community of men is located at Durilgai, with the big city nearby depicted as a parody of true community, a place which is associated with Thelma's social climbing and Ray's fall, and which is now the locale for Stan's experience of hell. His own past failures, especially his failure to take up the bearded man in the flood, mingle with Amy's, in the "swill pot" where drink affords no relief. It would seem that Stan has reached absolute bottom in the side street beneath a "Godless" paper sky: "He spat at the absent God then, mumbling till it ran down his chin. He spat and farted, because he was full to bursting; he pissed in the street until he was empty, quite empty. Then the paper sky was tearing, he saw. He was tearing the last sacredness, before he fell down amongst some empty crates, mercifully reduced to his body for a time"

(p. 333). At the milk bar belonging to Con the Greek, Stan senses that he has not yet reached the depths, and at the same time he is agonizingly aware of an irretrievable state of lost innocence. On the beach a little later, with the woman whose smell is "less fetid than his own condition" (p. 340), he does reach the depths as he attempts to strangle Amy's lust through bruising the throat of the cat-woman. Stan's psychic experience of death completes his third stage of life and the novel's Part Three. Returning to Amy he sees that a period has ended, that they have entered a fresh phase.

In the time of alienation from God which follows, years of resignation and suspended life, Stan experiences a freedom from God which is a parody of the freedom he is later to recover and which he vainly tries to explain to Lola after Ray's death: " 'Freedom. But prayer is freedom, or should be. If a man has got faith' " (p. 458). During the period of his own spiritual death, however, when Stan is "more or less resigned to that state of godlessness he had chosen when he vomited God out of his system and choked off any regurgitative craving for forgiveness" (p. 356), he experiences the same hollow parody of freedom which has ensnared Lola. His recovery begins after the accident where he just fails to shoot himself. The state of suspension ends, his emptiness begins to fill: "It is not natural that emptiness shall prevail, it will fill eventually, whether with water, or children, or dust, or spirit. So the old man sat gulping in. His mouth was dry and caked, that had also vomited out his life that night, he remembered, in the street" (pp. 422-423). Stan nourishes his new spiritual life by taking part in the communion service. The wine mingles with the vomit and bile of his hatred of Amy and his disbelief in God; Stan swallows both together, with humility and gratitude, confident that eventually he shall "receive a glimpse" (p. 432) of the transcendent reality he has always sought.[11]

[11] Cf. Jack Lindsay, "The Alienated Australian Intellectual," *Meanjin* XXII (1963), 57: "the world Patrick White describes is one of pure alienation"; and p. 58: "White's inability to conceive any answer, any defiance of alienation, beyond the spontanious harmonies of the crushed but unresentful soul, makes him unable to oppose effectively the thing that he so sincerely and fiercely hates." Lindsay seems to be blaming White for *not* doing things which are actually done magnificently in his novels.

We have seen how the theme is forwarded through narrative treated archetypally as ritual. The theme is also developed through a network of recurrent images. Although the image takes its meaning from its individual context, a continuity of association within subtly varied contexts is established. With repetition of the basic image, the metaphorical identification is confirmed. Some of the most important of these apocalyptic images in *The Tree of Man* are *ant* (identified with man's frailty), *fish* (identified with a transcendent divine spirit and the possibility of man's relation to this), *mandala,* and *square.* The patterns, of course, become clearer upon second and subsequent readings, a labour which White's novels richly repay. The fish motif in *Tree* begins with Mr. Gage, the postmistress's husband, whose paintings bring Amy Parker a moment of truth. Mr. Gage had been engrossed in a beautiful fish at the time of his first meeting with Mrs. Gage. Fish symbolism becomes prominent in Part Four, the section containing Stan's spiritual rebirth, where it is introduced frequently in a variety of contexts. A fish is one of Thelma's presents to her mother: "The fish was. He glittered. His being could not end in death" (p. 385).

The fish, as Jessie Weston demonstrates in *From Ritual to Romance,* is an ancient symbol of divine life, being identified with or considered sacred to those deities who were supposed to lead men back from death to life. Miss Weston maintains "that the Fish is a Life symbol of immemorial antiquity, and that the title of Fisher has, from the earliest ages, been associated with the Deities who were held to be especially connected with the origin and preservation of life."[12] Both the Buddha and the Hindu god Vishnu appear in fish avatars. For the early Christians the fish was the secret symbol of Christ, the apostles were commanded to be "fishers of men," and a sacramental fish-meal was celebrated in the catacombs by the primitive Christian Church. In the Mystery cults of the Mediterranean basin in the pre-Christian era, the fish was associated with the god-man and served as the holy food of their sacred meal. Some of the Christian mystics (par-

---

[12] Jessie L. Weston, *From Ritual to Romance* (New York: Doubleday Anchor, 1957), p. 125.

ticularly the Naassene sect) saw Christianity as the fulfilment of the earlier Mystery cults and attempted to fuse the mystic meal of the cults with the sacrament of the eucharist. In short, the fish serves as a universal symbol of deity, and of the possibility for man of a spiritual life begun in this life and continued in the next. In this context, it is found in Buddhism, Hinduism, various mythologies including the Celtic, the ancient Mystery religions of the Mediterranean basin, and Christianity. The universality of the symbol is evoked in *The Tree of Man,* as it is in *Finnegans Wake*[13] and *The Waste Land.* Nevertheless, White's use of the Methodist prayer meeting and the Anglican communion service at crucial points in the narrative structure of Part Four points to a Christian context for the fish image—and this, despite the apparent repudiation of the young evangelist at the time of Stan's death.[14]

The maiden name of Ray's wife, Tarbutt,[15] conceals the name of a fish. Elsie Tarbutt is an earlier version of Ruth Godbold, in *Riders.* She accepts Ray through a desire to undertake something too big for her, and as a more challenging and humiliating course than becoming a missionary. It is Elsie's son who is the child of promise, the inheritor of the birthright who remains when Stan has died. On the night of the rainstorm, when Stan has one of his moments of vision, the little boy sees life through the streaming windowpane as it would look " 'to a fish' " (p. 404). It is a revelation for the boy, but one which he cannot convey to the others. The boy's visual impression of life under water resembles a dream, and belongs to the inversions of reality and illusion effected in the novel. In the production of *Hamlet,* play and play-

---

[13] See Patricia A. Morley, "Fish Symbolism in Chapter Seven of *Finnegans Wake*: The Hidden Defence of Shem the Penman," *James Joyce Quarterly* VI (1969), 267-270.

[14] Zen Buddhism declares that any being reveals all beings, that *all* is ultimately *one,* but Christian mysticism has a far more personal character. The Christian faith of Doll and Elsie, and Doll's convent education, strengthen the novel's general Christian frame of reference.

[15] *Turbot* is a European flat-fish having a diamond shaped body, much esteemed as a food. Even the *kind* of fish chosen has significance, as the diamond shape relates to the square, associated with man's humanity in White's novels and in Jung's investigations of religious symbolism; and the edibility relates to the mystic meal where fish is identified with the body of the god-man.

ers suggest an inversion of the common perspective: real life is the dream, the pretence or play-acting from which death is an awakening to reality. Stan's thoughts of his submerged half continue the association of fish and spirit.

Madeleine, in youth the brittle heroine of Amy's "novelette," returns in Part Four as Mrs. Fisher, Thelma's friend. Her new name appears at first to be a parody of the usual context for fish symbolism, as these sterile women are contrasted with Amy's simplicity. The satire directed at the artificial sophistication of this woman and her society is similar to that found in the last chapter of *Riders* (the luncheon party of the Crab-Shell, the Bon-bon and the Volcano) or the scenes in *The Living and the Dead* with Muriel Raphael. The Armstrongs, the Forsdykes, and their friends suggest what Northrop Frye has called a chattering monkey-society. Unlike the comedy of manners in, say, Restoration drama, White's social satire is not of major importance in itself but serves to forward his main theme and to point up weaknesses in Stan and Amy Parker. Amy identifies Madeleine with all the luxury and the erotic experiences which Amy herself has not experienced; her desires are temporarily purged when she sees Madeleine retching on the ground, after the fire. Stan has been strongly tempted by lust in his rescue of Madeleine from the burning house.

Our last glimpses of Mrs. Fisher, however, reverse the suspicion that her name is simply a comic parody of the fish symbol. As Madeleine and Thelma are leaving Parkers', the narrator suggests that these were people "who had not realized themselves fully, but would perhaps, if time would stand" (p. 449). Madeleine speaks genuinely to Stan of the lovely smell of winter, which seems endless. And she is suddenly possessed by a yearning for bees, which are identified with her terrible nostalgia for lost possibilities. Here, as earlier in the novel, bees are identified with spiritual peace and with the sun (pp. 213, 450).[16] Solutions have eluded Madeleine so far. The last mention of her, however, describes Mrs. Fisher as one whose glances, towards

---

[16] Once again we find that White's most effective images are traditional rather than novel. Honey is a recurring biblical metaphor (Deut. 32: 13; Ps. 81: 16, Prov. 16: 24; 24: 13).

the end of her life, were directed inward. The suggestion that Madeleine's life constitutes another quite possibly successful quest illustrates the inclusive tendency of the comic structure.

The ant is identified with man's essential humanity, with his physical frailty and his eventual physical death.[17] Failure to notice the development of the ant pattern throughout the novel will restrict the impact of Stan's final epiphany, which begins with a leaf and the ants on the path. In his close attention to the natural world, Stan frequently observes ants; and on one such occasion the narrator comments that Stan makes these observations "from the dream state of the sleeper, in which he was slowly stirring and from which he would one day look out perhaps and see" (p. 216). When Stan goes to seek Ray in the city, people advise Stan with "antlike fidelity," as if receiving him "into their own ant-world" (p. 280).

A special pattern of ant imagery surrounds Amy, Mr. Gage, and his paintings. In the small clearing where her married life begins, Amy's childlike frailty seems to put her on a level with the ant. In Part Two, she encounters Mr. Gage spread out upon the ground, contemplating an ant. He is surprised that Amy neither questions nor criticizes his stance: "Because it is not usual for a human being to resist an opportunity to destroy. And she could have crushed with her foot such ecstasy as remained in his ant-body" (p. 103). (There are many times when Amy succumbs to "the queer pleasure she derived from sensing some hurt to her husband," p. 228.) Amy remembers this incident when Mr. Gage's paintings are discovered at the time of his suicide, and in her continuous preoccupation with what could have been her relationship with the dead man, she resembles the savagely simple woman of one of his paintings, reaching for the incandescent sun. In the painting's corner appears the skeleton of an ant filled with a fire as intense as the sun's. The painted woman, the ant, and Amy are thus identified, and depicted as aspiring to the transcendent absolute of the painting's sun.

The ant imagery is complemented by an assortment of images

[17] Mary Hare, in *Riders,* is distressed to observe some dying ants, accidentally crushed, which hang from her hand and from the bloodstone ring which confirms her ownership of Xanadu.

which are identified with man's spirit—bird, butterfly, fire, and fish. Although this polarized pattern resembles at times the bird-snake pattern of symbolism in D. H. Lawrence's *The Plumed Serpent,* the essential unity of White's vision is demonstrated by his use of the ant image alone at the time of Stan's death, and by the fiery ant of Mr. Gage's painting. Western literature has frequently associated the bird's freedom of flight with man's spirit. White uses this traditional association in *Voss,* in Palfreyman's profession of ornithology. In *Tree,* the man-child Bub is "both bird and ant" (p. 186) as he explores the ground and the tree-tops with wondering appreciation. The separation of spirit and animality is more distinct, more noticeable, in Bub than in a normal human being. The butterfly provides a variation on the bird image. In Chapter 21, where Stan attends a production of *Hamlet* and an early-morning communion service, the narrator refers to Stan's spiritual activity and his *communion* with the landscape. Following this, Stan stoops to watch some ants dragging a butterfly wing. On a sudden impulse, he twitches the wing away and tosses it into the sunlight, where it flutters and shimmers, "rightly restored to air" (p. 412). The wing, an image of the spirit, belongs by rights to the sun and air rather than to the ground and the ants. The connotations of the incident are similar to those surrounding the image of Bub as both ant and bird.

With reference to the ultimate vision of *The Tree of Man,* Manfred Mackenzie emphasizes the "quite unambiguous conclusion, when the dying Stan Parker is received into the 'One.' "[18] The identification of man and ant throughout the novel prepares us for Stan's final epiphany, when he expresses his belief in a leaf, in the cracks in the path and the painfully struggling ants: "But struggling. But joyful. . . . As he stood waiting for the flesh to be loosened on him, he prayed for greater clarity, and it became obvious as a hand. It was clear that One, and no other figure, is the answer to all sums" (p. 497). The paradox of suffering and joy is finally resolved into One joy, yet Stan's direct assertion of belief is not in this mystical One, but in the earth, the ants, the gob of spittle which, as he informs the young evangelist, " 'is God' " (p. 495).

[18] Mackenzie, "Apocalypse in Patrick White's 'The Tree of Man,' " p. 411.

The last five pages of Chapter 25, beginning "That afternoon the old man's chair had been put on the grass at the back" (p. 493), form a closely knit unit; the chapter's last page contains Stan's final epiphany, but these last five pages contain ours. Stan is shown at the centre of a mandala, which has formed out of the wilderness without man's conscious design: "It was perfectly obvious that the man was seated at the heart of it. . . . All was circumference to the centre, and beyond that the worlds of other circles. . . . The last circle but one was the cold and golden bowl of winter, enclosing all that was visible and material" (pp. 493-494). The golden-bowl image recalls the golden bowl formed by the brass rail of the balcony at the theatre, a bowl which had held all life in the form of the eternal archetypes of human fears and desires in Shakespeare's *Hamlet*. But whereas Stan, or man himself, is at the *centre* of this bowl that encloses "all that was visible and material," the *circumference* is not man in his ant-frailty, not man subject to death and physical decomposition, but some "last circle" beyond this—some absolute *with which man is intimately identified*.

Into this "large and triumphal scheme" comes the young evangelist, with his belief in the direct approach and his "steam roller" faith. His concern is not really for Stan's spiritual welfare but for himself, since his passionate exposure of his past sins is an "orgasm," an obsession which preoccupies the young man "even to the exclusion of his present mission, the old man" (p. 494). Once again, as so often in White's novels, we are reminded of the difference between what Kierkegaard described as subjective and objective truth, the former involving a valid personal relation to the truth.[19] The evangelist's faith is criticized subjectively, not objectively, as something held too easily. His faith is still untried in the furnace of doubt and suffering, nor does the novel support the youth's contention that the great glories may be had just by the putting out of a hand: "If you can understand, at

---

[19] Robert Bretall, ed., *A Kierkegaard Anthology* (Princeton, New Jersey: Princeton University Press, 1947), p. 192, comments as follows: "Having defined the truth as subjectivity, the *Postscript* proceeds . . . : since truth lies in the 'how' of the subject's relationship, *the fullest truth attainable by human beings will be that relationship in which the subjective element—the passion with which one holds to an object—reaches its highest intensity*."

your age, what I have been struggling with all my life, then it is a miracle, thought the old man" (p. 495).[20] In Part One, Amy has desired "the completeness, the safety of religion. But to achieve this there was something perhaps that she had to do, something that she had not been taught" (p. 28). The young man's story of life in the fettlers' camps serves to relate this critical point in the novel with an earlier one, where Amy has been confounded by Mr. Gage's painting of the "scrawny fettler-Christ" and the "jewels of blood" on Christ's hand, so that she has been brought to half-grasp "great truths" (p. 289). This painting, framed by Amy's speechless reverence and the shock and fear of the neighbour women, occupies a central position in *The Tree of Man* similar to Palfreyman's "crucifixion" in *Voss*.

Stan sees the kinship of "fair and foul," in Yeats's phrase, when the spittle appears to him as a "jewel" (p. 496) identified with the most sickening incidents of his life or the fetid character of his own condition when he fell down a city alleyway and "spat at the absent God." A. P. Riemer considers that Stan's discovery of God in a gob of spittle is "man's confirmation of his own divinity," and that this is "an intensely private intuition of divinity which has nothing to do with the conventional formulation of organized religion."[21] On the contrary, I suggest that this is a profoundly orthodox expression of the Christian doctrine of the divine transcendence as immanent in this created world, one which follows from belief in the Incarnation of God as man. Among the early Christians there were numerous heretical sects such as the Docetists, Patripassianists, and Sabellians who held that Christ's physical body was either a phantom or of celestial substance. Convinced of the evil character, or at least the ultimate unimportance, of the body and the natural world, these sects held that Jesus only *seemed* to have a human body; he did not really hunger and thirst, suffer and die, but only appeared to

---

[20] Olive Schreiner, in the novel from which White takes two of the epigraphs for *The Aunt's Story*, speaks of redemption as coming from within: "It is wrought out by the soul itself, with suffering and through time" (*The Story of an African Farm* [London: Ernest Benn, 1951], p. 229).

[21] A. P. Riemer, "Visions of the Mandala in 'The Tree of Man,' " *Southerly* XXVII (1967), 12-13.

do so in a kind of divine masquerade. Against this, the orthodox Christian faith has always upheld the full reality of both the humanity and the divinity of Christ. Stan's belief in a leaf, the ants, and his own spit, along with his understanding and acceptance of the most sickening incidents of his life, represents his profound acceptance of man's humanity, of his physical body and the natural world, of the necessity of this temporal flux within the economy of things eternal and of its final identity with the One which is "the answer to all sums."

The identity is expressed through an epithalamium mysticism,[22] not the unitive mysticism which negates the reality of the temporal. It is the same vision which underlies Willie Pringle's seeing the blowfly on its bed of offal as " 'but a variation of the rainbow' " (*Voss*, p. 441). There is, however, nothing "vacuous"[23] about White's artistic expression of this poetic vision. In *The Tree of Man* as in his other novels this identity between man, nature, and God is expressed by the radical metaphor, where two things are identified while each retains its own form, and by the anagogic perspective which sees the universe as the incarnate Word. The emphasis on immanence in *Tree* is balanced in the novel which follows by an emphasis on transcendence and divine grace, mediated to Voss through Laura and Mercy.

---

[22] See Denis de Rougemont, *Passion and Society,* trans. Montgomery Belgion (London: Faber, 1956), pp. 153-154.

[23] G. A. Wilkes, "Patrick White's 'The Tree of Man,' " finds that the novel insists upon "the acceptance of the workaday world," but feels that a certain awkwardness follows "from the embarrassing tradition of nature mysticism . . . and from the inherent difficulty of rendering mystical experience in terms that make it seem other than vacuous" (pp. 29-31). Cf. John Rorke, "Patrick White and the Critics," *Southerly* XX (1959), "the very difficulty of White's critics in dealing competently in artistic terms is partly explained by their almost total unfamiliarity with any depth of insight into moral complexity" (p. 69); ". . . the knowing and telling of the vast ambiguities of soul and world. These things White provides convincingly for the first time in Australian novel-writing" (p. 70).

"The great (and toothsome) sinners are made out of the very same material as those horrible phenomena, the great Saints. The virtual disappearance of such material may mean insipid meals for us."

C. S. LEWIS, SCREWTAPE PROPOSES A TOAST

chapter **8** A path through hell

Johann Ulrich Voss and Laura Trevelyan hardly qualify as the typical hero and heroine of romantic comedy. In terms of structure, however, *Voss* is a comedy which ranges over the full comic spectrum from romantic to ironic phases—a modern version of *The Divine Comedy*. In the Bonners' country house near Sydney, Voss looms like some giant crag over the huddled landowners. His own world is one of desert and dreams, and this same world is "his by right of vision" (p. 25). Although there *is* a sense in which Voss's experience is that of Everyman, nevertheless on the narrative level Voss is *not* the common man, whose fate is "his own fat paddocks, not the deserts of mysticism" (p. 340). In striving for the true knowledge which, as Laura suggests at the novel's end, may only come "of death by torture in the country of the mind," Voss may sometimes appear as the victim of tragic hybris, and much that is applicable to the traditional tragic hero is true of Voss, but he is essentially a comic figure.[1]

---

[1] See John Rorke, "Patrick White and the Critics," *Southerly* XX (1959), 71; and Geoffrey Dutton, *Patrick White*, Australian Writers and Their Work, ed. Dutton (Melbourne: Oxford University Press, rev. 1963), p. 33.

The structure of comedy may include a tragic episode within its larger framework, just as Christianity includes Christ's Passion within the larger scheme of redemption and resurrection: "The sense of tragedy as a prelude to comedy seems almost inseparable from anything explicitly Christian."[2] White's novel includes the sufferings of Laura, Voss, and the other characters within a larger comic framework such as this. Truly humbled at last, Voss is *nearest* to becoming God, the goal of his aspiration: " 'In the end, he may ascend' " (p. 381). His quest, despite the fact that it ends in his death, is successful. As in Dante's great epic, Voss's literal journey is both an allegory of the progress of the individual soul towards God, and a vision of the absolute towards which it strives.

The imagery in *Voss* is more intricately worked than in the *Commedia,* as the desert is identified with all three of the states in Dante's poem, Inferno, Purgatorio, and Paradiso. The characters in *Voss* move back and forth between these three states, with Paradise being glimpsed near the beginning of the novel as well as near the end. In its basic structural movement and emotional tone, however, *Voss* follows the threefold movement of the *Commedia,* as Voss moves from the inferno of pride, envy, and wrath (these being perversions of the natural instinct to love and desire goodness, as Vergil explains to Dante) through purgatorial suffering into final joy. The deaths of Voss, Frank, and Harry are preceded and illuminated by Palfreyman's death, and simultaneously accompanied by the crisis of Laura's illness.

In the Inferno to which the spirit of Vergil conducts the poet Dante in order to free him from temptation to sin, the seventh circle contains murderers, suicides, and blasphemers: those guilty of violence against others, against themselves, and against God and Nature. Woven into the theme of White's novel is the injunction that atheism is a form of suicide. Le Mesurier finally cuts his own throat, being unable to "wring out" hope for himself when Voss proves powerless. As for Voss, at many points in the first two-thirds of the novel his megalomania verges on blasphemy. Voss's removal from Germany to the world's

[2] Frye, *Anatomy of Criticism,* p. 215.

"underside" is perhaps a whimsical parallel of Dante's emergence from the Inferno at the earth's centre into the opposite hemisphere to begin the approach to the island mountain of Purgatory. The historic explorer Ludwig Leichhardt was also German, of course. But if White chose to emphasize the geographical movement in order to point up the literary parallel, he gave it a characteristic twist. Voss has *not* emerged into a different spiritual locale by moving to the world's underside; in Australia, "his boots sank into the same gritty sterile sand to which he used to escape across the *Heide*" (p. 10). Real freedom, the narrator subtly suggests, is not obtained by moving about on the face of the earth. The Australian desert to which Voss is drawn, however, is to prove needful to his destiny.

In the Earthly Paradise of Dante's *Commedia*, the poet meets Beatrice, who is associated with divine grace and revelation and has petitioned that Dante be granted this extraordinary tour which culminates in his experiencing the beatific vision. White's Laura combines the roles taken in the *Commedia* by Beatrice and Vergil, but her conception owes more to Petrarch than to Dante, as the name *Laura* suggests. (The names of White's protagonists are almost invariably significant,[3] and often yield layer upon layer of meaning, as does Mordecai Himmelfarb's name in *Riders in the Chariot*.) Petrarch's Laura is more human, less ethereal, than Dante's Beatrice or the *donna angelicata* of Petrarch's Italian predecessors. By emphasizing the romantic and Italianate character of Laura Trevelyan's appearance and surface personality, White underlines her relation to the Laura of the *Rime Sparse*. White's Laura has a "lovely throat" and "cool hand" (p. 6), a fine "Italian" (p. 70) style of handwriting which is elegant without being ostentatious, and "soothing, rather moody" clothes which suit her person. She is the literate member of the Bonner family.

In the case of Laura, as with White's use of archetypes and of literary parallels and conventions in general, his "sources" serve only to emphasize his true originality, which flowers from the

[3] See Thelma Herring, *"The Solid Mandala*: Two Notes," *Southerly* XXVIII (1968), 216.

root of cultural and literary tradition. Petrarch's Laura, despite the relative realism with which she is presented, is an *unobtainable* beauty, hence a cause of both joy and despair to the poet. In this respect, the *Rime* are in the Provençal tradition of *cortezia,* the idealization of sexual desire which forbade the physical consummation of love. The relationship between Laura Trevelyan and Voss, however, is both psychic and physical. Despite their geographic separation, the imagery clearly suggests the physical consummation of their love. In the relation of White's lovers, there is none of the *purposed* refusal to consummate love in order to heighten longing which underlies the literature of *cortezia.*

A second difference may be observed in the treatment of Laura herself. In the *Rime,* the poet is torn between his love for Laura (who is associated with fame, through punning upon her name and the laurel wreath) and his spiritual yearnings. White's novel contains a faint suggestion of a similar conflict between love and spirit when Voss fears that love may weaken him and hinder his quest, but as the novel develops he comes to understand that his relationship with Laura is a source of strength, not weakness. Eventually his aspiration is identified with his love. Thirdly, White's Laura takes the place of *both* Petrarch *and* his beloved Laura. In *In Morte di Madonna Laura,* the later lyrics which follow Laura's death, the poet's terrible grief is finally assuaged and the mood and tone become more spiritual, with a definite note of consolation. In the novel, a sharp change in mood occurs in Chapter 14, after Voss's death, where the tragic subplot begins to be seen within the larger structure of comedy. Here, unlike the *Rime,* it is *Laura* who survives, and who leads the reader towards a proper understanding of death. In general the analogies with Dante and Petrarch serve to emphasize the allegorical level of *Voss,* where Laura represents divine grace.

Laura Trevelyan's character and her relationship with Voss are crucial to the novel, both thematically and structurally. By being similar to Voss in many respects, Laura is able to help him. It is no accident that the novel begins and ends with Laura, not Voss. The reader is led to identify with Voss through Laura, who possesses his faults and virtues on a more human scale and achieves a self-knowledge which includes an awareness of the dangers of arrogance far sooner than does Voss. Laura's love operates to draw Voss back into the circle of humanity and out of the isolation into which he is driven by pride. As Mother Veronica Brady notes, Laura's belief in Voss is "the strongest argument in his favour."[4]

The similarities between Laura and Voss are evident in their first encounter. Both are introverts, for whom contact with other people requires effort. Laura receives the German reluctantly, obedient to her duty: "She would seldom have come out of herself for choice, for she was happiest shut with her own thoughts" (p. 3). Voss's distress is more noticeable, since Laura assumes a mask of social composure. With the return of the Bonners, Voss becomes "almost crazed by people. . . . How much less destructive of the personality are thirst, fever, physical exhaustion, he thought, much less destructive than people. . . . Deadly rocks, through some perversity, inspired him with fresh life. . . . But words, even of benevolence and patronage . . . would leave him half-dead" (p. 14).

Both are rationalists and religious sceptics, ready to value an intellectual equal but not really expecting to find one. In the absence of a rescue party, Laura feels, "she had to be strong" (p. 6). But the rescue party is already under way, for Laura and Voss are to rescue one another[5] from the isolation which has followed arrogance and pride. Laura and Voss have the virtues of their faults: strength, independence, and the refusal to yield can turn into stubbornness with a slight change in viewpoint. To Laura's "admirable self-sufficiency" (p. 5), the author has added the faintest hint of irony, noticeable in retrospect, as Laura and Voss are to discover what Connie Tiarks has attempted to make Elyot Standish realize: " 'We're not meant to live alone.' "

Laura and Voss are quite unlike in one respect. Laura is out-

---

[4] Mother Veronica Brady, "The Hard Enquiring Wind: A study of Patrick White as an Australian Novelist," unpublished doctoral thesis (University of Toronto, 1969), p. 88.

[5] On the level of narrative and "realistic" psychology, they rescue one another; on the level of allegory, Laura (as love) and Mercy (as divine mercy) rescue Voss (as man).

wardly "flawless" (p. 3) and composed, whereas Voss is socially unacceptable in appearance and manner, even "a bit of a scarecrow" (p. 12). His frayed trousers and distressed manner provoke in Laura almost a motherly pity, yet a pity mingled with admiration for his other qualities. Her early assessment of Voss as "one of the superior ones, even though pitiable" (p. 11) will continue to bear on Voss's character and quest throughout the novel. Despite this social inequality, Laura is identified with Voss's alienation from the society of "the established, the sleek or the ordinary" (p. 12). It is true that this society, although "ignorant," is also "innocent, and kind" (p. 5), and the sympathetic portrayal of Belle Bonner and Willie Pringle invalidates the charge that we find in White any simplistic denunciation of an entire class. In general, however, the Bonners' society, like their own residence, is a rich and relentless one which gives "no quarter to strangers" (p. 7). Both Voss and Laura are *strangers* to that society. A niece can become the archetype of the stranger, the outsider, more easily than a daughter. Laura remains something of a stranger to the Bonner family, despite their kindness, and in this way she is identified with Voss, "the shabby stranger" (p. 8), who is so unlike the young officers and landowners of the Bonner-Pringle society.

Voss, in his first appearance, engages the reader's sympathies, as he does Laura's, with his lack of social pretence and his sturdy independence. Even as a child he has preferred the freedom of the heath to the safety of the town. As an adult, he has rejected his parents' ambition to see him become a doctor or scientist. External freedom has led him, as it led Theodora and George Goodman, to wonder about the nature and purpose of that freedom, but this does not seem to be of immediate concern. In the first few pages, although the literary technique appears to be traditional, we have been subtly and skilfully introduced to Laura and Voss, and to the society to which they are strangers. So far, we sympathize with Voss's aspiration towards the infinite, preferring it to Mr. Bonner's earthbound gaze.

It is not until later in the chapter that the author-narrator effects a subtle change in point of view by introducing a second

point of view or frame of reference which operates simultaneously with the first: "At times his arrogance did resolve itself into
simplicity and sincerity, though it was usually difficult, especially
for strangers, to distinguish those occasions" (p. 19). This mention of arrogance recalls an image used earlier in describing
Voss's wresting of independence from his parents, that of "his
boot upon the trusting face of the old man his father" (p. 10).
As in *The Aunt's Story,* illusion and reality constantly change
places. Are simplicity and sincerity really arrogance and damn-
ing pride, or is it the other way round? The author warns us that
it may be difficult to distinguish between the two. The dual frame
of reference, the controlling point of view within which we see
the characters in this novel, involves pity and fear, sympathy and
ridicule, love and judgment.[6]

Our first impression of Voss is of his strength and self-sufficiency, his lack of fear for a desert land feared by others, and his
self-confidence in his ability to lead an expedition into this land.
He aspires to realize his own inner potentialities, and feels himself to be reserved for a peculiar destiny. The base-metal image
at the end of the first chapter exemplifies the subtlety, the refrac-
tory nature of White's symbols. This one serves, firstly, to link
Laura and Voss, setting them apart from the others and indicating the attitude of superiority which the others feel towards them,
an attitude from which the reader has already been led to disasso-
ciate himself. It does much more, however, since it involves the
narrator's frame of reference as well as that of the dinner guests
and, by implication, a prophecy of Voss's and Laura's fate. The
image recurs at the time of Le Mesurier's and Voss's death, at
which point we begin to see that the image actually contains the
theme. Northrop Frye describes the symbolism of alchemy as a
variant of apocalyptic symbolism, the purifying of the human
soul corresponding to the transmutation of earth or base metals
to quintessential gold.[7] Laura and Voss, in their initial arrogant
self-sufficiency, are the base metal awaiting transmutation.
Laura's realization (" 'It is for our pride that each of us is prob-

---

[6] See Frye, *Anatomy of Criticism,* p. 177.
[7] Ibid., p. 146.

ably damned' ") on the evening of the Bonners' party marks the point at which her own quest begins, her attempt to rescue Voss.

The second chapter clarifies our understanding of Voss's aspiration and the novel's theme, while reinforcing our sense that his character rests upon a paradox of strength and weakness. By contrast with the Bonners, Voss's weakness (his social humiliation) has appeared external and superficial. Now it appears as internal and profound, an "inherent helplessness" (p. 28) which may be more than physical. His knowledge seems a source of weakness beside the strength of Harry's innocence. Voss's purpose, as he explains it to Frank, is to discard the inessential and to attempt the infinite; he is prepared to pursue this idea through fire, torture, and death, knowing that " 'to make yourself, it is also necessary to destroy yourself' " (p. 31). This aphorism is ambiguous, and actually contains both the theme and its own demonic parody. In one sense, it suggests the New Testament theme of dying to sin in order to live unto God[8] which is further developed in "the paradox of man in Christ, and Christ in man" (p. 336). In another sense, however, it could suggest Voss's warning to Laura in the Bonners' garden, " '*Atheismus* is self-murder' " (p. 85), which provides a demonic parody of the New Testament theme. It is Voss's awareness of the dangers of the Idea being choked by the trivialities of existence[9] which makes him seek the desert, a place where it is easier to discard the inessential. Once again, the reader is attracted to Voss rather than to the contrasting Pringle society. Voss and Harry, the simple boy, are linked in their conscious acceptance of a terrain which others reject. In this way, Voss hopes, it is intended that he shall "justify" himself.

Voss's egotism has made him reject the "material world," where "men and women sat at a round table and broke bread together" (p. 32). The reference combines the eucharist symbol with the suggestion of mandalic roundness. Voss boasts that he will remake the desert into what he wishes, pay lip service to the

[8] See Luke 17: 33, and John 12: 24.
[9] In the parable of the sower (Luke 8: 14) the seed that fell among thorns is choked by pleasures and cares.

humility which he despises but others expect, and proceeds to imagine the desert as "a perfect abstraction" which will glorify his own name—but will offer that glory to himself rather than to posterity: "He had no more need for sentimental admiration than he had for love. He was complete" (p. 37).[10] In the dream which follows this discussion with his assistants, the granite monolith of Voss's idea is "untouched. Except by Palfreyman—was it?" (p. 40). Voss's ideal, in all this, is a *parody* of the traditional conception of a divine Being who is transcendent to as well as immanent in man, and whose nature is love rather than abstract perfection. And Voss's quest, had the novel been a tragedy with Voss as a tragic hero, would be a demonic parody of Arthur's quest for the Grail or of Christian's progress towards the Celestial City, with Voss's hybris evoking our pity and fear. Instead of this, Voss's proud self-sufficiency is altered by his relationship with Laura, so that his original megalomania[11] is contained within a comic structure in which his quest is finally successful. The novel does not stop with Voss's enforced "abdication." Laura's rescue party, unlike Colonel Hebden's, arrives in time to help Voss discover his need to love and be loved.

This structure depends upon an intricate network of triangular relationships, which may remind us of the structure of *Happy Valley*. The group composed of Voss, Harry, and Frank is contrasted with that composed of the "usurping" leader Judd, Turner, and Angus. The ornithologist, Palfreyman, hopes to maintain a "balance" between the two groups. The most important relationship is that of Laura and Voss, which is completed by the addition of "their" baby, the child of the servant Rose

---

[10] Cf. C. Hartley Grattan, "One-way Journey into a 'World of Desert and Dreams,' " *New York Times Book Review*, 18 August 1957.

[11] See Ian Moffitt, "Talk with Patrick White," *New York Times Book Review*, 18 August 1957, and Patrick White, "The Prodigal Son," *Australian Letters* I, 3 (1958), 39, where White explains (in slightly varying accounts) that his idea of a megalomaniac explorer was prompted by experiences in the Second World War, and also by accounts of the explorer Ludwig Leichhardt, who disappeared in 1848 while trying to cross Australia from east to west. White's reference to "the arch-megalomaniac of the day" is, apparently, to Adolf Hitler. A discussion of the relevance of Leichhardt's expedition to *Voss* may be found in M. Aurousseau, "The Identity of Voss," *Meanjin* XVII (1958), 85-87, and M. Clark, "Ludwig Leichhardt's Letters," *Meanjin* XXVII (1968), 405-408.

Portion. The child Mercy is important to the theme and the allegorical level of meaning, but less important in the narrative. In the Frank-Harry-Voss triangle we find the cynical intellectual, Frank Le Mesurier, and the simple boy, Harry Robarts, serving as Voss's "two dissimilar disciples. They were, indeed, an ill-assorted pair, alike only in their desperate need of him" (p. 35). These "dependents" are described as accepting even the crumbs that fall from Voss's mouth. Turner is " 'another convert' " (p. 38), in Frank's consciously ironic phrase, and Harry considers Voss his "saviour" (p. 34).

Later in the novel, in response to Voss's proposal of marriage, Laura refers to accepting "my destroyer as my saviour!" (p. 181). These references to disciples, converts, saviour, are part of a consistently developed pattern throughout the novel which leads to Laura's retrospective understanding of the meaning of Voss's life and death. Taken in isolation from the early chapters, these references have led the unwary to describe Voss as "a symbol of Christ."[12] But if the critic ignores the *demonic twist* to Voss's aspirations in much of the first three-quarters of the novel (ignores, that is, his megalomania), the resulting criticism is bound to be misleading. The *Oxford Dictionary* definition of megalomania (the term applied to Voss by White himself) as "the insanity of self-exaltation" aptly suggests the germ of the theme, but not the theme in its entirety, since megalomania is not Voss's final state.

In noting this comment by White on Voss, there is no question of the "intentional fallacy," since the authorial point of view is embodied within the novel itself: "With commentary ruled out, hundreds of devices remain for revealing judgment and moulding responses."[13] The modern preference for "objectivity" sometimes obscures the fact that the author is never silent or invisible. An author's voice, without recourse to direct commentary, is still dominant through his handling of dialogue, patterns of imagery and symbol, selection, sequence, and proportion.

[12] David Martin, "Among the Bones," *Meanjin* XVIII (1959), 54.
[13] Wayne C. Booth, *The Rhetoric of Fiction* (Chicago and London: University of Chicago Press, 1965), p. 272 and *passim*.

In *Voss*, White exploits the possibilities for apocalyptic imagery in Turner's oaths and drunken remarks. It is a drunken Turner, quoting a drunken Le Mesurier, who defines the narrative experience of the novel thus: " 'Contracted with a practisin' madman, you was, accordin' to your own admission, for a journey to hell an' back' " (p. 39). It is also Turner, or a common sailor very like him, whose anecdote helps Palfreyman to understand what his attitude towards Voss should be: "Voss, he began to know, is the ugly rock upon which truth must batter itself to survive. If I am to justify myself, he said, I must condemn the morality and love the man" (p. 94). This is the attitude towards Voss which the author-narrator asks of the reader,[14] using the other characters, especially Laura and Palfreyman, as emotional channel-markers for this purpose. Along with drunkenness, dreams, and the deliriums of fever and extreme suffering, the author uses Frank's conscious irony and Harry's extreme simplicity to justify apocalyptic imagery. *Voss* creates its own style, an effective fusion of form and content, as each successful work of art must do.[15]

Voss's initial remarks to Mr. Bonner introduce Harry in terms as simple as the boy himself (" 'He is good, simple' "), while Frank is described as one who has " 'great qualities, if he does not cut his throat' " (p. 17). Harry and Frank are Voss's first helpers and his last, staying with him until death. Whereas Harry is Voss's shadow, Frank's sophistications "could have been startling echoes of the master's own mind" (p. 356). Both Voss and Frank know what it is to wrestle with their daemon. Frank, disguised in cynicism and cloaked in irony, exemplifies what Voss

[14] Martin, "Among the Bones," p. 55, objects that "a novel isn't a prayer or rite. We cannot 'believe on' Voss. We have to believe in him." For this purpose, in this critic's opinion, the reader lacks sufficient factual information on Voss's youth and parents, as if the novelist were obliged to supply biographical and psychological case histories. While Voss's youth and parents are telescoped into the single paragraph to which David Martin objects, what Voss does to people and what people do to him *is* intricately illustrated throughout the long novel. The "act of faith" to which Martin objects is required of us, in one sense, by every work of art, whose hypothesis must be accepted (if only temporarily) in order to experience the work of art.

[15] Cf. Martin, "Among the Bones," p. 56: "*Ulysses*, because it is a new realism and a new allegory, creates its own style. But *Voss* does not create a new style, only a new muddle."

would have been without his arrogance *and* without the relationship with Laura which saves him from this arrogance. Frank is an unsatisfied rationalist, cynical rather than embittered, who has decided in advance that his search for the meaning of life will be fruitless. He is fond of considering God as a metaphysical problem, "ploughing through the dark treacle of seductive words and getting nowhere at two o'clock in the morning. Getting nowhere" (p. 30). Since Frank is also vain, he is tempted and flattered by Voss's talk of attempting the infinite, but the land which Voss has every intention of knowing with his heart, Frank is determined to consider as " 'a bad joke' " (p. 36). Frank's suicide fulfils Voss's jesting prophecy to Mr. Bonner, and Frank's life expresses the novel's theme in its demonic form: " '*Atheismus* is self-murder.' "

Harry is another of God's fools, "strong with innocence" (p. 28). The narrator tells us that Voss's form contains all possibilities for the boy who follows Voss like a faithful shadow, weak in wit but strong in spirit and physique. He gives himself to others (especially to Voss) unreservedly, as his simple nature finds purpose only through service, and he eventually fulfils his own prediction: that he will learn Voss's unique language and " 'stick closer than anyone, in the end' " (p. 242)—mad talk, according to Judd. Frank Le Mesurier, recognizing in Harry the innocence of his own childhood, hates what he cannot recover. The land, and the comforts of " 'havin' your belly full' " (p. 36), are accepted by Harry, who would have understood Holstius' advice to Theodora. Harry is too innocent himself to perceive moral deficiencies in another: "Like all those in love, he would misinterpret lovingly" (p. 37). This is illustrated at Rhine Towers, where Voss appears for a time to be as benevolent as Mr. Sanderson himself: "Harry Robarts accepted gladly that *his idol*[16] should deceive their host by borrowing the latter's character. This was not theft, that Mr. Voss had demonstrated to be honest" (p. 123, italics

---

[16] Harry's loyal and loving devotion to Voss throughout the latter's diabolic megalomania is paralleled by that of the young prince Emeth, in C. S. Lewis' symbolic romance for children, *The Last Battle*. Emeth discovers that his service to Tash, a devil-figure, has been accepted by Aslan the Good, because of the truly loving nature of the service.

mine). But that which Harry can accept so easily ("that man is right") is for the educated Palfreyman both a torment of doubt and an instinctive craving.

At his first meeting with Mr. Bonner, Voss has informed him that Palfreyman[17] is a man of great principles, "a Christian." Both Voss and Palfreyman are physically weak, but Voss's arrogance contrasts with Palfreyman's humility, and Voss reacts to the latter's reference to the will of God as if it is necessary to protect himself from some unpleasantness. Voss encounters this man, whom he has termed "exceptional," in the Botanic Gardens, where Palfreyman's neat but unpretentious grey contrasts with Voss's black: "the German's hot coat and black, sculptural trousers had an air of monumental slovenliness" (p. 41). Voss's appearance suggests that of Goethe's Mephistopheles or the shabbily debonair devil-figure of Ivan's nightmare in *The Brothers Karamazov*.[18] Whereas Palfreyman can find happiness in attending to insects, birds, and other life outside himself, Voss, like Waldo Brown in *The Solid Mandala*, is entirely self-obsessed. Palfreyman's references to furthering "His Grace's" interests allude, on the realistic level, to his English patron, the peer who has commissioned him, and on the allegorical level, to his existential patron, God. Much of White's wit and humour will be missed if we ignore the various levels of meaning.

The encounter with Palfreyman in the Botanic Gardens reminds Voss of his visit to the Moravian Mission[19] earlier that year at harvest time. This pastoral idyll prefigures the longer one with Sanderson at Rhine Towers (Chapter 6), affording an archetype of the earthly paradise. In its timeless aspect of placid

---

[17] *palfrey*: a saddle-horse for ordinary riding, as distinct from a war-horse; especially a small saddle-horse for ladies (*Oxford Universal Dictionary*). Palfreyman's name, which denotes humility, is like the allegorical names in Bunyan's *Pilgrim's Progress*.

[18] See Dostoyevsky, *The Brothers Karamazov* II, trans. David Magarshack (Harmondsworth, Middlesex: Penguin, 1967), 747.

[19] The Moravian Brethren are a pietistic sect based on a fifteenth-century evangelistic movement led by the Bohemian reformer John Huss. It was restored in 1722, after centuries of persecution, in the Silesian town of Herrnhut, which became a sanctuary for religious refugees from Moravia and Bohemia. The eighteenth-century German Pietists considered purity of acts and emotions to be more important than rationalism and religious formalism.

permanence the scene appears "carved," yet the harvest ritual
suggests a cyclic or living permanence. The peace and goodness
of the earthly scene, which seem to emanate from Brother Müller's soul, contrast strongly with Voss's restlessness. The Brethren, however, accept his frenzied movements when he joins in the
harvesting, "taking it for granted that even the apparently mis-
guided acts obey some necessity in the divine scheme" (p. 45)—
another example of authorial control of point of view without
actual commentary. Laura's realization of Voss's problem in the
Bonners' garden in Chapter 4 is anticipated here by Brother
Müller: " 'Mr. Voss', he said, with no suggestion of criticism,
'you have a contempt for God, because He is not in your own
image' " (p. 45). But Mr. Voss, explorer, is not yet ready to
agree.

We have noted that the internal point of view in the novel con-
trols the reader's attitude towards Voss, and that emotional response ranges between the opposite poles of sympathy and ridicule. The early chapters tend to evoke one emotional response *or*
the other, although both are usually present in varying degrees.
Thus the first chapter presents Voss as sympathetic, with the
Bonner society ridiculous by contrast. Chapter 2, where Voss is
sometimes ridiculous through the grandiose nature of his aspirations, ends with Brother Müller's comment, noted above. The
third chapter re-establishes our sympathy with Voss, both by
contrasting him with a society predominantly ridiculous and by
involving us in Laura's concern for his welfare.

The Pringle picnic provides the setting for some of the bitterest social satire in White's novels. The merchants and landowners, with their dialogue "of almost mystical banality"
(p. 56), are "mediocre, animal men" (p. 57) compared to Voss,
men who are ignorant of the power of rock and fire with which
Voss is associated. There is a double irony in the fact that these
men should find Voss's words "demoniac" *at this point*, simply
because his aspirations, poetically phrased, counter their materialism. Voss is ready to agree that Woburn McAllister, the
owner of a valuable property in New South Wales, is " 'obviously
one of the cornerstones' " (p. 62), a parody of the New Testa-

ment description of Christ. It is now clear that Voss and Laura are alike; walking in the Pringles' garden, they appear to be of equal stature and their expression is conspiratorial. On the return trip in the Bonners' carriage, with Voss as uncommunicative as usual, Laura realizes that Voss's almost unlimited arrogance is the quality which "just saves him, terrible though it is" (p. 68). Laura, identifying with the German through consciousness of her own arrogance, feels the need to "expiate" his guilt. This incident is effective on the first level of psychological "realism," while its other levels become clearer as the Voss-Laura relationship develops.

Sanderson's station at Rhine Towers (Chapter 6) is an archetype of the earthly paradise, like the land of Beulah in the writings of Bunyan and Blake. Before the meeting with Mr. Sanderson, Turner has flung his knife into the waves, symbolically purging the party, albeit temporarily, of the knives which are connected throughout the novel with suffering and cruelty. In the *Commedia,* the Earthly Paradise is the place where Dante meets Beatrice; in the novel, Voss writes at this time to Laura to propose marriage, "compelled" to do so by the peaceful beauty of the land and the idyllic atmosphere at Sanderson's station.

The prototype for both Mr. and Mrs. Sanderson may be found in the Knight of Faith of Søren Kierkegaard's *Fear and Trembling,* a figure which Kierkegaard contrasts with the Knight of Infinite Resignation. The latter, like the ancient Stoic or modern Romantic hero, is willing to renounce everything—willing, that is, to forswear the finite in hopes of the infinite. The Knight of Faith, unlike the aloof and philosophic Knight of Infinite Resignation, is simple and inconspicuous in outward appearance. By virtue of the absurd, he is ready *to receive back* all that he renounces in the first movement of faith, the infinite resignation. This describes White's Sanderson, an English gentleman and devoted husband who accepts the circumstances which preclude his being monk or hermit: "Sanderson tended his flocks and herds like any other Christian. If he was more prosperous than most, one did not notice it unduly, and both he and his wife would wash their servants' feet in many thoughtful and imperceptible ways" (p. 122). We will meet the figure of the Knight of Faith again in *The Solid Mandala,* in the persons of Leonard Saporta and Mr. Allwright.

An aura of timelessness envelops the inhabitants of the station, just as the Moravian scene had appeared to be carved. In the gentle, healing landscape, "the world of gods was becoming a world of men" (p. 120). By Sanderson's hearth, home and family are "enchantments" which cast a spell for good. The name, Rhine Towers, relates to Voss's yearning, described in Chapter 4, to experience another German summer, with flowing rivers, slowly sloping fields and trees that are green even under dust.[20] Sanderson's station symbolizes Voss's land of heart's desire, so that he experiences a "sense of homecoming" (p. 123). But what is real for Sanderson is, at this time and place, a mirage for Voss, who is desirous of it but unable to accept this solution to his quest. As Voss remarks to Sanderson, it is not in his nature to build a solid house and live in it the kind of life that is lived in such houses.

Le Mesurier realizes that "the serpent has slid even into this paradise" (p. 125), when a perverted impulse in Voss begins to manipulate the situation towards tragedy. Palfreyman's collapse rescues the party from their impasse, so that Voss's strange objections may be ignored: "It was possible that he himself had forgotten, until such times as he would torment himself by reviving painful memories of all his past perversities" (p. 126). Le Mesurier himself begins to change at Sandersons', where landscape and children conspire to penetrate the wall of isolation which his ironic scepticism has erected. But the breach so made proves inadequate to reverse the mental and emotional habits of Frank's entire adult life, and the images in this chapter, of a broken clock which lacks something essential and a wild dog which Sanderson failed to tame, prefigure Frank's end. Earlier, Le Mesurier described himself as "a man of beginnings," always

[20] At the sight of the rocks or towers which resemble a castle on the Rhine, Voss almost drowns in bliss, and finds it "the more intolerable that he might not finally sink, but would rise as from other drownings on the same calamitous raft" (p. 124); the "calamitous" raft prevents his sinking or drowning in life. The imagery is typical of White's inversion technique.

just about to act positively: " 'And this colony is fatal to anyone of my bent' " (p. 95).

Brendan Boyle of Jildra, the man who dislikes only himself, provides a variation in slow motion on the motif of self-destruction. Whereas Le Mesurier is destroying himself by cynicism and will finally cut his own throat, Boyle has chosen to rot slowly in filth.[21] His station at Jildra is a perfect inversion, a demonic parody, of the Sanderson estate. Its chaos contrasts effectively with the harmony at Rhine Towers, where everything is healthful, beautiful, peaceful, creative. In the slatternly settlement at Jildra, all is confused, noisome, ugly, discordant and destructive: "the station-owner had torn the boards off Homer to chock the leg of the table, and such other books as he had inherited, or even bought in idealistic youth, now provided material for spills, or could hope at best to be ignored, except by insects, dust and mould" (p. 162). At Rhine Towers the members of the expedition had experienced innocent dreams, but at Jildra Voss suffers from sleepwalking, and the apparition of his naked body becomes a torment for Palfreyman, suggesting to him that Christ is an evil dream, his lifelong deception.

Boyle's personal quest is also a parody of Voss's. As Voss seeks to discover the divinity within himself, Boyle is as urgently engaged in exploring the depths of his own repulsiveness. He tells Voss that each man has his own obsession, and that Voss's apparently is to overcome distance—but in much the same way as himself, Boyle adds, and with similarly disastrous results. He anticipates that Voss will celebrate " 'a high old Mass . . . with the skull of a blackfeller and his own blood, in Central Australia' " (p. 163). This prophecy, unlike Voss's jesting prediction of Le Mesurier's suicide, is fulfilled, but only after being inverted; a high mass, that is, *is* celebrated in Central Australia at the time of Voss's death, but the demonic or black mass anticipated by Boyle is changed back into a true eucharist.

The Sandersons are treated briefly in order to preserve the purity of the archetype. Much of Chapter 6 is devoted to intro-

---

[21] The pun concealed in Boyle's name ("boil") suggests his personality and way of life.

ducing the emancipist Judd, whose penal record is turned into an image of man's nature. In the first chapter, Voss notes that most men have committed murders; and, in the last, Laura knows that she must stand on trial with Judd. The former convict is a massive man, large and strong yet kind and gentle, one whose gifts are for practical things. Tempered in hell by his past sufferings, he is now like one "risen from the tomb of that dead life" (p. 129). Far from appearing as the Judas of one critic's description,[22] he appears to be almost a Christ-figure, a rougher version of the emaciated saintliness of the ornithologist. Palfreyman makes the association himself, referring to the "almost Christlike humility" (p. 146) with which the convict has tended one who, as a member of the English upper classes, is identified with those responsible for his sufferings. Much of the imagery which surrounds Judd in this chapter reinforces this association with Christ: his wounds, the lambs' blood, the secret spring. Even Voss, who detests humility, is reminded by Judd's form of "a mass of limestone . . . filled with a similar, slow, brooding innocence" (p. 131). In the desert it is Judd who insists, when Palfreyman fears to speak up, that the party celebrate Christmas, and it is Judd who becomes covered with the blood of the sheep he kills for their celebration. The emancipist "had aspired longingly at times to be reborn" (p. 190). If, however, we imagine that Judd *is* a Christ-figure, his role as the usurping leader becomes incomprehensible. Appearances may be deceptive, like Judd's mock Christmas-pudding made up under desert conditions. Judd is one who is "wedded to earthly things" (p. 239) and who craves "earthly love" (p. 240). His mutiny must be understood as the repudiation of Voss's willingness to risk all for the sake of his soul, a quest for the absolute or thirst for the kingdom of heaven which leads to Voss's ultimate union with Christ.

The discussion between Turner and Angus which follows the great desert storm (Chapter 10) helps to define the structure of relationships among the men of the expedition—a structure which is intimately connected to the theme. Angus and Turner are loyal to Judd as Frank and Harry, to Voss. Both groups com-

22 Martin, "Among the Bones," p. 54.

pose a triangle (and the latter group, a "trinity"[23]) with each leader being flanked by two dissimilar or ill-assorted disciples. The archetype for this relationship, as Samuel Beckett reminds us in *Waiting for Godot,* is the crucifixion of the two thieves on either side of Christ, where one of the two is lost and one is saved.[24] Angus and Turner, who remain with Judd when the party splits in two, are linked in mediocrity, but Angus believes in God while Turner finds it impossible to believe in anything he cannot see.[25] Le Mesurier's nightride through the storm, to bring the message that the sheep must be abandoned, has verified the suspicions of "the cave-dwellers," Turner and Angus, that "the rider was not of their own kind" (p. 249). Turner proceeds to liken the two groups (Judd's and Voss's) to *oil* and *water,* to illustrate their essential difference, their refusal to " 'run together, ever' " (p. 250). Earlier, at Sanderson's station, Judd and Voss have been compared to two rocks which cannot come together except in conflict.[26] On the allegorical level Judd, who is repeatedly characterized as the common man, represents man in his natural state, without the mediation of any external grace, while Voss, through his aspiration to something more than common joys and satisfactions, represents man's desire to relate to some absolute or transcendental Being—a desire which is unnatural to man as a practical rational animal.[27]

White's use of oil and water in this context of apocalyptic

---

[23] Frank, Harry, and Voss are described as enjoying their "trinity" (pp. 354, 372) after the departure of the mutineers.

[24] *Waiting for Godot* (London: Faber, 1967), p. 12. See Luke 23: 43.

[25] The connection between Turner and the thief who was lost is suggested in the description of Turner's eyesight: "The seedy Turner, who could not see straight except by squinting, and then was crooked in his final vision" (p. 248).

[26] The pattern of rock imagery associated with Voss suggests the pattern found in the Bible which associates Christ with rock or stone, especially as the rejected stone which becomes the headstone of the corner: Ps. 118: 22; Matt. 21: 42; Mark 12: 10; Luke 20: 17; Acts 4: 11; 1 Peter 2: 7-8; and the stumbling block or rock of offence: Romans 9: 33; 1 Peter 2: 8. This suggests the dying-in-order-to-live motif (Romans 6: 8-10, 1 Cor. 15: 36) which underlies the novel's paradoxes of strength and weakness, arrogance and humility, death and life.

[27] The *naturalness* of the desire to reject the desert is emphasized in the "animal spirits" let loose when Colonel Hebden decides to abandon his rescue mission. The men behave like the horses which have struggled back each night, despite

imagery follows a similar usage in the Bible. The Old Testament contains hundreds of references to oil, which was important in the daily life of the time. It was used to anoint the heads of guests at a festive meal, and came to be associated with joy and gladness. Isaiah uses the olive berry, source of oil, as a symbol of spiritual life.[28] The New Testament parable of the wise and foolish virgins (Matt. 25: 1-12) establishes a similar context for the symbol, identifying oil with the grace of God. Kierkegaard's interpretation of this oil as "the infinite passion of expectation" (i.e. an infinite desire for God) aptly describes the limitless aspiration of Voss. With reference to the bridegroom's refusal to admit the foolish virgins who come without oil, Kierkegaard writes: "the bridegroom said: 'I do not know you.' This was no mere quip . . . but the sober truth; for they had made themselves strangers in the spiritual sense of the word, through having lost the infinite passion."[29]

Pilgrim's Progress, like *Voss,* uses water in both an apocalyptic and a demonic context. Bunyan's pilgrim, in the House of the Interpreter, finds water being used to cleanse the soul of the "dust" of sin—the baptismal context commonly found in Western literature. Then, with a transformation similar to that which takes place in *Voss* (between the spring-water of Chapter 6 and the oil-and-water context of Chapter 10), Christian sees water being used by devils in an attempt to extinguish a fire. The Interpreter explains that the fire symbolizes the work of grace in man's heart, and is maintained by the *oil* of Christ's grace.

"Grace," in the Old Testament, frequently denotes the graciousness of a superior towards an inferior; in the New Testament, grace connotes God's love and mercy towards man. On the allegorical level of meaning in *Voss,* this grace is mediated to Voss by Laura. The baby Mercy is Laura's means to divine grace, as Laura is for Voss; through her relationship with Rose, Mercy's mother, Laura has learned humility. Judd's wife, by contrast, is

---

hobbles, in the direction from which they have come. Similarly, the animality of Turner, Angus, and Judd has been emphasized in Chapter 10, just before the separation into two parties.

[28] Isa. 7: 4, 6.

[29] Søren Kierkegaard, *Concluding Unscientific Postscript,* trans. D. F. Swenson, Introduction and Notes by Walter Lowrie (Princeton: Princeton University Press, 1944), p. 20.

"a heavy woman, in whom purpose took the place of grace" (p. 140). Literally, that is, she lacks feminine gracefulness; allegorically, both she and Judd represent man in his natural state.

Judd's allegorical function, as the natural man, is clearly established in Chapter 12. After obeying Voss's request to shoot the dying horse, he remains to stone the dead beast, slowly and viciously, an apparent folly which contrasts with his earlier actions. It terrifies Harry, who recalls Judd's many acts of kindness; these appeared the more poignant "since all human ties must be cut" (p. 332). That night Judd admits to no longer knowing where the party is heading, unlike former times, when he knew his way and his strength. The narrator suggests that this is "possibly an unearthly situation" (p. 333) and, a few pages later, that Judd's yearnings for "his own fat paddocks, not the deserts of mysticism" are the yearnings natural to the "common man" (p. 340). Judd's assertion that he can trust his own self, and his scorn for the lost compass whose broken needle had pointed to the ground where Palfreyman was buried, are part of the allegorical as well as the literal level of meaning.

The difficulty for the reader is posed by the contrast between, on the one hand, the meaning on the narrative level (where Judd's humility and genuine compassion are morally superior to Voss's arrogant selfishness) and, on the other hand, the meaning on the allegorical level (where the two groups represent the difference between *nature* and *grace*).[30] The reader may be puzzled by the apparent denunciation of Judd, in the last quarter of the novel, as the usurper and the mutineer, since Judd is so obviously a better man, morally, than Voss. While the allegory is perfectly consistent within itself throughout the novel, it is partly divorced from meanings established through narrative and "realistic" psychology.

I am reluctant to call this a weakness in the novel, since it is inseparable from the novel's theme and from the poetic truth of the novel *as a whole*. In most of White's novels, however, the various levels of meaning are perfectly fused. Contemporary readers, unused to allegory, are likely to find *Voss* difficult. It is

---

[30] See Francis A. Schaeffer, *Escape from Reason* (London: Hazell, Watson and Viney, 1968), p. 9.

perhaps the most difficult of White's novels, although its difficulties are always *valid*; its form is the natural and inevitable expression of its particular matter, its ideas are ultimately inseparable from the rhetoric or technique used to express them. The
intricate relation among its various parts (narrative, character,
patterns of imagery, motifs, and so on) perfectly exemplifies the
necessity of our understanding a novel as a whole. The inversion
of the traditional connotations of certain symbols, such as *water,*
makes it particularly dangerous to isolate remarks or images
from context.

Numerous references in Chapter 12 point to the situation as
being unnatural, the divine grace being something outside the
framework of the natural world. From the points of view of
Angus, Turner, and Judd, whose hopes are earthbound, Voss's
aspiration towards an absolute is " 'a form of madness' " (p.
250). In this respect, then, Judd's party is not unlike the Bonner-
Pringle society which chooses the apparent safety of home to the
dangers of the desert. After Judd's initial kindness and humility
and Voss's megalomania, events force us to make a volte-face in
our attitudes towards both men. In this way, White compels us to
face the paradoxes of nature and grace, "of man in Christ, and
Christ in man" (p. 336).

Voss's expedition is continually forcing a reappraisal of the
illusion of reality and the reality of illusion. In *Voss,* as in all
White's novels, there is a constant inversion of failure and success, appearance and reality, madness and sanity. This is a motif
in Chapter 9, where the narrative deals with Mercy's birth and
Rose Portion's death. Death points to the illusory nature of
earthly safety. After the initial shock of fear, however, Laura is
exhilarated by the possibilities which lie beyond this illusory
safety. The inversion of madness and sanity is strongest in Chapter 10, where the splitting of the expedition into two parties is
emphasized. Judd, the natural man identified with water, has
termed "madness" Harry's aspirations to learn his master's special understanding. Harry relates this understanding to his own
inner knowledge, for which he cannot find words. Laura's reference at the novel's end to Voss's *failure* in his struggle against

evil is one of the most ironic examples in this pattern of paradox and inversion. Earlier, in speaking to Voss of their common daemon, Le Mesurier has described both Voss and himself as failures. But Voss's failure is like that of Palfreyman ("He had failed evidently," p. 337) and of the crucified Christ; namely, one which another perspective reveals as the ultimate in success. All White's protagonists experience failure in this sense. The exploration of what is called in *Riders* the "mystery of failure" belongs to White's great theme, the mystery of unity, in which the apparent cleavage and pain of the temporal world is transformed into joy.

The desert symbol, basic to Voss's quest and to the novel's theme, is itself paradoxical or two-sided, as we so frequently find in White's work. On the one hand the desert, with its associated images of sand, rocks, oases, and so on, is desirable though terrible, as the only possible route to the absolute of Voss's desire, his quintessential gold or " 'inland sea' " (p. 141). In this harmonious aspect, the stark land of "desert and dreams" (p. 22) is the hero's way. Its stones of humiliation belong peculiarly to Voss, Laura, and the few stubborn ones who will "blunder on, painfully, out of the luxuriant world of their pretensions into the desert of mortification and reward" (p. 70). The desert is a place whose bareness, then, is helpful, a place where humans are reduced to bare essentials. It is this desert that Voss enters in joyous anticipation, even before the actual expedition, taking possession by a spiritual *droit de seigneur*. It is this same aspect which underlies Laura's summation at the novel's end: " 'Perhaps true knowledge only comes of death by torture in the country of the mind' " (p. 440).

On the other hand the desert is *detestable,* not merely in the awesome or terrible quality of its desirable aspect, but as the symbol of isolation, prejudice, and hatred. It is for this reason, as Laura tells Voss, that it fascinates him: it is a place where his own characteristics seem to be " 'taken for granted, or more than that, exalted' " (p. 83). And she warns Voss that he will be offended by this truth. Voss's egotism underlies the desert as chaos, a wasteland of fiery fevers, where black shadows terrify and men and beasts lie down to die. This feeling of tension or movement between the desert as desirable and detestable is also found in Isaiah and the Psalms, which contain the promise that the desert shall blossom as the rose.[31] *Voss* contains similar images of the desert as a fertile garden, when Voss thinks of Laura beneath a flowering sky (p. 208) or amid a "marriage" (p. 185) of light and shadow, and when the glory of the desert sunset is a "celebration of the divine munificence" (p. 330).

Early in the novel the desert symbol begins to widen into an image of all human life. When Laura tells Voss that *he* is her desert, both the desirable and the detestable aspects just discussed are suggested, although Laura avoids some of the dangers of the latter by choosing a "desert" (Voss) which is itself a relationship rather than a cause of isolation. Later, Laura's desert includes the suffering of her illness and her concern for the child, while she is Voss's spiritual companion in that other desert. Their loving relationship is the "gold" (p. 211) that Voss finds in the desert. The wider connotations of the desert symbol are suggested as Palfreyman wonders that Laura should envy them their journey "of dust, and flies, and dying horses" (p. 102). *Life* is the journey into the dust of death, a journey in which, as Laura remarks, the chances are equal for everyone and during which hope must be wrung out for oneself. Laura's remark (p. 103) anticipates Voss's reply to Le Mesurier's plea for hope: " 'I suggest you wring it out for yourself, which, in the end, is all that is possible for any man' " (p. 374).

Between the two groups of three and the two leaders (or leader and usurper), Palfreyman stands aloof: "He would most willingly have maintained a balance, indeed, it was his one thought and desire, who was a small, weak, ineffectual man" (p. 277). He sleeps equidistant from the two fires around which the other two groups are ranged. After attempting to disclaim association with any party, he rephrases his position so as to claim a share in *all* parties. If this involves martyrdom, which Voss suggests will be an inevitable result of such catholicity, then Palfreyman is prepared to accept this too. In *Riders,* Himmelfarb makes

[31] Isa. 35: 1-2; Isa. 51: 3.

a similar remark before his mock crucifixion; his determination to take "Providence" and Everyman as his "mate" shocks the foreman. The divine grace, that is, belongs to no single party but is accessible to the Judds and to the Vosses.

Palfreyman's association with Christ in Chapter 12 is prefigured in Chapter 10, not only by dialogue but also in the radical metaphors which describe the desert landscape. The passage depicting Palfreyman's desire to maintain a balance is followed by imagery of creation (with each new morning as a new creation) and of baptism: "For the sun was rising, in spite of immersion. It was challenging water, and the light of dawn, which is water of another kind" (p. 277). Darkness is identified here with water, as the sun rises out of, or overcomes, both darkness and water.[32] A continuous allegory of nature and grace, or the natural man and man infused with some transcendental quality, underlies this chapter. Central to it are the symbols of oil and water to which Turner draws attention, with water being identified with the natural man, or man as a rational animal. Water is set in a similar context in Christ's injunction that it is necessary to be born "of water and of the spirit" (John 3: 5).

Chapter 10 includes the crossing of the river to reach the shelter of some caves, a "mystic crossing" of "this most personal river" (p. 273) which must be suffered by each of the members of the expedition. This mystic crossing in *Voss* has many parallels with the river which Bunyan's pilgrim must cross before approaching the Celestial City. Palfreyman, although distressed by the loss of his specimens and by his leader's behaviour, believes that a more ultimate test than these is yet to come. Palfreyman and the spirit of Laura wait in selfless devotion for Voss "to soar with them. But he would not be tempted" (p. 284). The *temptation* to good (later, there is the *expiation* of innocence) illustrates the stylistic device of inversion, a favourite with White. As Voss still aspires to be his own God, he is determined to consider love as a weakness or failing and hence, a temptation.

---

[32] A similar identification of darkness and water is found in John 1: 5, where "the light shines on in the dark and the darkness has never quenched it" (New English Bible).

Chapter 12 is based upon the crucifixion, an archetype of redemptive suffering prominent in all White's later novels. It contains the allegory of nature and grace which underlies Chapter 10, since it is the split into two parties which results in Palfreyman's death. Voss's choice of Palfreyman as ambassador follows from Judd's jealousy when Voss made his earlier overtures to the aborigines. The "unbiased" Palfreyman declares his hope that he may "acquit" himself truly, words suitable to going into battle or embarking on some ordeal. Indeed, this is for Palfreyman the ultimate test which he had expected. Palfreyman goes, unarmed and trusting to his faith, wearing a cabbage-tree hat. The cabbage-tree recurs in the last chapter as a vision which refreshes Belle.

Watching Palfreyman, "all remembered the face of Christ that they had seen at some point in their lives, either in churches or in visions, before retreating from what they had not understood, the paradox of man in Christ, and Christ in man" (p. 336). This paradox, used with reference to Palfreyman's willing sacrifice of himself for the sake of the other members of the expedition, will be recalled when Laura speaks of the three stages: "Of God into man. Man. And man returning into God" (p. 380). *Voss* is based solidly upon this paradox of man in Christ, and Christ in man, which includes within itself all the other paradoxes of the novel. Palfreyman's apparent failure must be seen within the pattern created by the working out of these paradoxes in each of the main characters, whose failures, like Palfreyman's skin in the morning light, are "transfigured" (p. 337).

The entire twelfth chapter supports this archetypal "Christ-picture" which so infuriates Voss. It occurs in the spring, when the party emerges from wintering in a cave and prepares to re-enter the desert. The small grey bird which undermines the men's self-confidence in their ability to control their own fate serves to recall Laura's words in the previous chapter, her conviction that her life is utterly beyond her own control.[33] Palfrey-

---

[33] Palfreyman's compassion for the dead bird recalls Christ's words, that not a sparrow falls without God's knowledge and concern. Many small details ("sponge," "scourging") serve to reinforce the main crucifixion scene which dominates the chapter.

man is described as being *too honest* to take refuge in illusory self-importance, an honesty which, as the imagery suggests, will lead to the crucifixion of its possessor.[34] The landscape embodies the failure/success paradox, being first shown in its desirable and victorious aspect as the desert of Isaiah's promise, the desert which shall blossom like a rose. In this context of apocalyptic imagery the entire landscape, full of vibrant green beauty and numerous signs of "victorious life" (p. 328), becomes a daily eucharistic celebration.

With a sudden twist, as Turner balks at the prospect of re-entry, the desert becomes "the approaches to hell . . . this devilish country . . . chaos" (p. 331), reflecting Palfreyman's imminent martyrdom and the dark night of the soul before death. This formidable desert, as Ralph Angus observes, is a place which no sane man would enter—and, by the chapter's end, the three "sane" or "common" men have realized this, and turned back. Each man, however, is to encounter the desert sooner or later, as the ultimate and unavoidable test: "There was no avoiding chaos by detour" (p. 331). Their problem is to find the path through hell.

After Palfreyman's death, each survivor feels that part of him has died. In the continuous allegory which is but one of the many levels upon which *Voss* operates, Palfreyman represents not only an archetypal Christ-figure but also the necessity of each man's sharing in this death in order to acquire a share in a greater form of life.[35] The narrator suggests that it is the simple Harry who best understands the meaning of Palfreyman's death. The broken remnants of the one compass which had remained to the company after the river crossing and had been stolen by the blacks

---

[34] "There comes a moment when an individual who is too honest to take refuge in the old illusion of self-importance is *suspended agonizingly* between the flat sky and the flat earth, and prayer is no more than a slight gumminess on the roof of the mouth" (p. 327, italics mine).

[35] Palfreyman is also, of course, fully realized as a human being, kind but weak, a man who, as Voss realizes, "could never rescue him" (p. 260). James Mc-Auley, in "The Gothic Splendours: Patrick White's 'Voss,' " *Southerly* XXV (1965), 43, notes White's superiority to Pasternak's *Dr. Zhivago* in this respect: "White . . . has been able to combine his symbolist intentions with the presentation of characters that are realized in some psychological depth and with great visual clarity."

are now discovered upon the ground, with the arrow pointing to the bare earth where Palfreyman lies buried, indicating the necessary route for the successful completion of a quest such as Voss's. It is after Palfreyman's death that the division into the two parties, symbolized earlier by oil and water, is openly declared, and *from the site of Palfreyman's grave* the two parties ride in opposite directions.

In the next chapter, Voss's death and the crisis of Laura's illness are based upon "the paradox of man in Christ and Christ in man" of Palfreyman's martyrdom. Previous chapters have dealt largely with *either* the desert expedition *or* the society which has remained at home.[36] In Chapter 13 these two locations are fused, not only through Laura's psychic accompaniment of Voss, but through the widening of the desert symbolism to embrace all levels of human experience. There is a similar convergence in *Happy Valley,* as the intricate interrelationships become apparent. The emotional gamut in *Voss* ranges between the two comic poles of sympathy and ridicule. In Chapters 12 and 13, emotion tends to converge into a feeling of calm *acceptance,* corresponding to the catharsis of tragedy. These chapters contain the burning core of the novel in an atmosphere of ritual, vision, and dream. Voss's failure to mount his horse is an incident which might have made him look ridiculous in the past: "But the black men did not laugh" (p. 360). Nor does the reader.

The desert now has its hellish aspect (pp. 356, 358), as it did before Palfreyman's death. Voss's two disciples have come to very different conclusions through similar experiences. Harry's claim is that Voss has taught him " 'to live,' " and Frank's, " 'to expect damnation' " (p. 355). Voss rejoices in Harry's answer and in the boy's devotion, while renouncing claims to be his "Lord," since Laura has taught him to renounce his strength. Hartley Grattan, reviewing *Voss* in 1957, wonders if Voss's

---

[36] Cf. Grattan, "One-Way Journey": "Mr. White poses the classic distinction between the urban Australians, then as now the vast majority, and the lovers of the 'real' Australia (i.e. the outback)." Mr. Grattan fails to note that White goes beyond this distinction, common to Australian literature, by *universalizing* the desert experience into something which faces every man. Precedents for this treatment of desert symbolism extend back through English literature into Isaiah and the Psalms.

peculiar wholeness is merely eccentric or rather exemplary for all, and answers his own query by asserting that the novel provides no answer to this question, that White does not know the answers, but that it is enough that he asks the questions. I suggest that Grattan underestimates his author. The novel shows that Palfreyman's death and Laura's suffering *are* exemplary for all, and that Voss's death belongs to this context—as Harry has understood.

Christianity is not the only religion which finds an explanation for human life in the idea of an incarnate and suffering God. Aeschylus based his drama, the *Eumenides,* upon the idea of the reconciliation of man and God being effected through a suffering Zeus. The Mystery religions of the Mediterranean basin are based upon faith in a similar divine Man or human God, such as the Egyptian Osiris, the Syrian Adonis, and the Phrygian Attis.[37] White has chosen, however, to base his novel upon "the paradox of man in Christ, and Christ in man." Voss becomes whole only when he realizes his incompleteness, that is, when he relinquishes his claim to be his own God. As James McAuley suggests, White's theme is not simply the fantastic and eccentric egomania of a single individual, but an imaginative interpretation of "a tension within modern civilization, perhaps the ultimate problem of that civilization."[38]

The doctors who attend Laura in her feverish illness afford an opportunity for social satire reminiscent of G.B.S. at his best.[39] More important, Dr. Kilwinning's sceptical antagonism is an important technical device for controlling the point of view. As the doctor becomes an object of ridicule in his arrogant assumption

---

[37] See Jessie L. Weston, *From Ritual to Romance* (New York: Doubleday Anchor, 1957), p. 153. Miss Weston quotes from G. R. S. Mead's translation of the Hermetic writings, *Thrice-Greatest Hermes,* to support her argument that the essential kinship between Christianity and the pagan Mysteries contains the key to the secret of the Grail romances. There are many parallels between *Voss* and the quest of the Grail.

[38] McAuley, "The Gothic Splendours," p. 40.

[39] "Alas, his status as fashionable physician failed to protect him from a great many unpleasantnesses. If anything, the fees he charged seemed, rather, to make some individuals aspire to get their money's worth" (*Voss,* p. 362). Dr. Kilwinning reminds us of characters in Virginia Woolf as well as Bernard Shaw; his character and name suggest a combination of Dr. Bradshawe and Miss Kilman in *Mrs. Dalloway.*

of superiority and the grossness of his self-satisfaction, the reader's sympathy for Laura and the Bonners is increased. With Laura's illness, the Bonner house has become the desert, made endurable by "oases of affection" (p. 352); and the character and appearance of its inhabitants, like that of the members of Voss's expedition, have been changed by suffering and love. The Bonners have "wizened in a few days" (p. 362). Mrs. Bonner shares with Laura, as Laura with Voss, "the same hell, in their common flesh" (p. 358). Mrs. Bonner looks after Mercy during Laura's illness, but if her care begins in expiation, it ends in love.[40] It is comic that she is forced into deception and cunning to hide this new love for Laura's child. When Laura decides that only the supreme sacrifice will save Voss, by convincing him " 'that he is not God' " (p. 365), she is prevented by Mrs. Bonner from carrying out her intention to give Mercy away, as Abraham was prevented from killing Isaac. After Laura has passed the crisis of her illness, she hopes that failures are accepted in the light of intentions. Like Palfreyman's death, this belongs to White's pattern of the mystery of failure.

Laura's spiritual suffering, in her concern for Voss, is reflected in the physical illness, climaxed by the leeching and fever. When Laura claims to understand at last the sufferings of Christ, and when she wonders who will love man, " 'so shoddy, so contemptible, greedy, jealous, stubborn, ignorant' " (pp. 380-381) *when she is gone,* White is drawing once again, as with the death of Palfreyman, upon the crucifixion as the archetype of redemptive suffering. Meanwhile, in that other desert, the trinity of white men approach their death, attended by a great comet, a marvellous phenomenon which the aborigines fear as the Great Snake, but which Voss finds beautiful and desirable. As Mrs. Bonner is wrestling with her conscience over Laura's desire to "sacrifice"

---

[40] Mrs. Bonner "was continually washing her hands, but could not cleanse herself of all her sins" (p. 363). Following the account of Pilate's washing, Western literature has frequently used the washing of hands as a symbol of the *ineffectual* attempt at spiritual cleansing (as, for example, in Shakespeare's *Macbeth*) and White is continuing this tradition in *Voss*. There is, however, another symbolic context for this action, following an even older tradition, where the attempt at spiritual cleansing is treated as being successful: cf. Ps. 26: 6.

Mercy, the sight of this same comet strengthens her resolve to keep the child.

Voss has changed from his earlier self-absorption in his own magnificence. He is suddenly sobered by Jackie's belief in the superior power of the Snake, and tells Le Mesurier that he has no plan except to trust to God. Thus "the man who was not God" *is withdrawn,* and can only suggest to his pitiful disciple that he must wring out hope for himself, " 'which, in the end, is all that is possible for any man' " (p. 374). Voss has given up his claim to transcendental status. Le Mesurier, although he has always anticipated Voss's "abdication," cannot bear to find that gold has tarnished into the baser metals (p. 375) of ordinary humanity. This symbol, which marked the end of the first chapter, has expanded to contain the theme: the paradox of failure and success, life and death, and the three stages of man's relationship to God. The alchemical symbolism is continued in the rest of Voss's life, as the "base metal" of his humanity begins to be transmuted into gold, or the second stage to move into the third.

Through Voss's last days, Laura keeps constant vigil. The eucharistic ritual celebrated by the aborigines exemplifies what Northrop Frye calls " 'demonic modulation,' or the deliberate reversal of the customary moral associations of archetypes."[41] Here, however, we have a modulation of a modulation, or the reversal of demonic imagery back into its angelic or apocalyptic form. Although the "priest" is an old blackfellow, the "wafer" is a witchetty grub, and the place is a filthy hut, this is no black mass but a true eucharist. Men, to the native mind, are no more than witchetty grubs in the hands of children (p. 374). Thus, in swallowing the grub "that absorbed the unworthiness in his hot mouth" (p. 382), Voss identifies himself with man and God. His last suffering is his consciousness of the animals' fear and pain, as they are massacred by the aborigines. A second eucharist is celebrated in dream just before Voss's death, in an atmosphere of joyous calm, with white lilies of prayer and love serving as communion wafers. These "nourishing blooms" are to serve as food on "the long journey back in search of human status" (p. 387),

[41] Frye, *Anatomy of Criticism,* p. 156.

a restatement of Laura's apocalyptic utterance at the height of her illness: " 'When man is truly humbled, when he has learned that he is not God, then he is nearest to becoming so. In the end, he may ascend' " (p. 381). The experience of each character in the novel illustrates the three stages posited by Laura in her fever: God into man; man; and man returning into God. As James McAuley notes, Voss's ambition is to be fulfilled in the way that he had rejected, through love and humility, for as Laura sees, the Christian way is also a deification of man.[42]

The continually growing knives of Voss's visionary dream just before death form part of a pattern of knife imagery which is identified in the novel with human suffering and frailty. This pattern is developed most noticeably through Jackie, the black boy who decapitates Voss with the knife which Voss has given him, thereby expiating his innocence.[43] Jackie has been taken into the aboriginal tribe which had captured the white men, and been given a wife from the tribe, shortly before Voss's death. His murder of Voss is obviously required of him by the tribal elders as a ritual which marks his adult status and his member- ship in the tribe. Jackie exchanges the unimpaired innocence, which has caused Voss to love the black boy best among his followers, for "increasing but confused manhood" (p. 388). Like Theodora Goodman, that is, he moves through at least three levels of experience, beginning with the Edenic innocence of childhood and passing into adult experience.

With the torments that follow his murder of Voss and his chosen isolation, Jackie passes rapidly into the third state of suffering or descent into hell. It is ambiguous as to whether or not Jackie reaches the fourth state of recovered innocence, but there are faint suggestions that he may do so, in the imagery con- nected with the "splendour" (p. 413) of the harness. In Chapter 15, Jackie is described as having experienced too much too early.

[42] See McAuley, "The Gothic Splendours," p. 42.
[43] "Terrible knives of thought, sharpened upon the knives of the sun, were cut- ting into him" (p. 413); " 'Man is God decapitated. That is why you are bleeding' " (p. 358); ". . . driven the knife into His image, some other man" (p. 190). Note the inversion technique, in "expiating" innocence rather than guilt.

The psychic torments of his last days, when he acquires among the aborigines the reputation of a prophet, suggest the descent of Odysseus into Hades to learn wisdom from Tiresias, or the similar mission of Aeneas in the sixth book of the *Aeneid*. This archetype of the "night journey" or descent into Hades has been common to Western literature since the epics of Homer and Vergil. It may be interpreted psychologically as the descent into the unconscious in search of truth and self-knowledge, at the cost of suffering. Like Conrad's story of Marlow's encounter with Kurtz in *Heart of Darkness*, White draws upon the imagery of the traditional voyage into Hades in Jackie's journey through the country of the dead, his communion with the souls of those who had died, and his resulting increase in wisdom.

In the relationship between Colonel Hebden and Mrs. de Courcy, those tentative explorers, we have a humorous parallel of the relationship between Laura and Voss, a little echo of the dominant motif. Mrs. de Courcy regarded everything as "inevitably humorous" (p. 403), and neither she nor the colonel has aspired to the desert quest. Although reduced in scale, their characters are similar to those of Voss and Laura but with the *gender reversed*. Mrs. de Courcy has Voss's tenacity and will, his relentless thirst for conquest. She is described as both ruthless and cruel. The colonel tells her that if she had been a man, she might have become an explorer: " 'You are sufficiently tenacious. Your thirst for conquest would have carried you over the worst of actual thirst' " (p. 402). The colonel, although a tentative explorer by his own admission and the leader of an actual expedition in search of Voss and his party, has something of Laura's humility and sensitivity, so that he plays Laura to Mrs. de Courcy's Voss. Colonel Hebden reminds Mrs. de Courcy of human frailty, warning her that she " 'must learn to accept the deficiencies of human beings' " (p. 404).

Subsequent to his mutiny, Judd proves to have been correct in assessing that there is " 'hell before and hell behind' " (p. 340), but wrong in believing that it is possible to evade this suffering. It belongs to the theme of *Voss* that the descent into Hades is an unavoidable stage in man's eternal quest. Judd returns alive, but his nearness to death has altered the trust in his own strength which controlled his actions at the time of his mutiny. And he returns only to find, like Job, that his wife and sons are dead and his property lost. Judd must endure the desert in the years of suffering which follow. His last appearance reinforces the archetypal quality of his past record as a convict, for Laura realizes that "she must stand on trial with him" (p. 436). His recollections of the expedition mix together the actions of Voss and Palfreyman; the novelist's technique makes use of the muddled memory of an old man, as earlier it used drunkenness, fever, and dream, to support the novel's theme of the *three stages,* and the paradox of Christ in man and man in Christ. As Laura puts it, "Voss had in him a little of Christ, like other men" (p. 438).

In literature which is roughly contemporary with *Voss,* the novel which suggests itself for comparison is Malcolm Lowry's *Under the Volcano.* The fact that this is a tragedy and *Voss* is a comedy helps to point up the difference in the way White develops a somewhat similar theme. The protagonists in the novels are engaged in an exploration of hell; Geoffrey Firmin thinks of himself as "a great explorer who has discovered some extraordinary land from which he can never return to give his knowledge to the world: but the name of this land is hell."[44] Unlike Voss, the consul is weak in will but developed in self-knowledge; he knows of the path through hell of which Blake wrote, but feels unable to take it. The relationship with a beloved woman is vital to both the consul and Voss, and both novels use letters between the protagonist and his beloved to reveal thoughts too personal and deep to be spoken aloud. The consul's need of Yvonne is a constant refrain in Lowry's novel, but whereas Voss is enabled to find the path through hell in his relationship with Laura, Yvonne seems relatively powerless to help the consul. Thus *Voss* has the threefold movement of the *Divine Comedy,* while Lowry's early death prevented his completing the novel with a

---

[44] Malcolm Lowry, *Under the Volcano* (Harmondsworth, Middlesex: Penguin, 1963), p. 42. The quotation at the end of my paragraph on Lowry is from *Under the Volcano,* p. 137.

Paradiso movement, planned as a complement to the Inferno and Purgatorio movements of *Under the Volcano*. Both Voss and the consul, initially, are lonely figures, terrible in their isolation; but Voss is enabled to move beyond this into the fulfilment of love. The "atheism is self-murder" motif in *Voss* is paralleled in *Under the Volcano* by the image of the "artist with a murderer's hands," seen on the movie poster. Geoffrey Firmin, like Frank Le Mesurier, finally destroys himself. Both novels make constant use of archetypes and apocalyptic imagery, and exploit the possibilities in drunkenness, dream, and vision for this purpose: as the drunken consul tells his self-satisfied neighbour, Mr. Quincey, perhaps Adam was not really banished from paradise at all, but punished by "his having to *go on living there,* alone, of course— suffering, unseen, cut off from God." But the way out, the path through hell, has been found by Voss.

We have already noted many associations between *Voss* and earlier literature of all ages, including Dante, Petrarch, Bunyan, and Vergil. Voss's journey " 'to hell an' back' " is deeply rooted in Western literature and tradition. His aspiration to know and experience everything belongs to the Faust legend treated by Marlowe, Goethe, Mann, Lowry, and others. Since Voss is his own tempter, he combines in one figure Faust and the tempter Mephistopheles. His journey is also a quest of the Grail, like Theodora Goodman's. Structurally, however, *Voss* and *The Aunt's Story* are comedy, not romance, and both Voss and Theodora contain the dragon to be slain *within themselves*. White's use of dream and vision has a medieval precedent in the technique of the "vision" poem. Like *Piers Plowman, Voss* combines social satire with a spiritual allegory of the search for salvation.

Bunyan's *Pilgrim's Progress* uses a similar convention, presenting the pilgrim's journey from the City of Destruction to the Celestial City on Mount Zion as the dream of the narrator. The pilgrimage of Christian, Bunyan's hero, is derisively called his "desperate journey" by those who stay behind, just as the Bonners speak of Voss's expedition. There are many parallels between the journeys undertaken by Voss and Christian, with episodes in White's novel, such as the sojourns with Sanderson and with Boyle at Jildra, resembling the situations encountered by Bunyan's pilgrim. Names such as Palfreyman, Mercy, and Rose are straight out of the tradition of medieval allegory. There is, of course, no question as to the enormous advance in subtlety and complexity between a naive allegory such as Bunyan's and a novel such as *Voss*. But a look at the literary and cultural roots enriches our understanding of the twentieth-century work. The path to the Celestial City, in *Voss* and *Pilgrim's Progress,* lies through the Valley of Humiliation and the Valley of the Shadow of Death, and both White and Bunyan appear to be drawing much of their imagery from the Old Testament, especially in the desert or wilderness symbolism which is of basic importance to the theme. Bunyan takes his description of the Valley of the Shadow of Death from the prophet Jeremiah: "A wilderness, a land of drought, and of the Shadow of death; a land that no man (but a Christian) [*sic*] passeth through, and where no woman dwelt."[45] The terrain is familiar to one who has travelled with Voss.

---

[45] Cf. Jer. 2: 6.

And I looked, and, behold, a whirlwind came out of the
north, a great cloud, and a fire infolding itself....
Also out of the midst thereof came the likeness of four living
creatures. And this was their appearance; they had the
likeness of a man.
EZEKIEL 1: 4-5

chapter 9 The quaternity

Riders in the Chariot invites the reader to examine the relation
of good and evil, and to "admit the possibility of redemption"
(p. 162), as Himmelfarb asks of Miss Hare beneath the flowering plum tree. The novel's central symbol, the fiery Chariot of
God with its Four Living Creatures as Riders, belongs to this
theme, and the Riders are finally revealed as those involved in
the work of redemption.

The structure required to support this great theme is both intricate and, in the last analysis, simple. Like some vast, gothic
cathedral whose intricacy of detail is built upon the shape of the
cross which forms its ground plan, so the wealth of detail in the
novel supports an equally simple but profound design. All the
events in Sarsaparilla drive towards the "crucifixion" of Himmelfarb and the effects of this upon the characters in the novel. This
climax provides a focus through which the outer events and inner
experiences of the four main characters, whose background is
given in such detail, are completed and are understood. The
structural principles include the four stages of man's spiritual

development (innocence, experience, suffering, and rebirth); cyclic patterns of natural growth, decay, and recurrence; and biblical typology, the figurative interpretation of the historical events. All these techniques are found in the novels which precede *Riders,* but not on the same heroic scale.

Riders is based, structurally and thematically, upon the Scriptures and litanies of both Jew and Christian, and effects a *fusion* of the quintessence of these religions.[1] The novel's ironic treatment of the conversion of Moshe Himmelfarb and the Rosetree family to Christianity (for reasons of social and economic convenience and security) and Mordecai Himmelfarb's own continuance in the orthodox Jewish faith must be seen within the total context of the experience and interrelationships of the four Riders and the pattern established by archetypes and apocalyptic imagery. The climactic Part Six represents *both* Passover and Easter, as its first words tell us. The novel takes its ultimate meaning and its unity from the identification of the events celebrated in these religious feasts, the identification of seder meal and Christian eucharist. Religion is the coat which the naked soul puts on at birth and must take off at death. Ultimately, as Mrs. Godbold tells Haïm Rosetree, " 'it is the same' " (pp. 480, 482).

A brief look at the four protagonists—Jew, mad spinster, half-caste artist, and washerwoman—reveals the true universality of White's vision. The Riders include two women and two men; two formal adherents of recognized religions, and two who seek the deity independently, in nature and in the truth of art. Their geographic origins, and varieties of racial type (Jew and Gentile, Anglo-Saxon, European and aboriginal Australian), are sufficient to suggest all men and all countries of the world. The social spectrum represented by their backgrounds is equally inclusive, ranging from the privileged aristocracy (Miss Hare), through the upper middle class of merchants and intelligentsia (Himmelfarb) to the "respectable poor" (Ruth Godbold) and the social

---

[1] Colin Roderick, "Riders in the Chariot," *Southerly* XXII (1962), 62, suggests that the novel owes "very little to Christian dogmas except as a *deus ex machina.*"

outcast (Alf Dubbo). These original differences are unimportant
in the relation which is established between them, and are ultimately nullified in the humility of each. Each has become an outcast from established society, the outcast or archetypal stranger
for whom the seder door stands open. But none is a stranger to
the faith or vision symbolized by the Chariot.

Each of the four whom we come to recognize as Riders in the
Chariot of God has personal knowledge of the fiery Chariot, seen
with the eyes of faith. Himmelfarb's explanation to Miss Hare of
the hidden zaddikim, or holy men, who secretly pursue their
good deeds of healing and interpreting, contains one of the most
explicit references, and suggests that the zaddikim themselves,
filled with the creative light of God, *are* the Chariot.[2] The Riders'
ignorance of their own role is necessary if they are to avoid spiritual pride—the subtlest and strongest temptation, as T. S. Eliot's
Becket (in *Murder in the Cathedral*) well knew.

Each, however, is able to recognize the *other* as "an apostle of
of truth" (p. 63). The meaning of what Himmelfarb calls "the
Chariot of Redemption" (p. 142) is clarified for him by the
ancient cabalistic and Hasidic works discovered in Rutkowitz's
shop. The light which issues *from* the ecstatic and remains *with*
him is the light of God, his Creator, to whom he has willingly
bound himself " 'with ropes of love . . . even when most hindered
the love of service burns in his heart, and he is glad to fulfill the
will of his Creator' " (p. 141). This is the light recognized by
and reflected from the illuminates, the same light which will be
reflected out over the community by the quiet and loving spirit,
as the dyer assures Mordecai at the time of his wedding.[3] *Lovingkindness* is the light "which might redeem, not only those in
whom its lamp stood, but all those who were threatened with

---

[2] The Chariot, in turn, is identified in Jewish Merkabah mysticism with the
divine throne and the Godhead. This Jewish tradition, identifying the zaddikim with the Chariot and the Chariot with God, may be compared with the
Christian tradition of the company of Christ's followers as composing the
body of Christ.

[3] Once again, the Jewish tradition is paralleled by a Christian one, of Christ's
witnesses as the light of the world, a light set on a hill or on a candlestick:
Matt. 5: 14-16; Phil. 2: 15. The pattern of imagery is completed by representing the godless life as darkness.

darkness" (pp. 321-322). The Riders are fellow-travellers in quest of the answer to the problem of the redemption of all men; as such, they are engaged in a "similar mission" (p. 327) and involved in the "same madness" (p. 329).

All the Riders sustain the paradox of strength in weakness. Although powerless in the eyes of the world, they have acquired an inner strength, the core of rock which Miss Hare knows is necessary to match Mrs. Jolley and her like. All are physically ugly, possessing at best a "botched" beauty which the world will not acknowledge. Mary Hare's ugliness, as a child, has made her the "servant of servants," scorned even by the family maids. Himmelfarb develops from a waxen little boy into the "ugly Jew" of Jürgen's phrase, hideous in external appearance. The Riders are society's untouchables, lowest of the low, "fellow flotsam" (p. 332) rejected even by other social outcasts such as the Khalils. The concept of the spiritually elect as ugly and apparently undesirable recalls Isaiah's prophecy of the Messiah or the suffering servant: "he hath no form nor comeliness; and when we shall see him, there is no beauty that we should desire him."[4]

Finally, all are in some sense sacerdotal figures: Miss Hare's "many little rites, both humdrum and worshipful" (p. 36) form a curious analogue to the strict observances performed daily by the orthodox Jew. There are some who, like the snake, fail to sense this "sacerdotal authority" and remain to be converted. It is also important to realize the close relation between the Riders and the common man, through the bond of suffering. White's vision is by no means esoteric or concerned only with an elect, a spiritual elite. As Himmelfarb assures his wife, when she links herself with "the ordinary ones" in an unusual mood of despair, " 'there is no distinction finally' " (p. 149).

The names of White's characters are always significant, and sometimes contain the theme in microcosm or reflect some aspect of it. In *Riders* and *The Solid Mandala* the double names Martin-Mordecai and Aaron-Arthur suggest that the dual heritage of Christianity and Judaism forms an essential unity. The religious synthesis is effected not by didactic statement but by the artistic

4 Isa. 53: 2.

techniques of the novel, and remains valid within the total "statement" made by the novel as a work of art. Mordecai's father, who hopes to see the barriers between Jew and Gentile dissolve before the smiling face of sweet reasonableness, chooses the Gentile name of Martin for his son. There is an unconscious irony in his choosing the name of one of the greatest men of faith, Martin Luther. Since the boy's mother asks only " 'that Mordecai shall be remembered as a man of faith' " (p. 106), the name by which his father attempts to divorce him from his Jewish tradition only serves to reinforce it. Through narrative, character, myth, and image, the novel reveals the essence of the two religions, Judaism and Christianity, to be truly *one faith*.

There are other connotations in Himmelfarb's name. Mordecai, in the book of Esther, was the father of Esther, Xerxes' favourite, through whom a major persecution of the Jewish people was averted. And from the German (*himmel* 'heaven', *farbe* 'colour'), his name suggests God's colour, the light of heaven. As Miss Hare is covered and protected by her large wicker hat (which is repeatedly described, thus drawing attention to its mandala form and its resemblance to the shield of faith of Pauline imagery), so Himmelfarb is "furnished" with his faith: "As the coverings of the Ark were changed, in accordance with the feasts of the year, so his soul would put on different colours" (p. 131). The unconscious corruption of his name to "Himmelson" ('heaven's *son*') by the factory typist directs attention to his name while adding a new dimension to it. Jürgen Stauffer, his German friend, gives us another variant as the boys wrestle together: " 'Old Himmelfurz!' " (p. 109). Himmelfarb, that is, is God's foot or footstool,[5] the lowliest of his servants— or is it the most precious of his jewels?

Mary Hare is small and freckled, with sandy skin, "speckled and dappled like any wild thing native to the place" (p. 12). Her outward appearance thus suggests her namesake, and in Part One the name is brought to our notice by the reference to her mother's *catching* a Hare as husband. In Part Two Himmelfarb,

---

[5] German *furz* 'foot': Reha, his wife, later calls herself his footstool, or cushion. Similarly, Miss Hare has described herself as the servant of servants.

delighted with her name, explains that the hare is the animal which offers itself for sacrifice. To Mary's objection that there is already too much cruelty in the world, Himmelfarb replies: " 'The concept of the willing hare is surely less painful than that of the scapegoat, dragged out, bleating, by its horns' " (p. 98). At the ball which marks Mary's social debut, she is the sacrificial victim, appropriately dressed in white.

Himmelfarb, who has been made an unwilling scapegoat in Nazi Germany, becomes the willing sacrificial hare or ram in Sarsaparilla. For Hindus the hare is a sacred animal associated with the moon. White's last three novels reveal an increasing interest in eastern symbolism and tradition, as in the use of the lotus (the eastern counterpart of the rose) and the mandala. In Chinese art the hare is a symbol of longevity, a creature of the moon which mixes the elixir of life and the pill of immortality.[6] This concept belongs to the mood of continuity in Part Seven. The Godbolds' conviction that Miss Hare's spirit remains nearby, despite her physical disappearance, is part of the general feeling of restoration and unending growth which dominates the final part of the novel.

Mary Hare is a nature mystic who experiences a sense of union, not simply communion, with natural objects and creatures. She feels that she is part of everything around her, being able, as she tells the unbelieving housekeeper, to *enter into* water and become like it. She recalls "occasions when she had lost her identity in those of trees, bushes, inanimate objects, or entered into the minds of animals, of which the desires were unequivocal, or honest" (p. 83). Her mother's journal, uncovered by the destruction of Xanadu, records Mary's experience of an altered state of consciousness, a psychic journey. Her thoughts are as alive, changing, growing as any natural object. Something of her simplicity and her special powers are prefigured in characters

---

[6] Robert Graves, *The White Goddess* (enlarged edition; New York: Noonday, 1966), p. 29, notes that, despite the taboo against the pig and the hare in Leviticus, both animals were sacred as well as taboo in ancient Britain, where the hare was a royal animal: "The position of the Hare constellation at the feet of Orion suggests that it was sacred in Pelasgian Greece too." In Dubbo's final painting of the Chariot, Miss Hare is depicted with a pig's snout. The mystic hare is associated with both madness and melancholy.

such as Theodora Goodman, Bub Quigley, and Stan Parker, in White's earlier novels. In *Riders* the simplicity of a very minor figure, William Hadkin, is described as knowledge of a different kind. It is Mary Hare, however, one of the four Riders, who is the divine fool of this novel.

There is a great deal, as she tells Mrs. Jolley, that she truly loves. As the housekeeper persists in enquiring into her beliefs, she confesses to believing in a thunderstorm, wet grass, patches of light, and stillness: "There is such a variety of good. On earth. And everywhere" (p. 57). The whorls of hair on Himmelfarb's neck excite "her love for all living matter" (p. 96). These ecstatic states are primarily a religious experience for Miss Hare, the source by which her spirit finds refreshment and renewal— her eucharist, as it were: "she would recognize the Hand in every veined leaf, and would bundle with the bee into the divine Mouth" (p. 61). Her experience thus eliminates the division which is arbitrarily posited by some psychiatrists between nature mysticism and the ecstatic experience of a religious mystic.

Whereas it is generally those who reject or despise the Rider characters who call Mary "mad," the narrator frequently draws attention to her resemblance to a child or animal. The secret and shorter path she takes to Xanadu suggests the short cut which her child-nature allows her to take to grace.[7] As Mary traverses the paths of her little kingdom, she is both stroked by ferns and scratched and slapped by rougher growths. She considers that this is only to be expected "once her feet were set upon the paths of existence" (p. 9). Obviously we are in the presence of another quest. In childhood Mary resembles a little, wondering fish; not content with the shallows, like her mother, her instinctive knowledge draws her to seek the depths. In old age "the seeker" (p. 82) suspects that her extended consciousness, her ability to identify with natural things, may quite possibly count as her *contribution*. But her continuing problem, and in some sense the goal of her quest, is "how to distinguish with certainty between good and evil" (p. 82). She also seeks to discover what is at her

---

[7] The Godbold children temporarily share the secret but are later shown embarking on the adult stages of experience and suffering.

own centre, and trusts that this will be revealed when enough of her is "peeled away" (p. 51). Like Stan Parker, in *The Tree of Man,* the quest turns inward.

Mary is human as well as animal, although her animality is more noticeable, her rationality less, than in the "normal" person. Her search for truth has made her dimly suspect "that she, too, contained something evil which could take control at times? Some human element" (p. 83), a realization that makes her long for the mystic state which removed her from the human frame of reference. Provoked by Mrs. Jolley, Miss Hare becomes "half ashamed for her own powers of emulating the cruelty of human beings. 'It is I who am bad' she sighed half aloud" (p. 85).[8] Earlier, the reader has tended to reject, with amused indignation, the same verdict recorded by Mrs. Jolley on the cake.

The very success of White's contrast between the four protagonists and the evil trio tends to blind us to something which is an important part of the total design—namely, that the nature of each of the Riders contains at least some small measure of the cruelty or evil which finds expression in Blue and Mesdames Jolley and Flack. Even Mary, the mad innocent whom Peg finds both different and the same, is frequently snared by arrogance: "Mary Hare loved Peg, but she loved her own arrogance. It was her great pride" (p. 48). And it is Peg, not Mary, who is here described as *blameless.*

Mary's capacity for cruelty or evil is obviously slight. Even in the passage describing Mary's self-doubts, the use of the verb *emulate* tends to dissociate her from the human race and its cruelty. Two images are used to suggest Mary's near-innocence or purity. The first is her animality: the animal is morally irresponsible, and Mary is "at most an animal, at least a leaf (p. 502).[9] The second image is the foetus or the unborn soul. Just before his death, Mary's father calls her " 'ugly as a foetus.

---

[8] Theodora Goodman, provoked by her mother's behaviour, reaches a similar conclusion.

[9] In Part Two, Himmelfarb feels that in relating his story to Miss Hare, "it was like addressing some animal, or not even that. He remembered seeing fungi which suggested existence of the most passive order. And she could become perfectly still. It was only later that he recoiled from such an attitude, as if he had been guilty of treading on life" (p. 100).

Ripped out too soon' " (p. 55); previously, he has described the unborn soul as whole and pure, asking Mary if she considered herself " 'one of the unborn' " (p. 34). The apparently cynical statement of Mary's father that all human beings are decadent, that degeneration begins at birth, contains a facet of the vision which underlies all White's novels. But Norbert Hare, that suspect visionary, has only a *part* of White's vision. He stops in the middle, as it were, of Laura Trevelyan's three stages: "Of God into man. Man. And man returning into God." His despair seems to issue from the judgment which he passes on himself: "Whatever the source of his experience, he was, however, aware of a splendour that he himself would never achieve except by instants, and rightly or wrongly, came to interpret this as failure" (p. 54). Norbert recognizes man's fall from innocence but fails to "admit the possibility of redemption" (p. 162) or spiritual rebirth—the postulate upon which White's novels rest.

It is not surprising, after the unhappiness of her childhood, that Mary should love natural objects and animals, for nothing in her early experience makes it possible for her to like human beings. Her mother's superficial affection and rational kindness is only a little more acceptable than her father's outright rejection. From the depths of his alcoholic and despairing state, Norbert Hare's resentment of his daughter's awkwardness and ugliness explodes violently from time to time. But Mary's red, blotchy skin is the same colour as the evening light: "So splendid that even she, a red girl, had no need to feel ashamed of the correspondence" (p. 20). The little girl remains as shy of people as any wild creature. She learns that love is something brittle, which must be avoided as too precious for daily use; thus she learns to love, in her own way, the greenish rooms and golden stones and the tunnels through the shrubberies.

Xanadu, not humans, becomes the object of her "noble love" (p. 13), and upon animals, birds, and plants she expends her great but pitiable love. Husbandless and childless, like Theodora Goodman, she takes the wild creatures to her heart and rears a nestling in her bosom. The novel shows this alienation from man and closeness to nature to be her weakness and her strength. She herself insists that one can do anything, provided one wants to sufficiently, "but there were an awful lot of things you did not want enough. Like learning to love a human being" (p. 15). Through her relations with the other Riders, Mary does learn to love human beings. But her own special gift is to discover " *'lovingkindness* to exist at the roots of trees and plants, not to mention *hair,* provided it was not *of human variety*' " (p. 504), as her mother had confided with horrified emphasis in the old diary.

We see Xanadu first as it apears to Mary, a paradise, her "vision" and her spiritual home. Begun as "Norbert's contribution to the sum of truth . . . created in the first place for its owner's *pleasure*" (p. 16), Xanadu is an archetype of Eden, exquisite and exotic with its park, its little woods and rose garden.[10] Even in Norbert's time, the greenish beauty of the garden is reflected in the house. An ironic contrast is provided by the materialism of the landowners, who want only what purports to be useful and who consider as flash and un-Australian that which is intended "to please, not to say glorify" (p. 16). Clearly, the narrator is endorsing the latter purpose. Yet the first chapter has shown that Norbert Hare's attempt to create a Xanadu, a Pleasure Dome, has been opposed by the "native cynicism" (p. 11) of the grey scrub, and that his wilfully created park has failed.

The true Xanadu is not the artificial and fragmentary one attempted by Norbert, but the natural wilderness reverenced by Mary,[11] an archetype for the whole natural world. Nature has taken over inside the house as well as outside; a carpet of twigs and insects overlays the Aubusson and the elm branch saws in the dining room. To Mary, whose ownership is confirmed by her father's bloodstone ring, it has become the paradise her father hoped to create. Unlike Norbert, who prefers the fragment to the whole, but like Theodora Goodman, who accepts the slug at the

---

[10] Cf. Malcolm Lowry's use, in *Under the Volcano,* of the little park as an Edenic archetype. The park, like Xanadu, is intended for man's pleasure; its little sign warns that those who misuse it will be evicted. Similarly Mrs. Hare, attempting to instil carefulness into the child, warns Mary that the beautiful things are to be enjoyed, not thoughtlessly smashed. Xanadu is the site of the Khan's pleasure garden in Coleridge's *Kubla Khan.*

[11] She finds the *kneeling* position necessitated by the shrubbery tunnels to be one that is natural in the act of worship.

heart of the rose as something belonging to the whole, Mary relishes the perfection of every part of Xanadu: "In all that dreamy landscape it seemed that each particle, not least Miss Hare herself, contributed towards some perfection. Nothing could be added to improve the whole. Yet, was she not about to attempt?" (p. 4).

The inference is that the present appearance of perfection may be illusory. Miss Hare's knowledge of evil, as the narrator explicitly states, is extremely limited. It is soon to be expanded, through her experience with Mrs. Jolley, Mrs. Flack, and Blue. Their entrance into Xanadu marks the beginning of its end. The paradise which contains the forces embodied in this trio is a fallen Eden, ultimately "the stage set for a play of divine retribution" (p. 501), the archetypal apocalypse. Xanadu, identified with the human body as well as with the entire natural world, is revealed as both man's doom and his inheritance of splendour. Its essential mystery and glory seem to survive its destruction. This is what Miss Hare had hoped the Jew would understand: "Yes, glory, because decay, even the putrid human kind, did not necessarily mean an end" (p. 99). After Xanadu has been demolished, Ruth Godbold and her children and children's children, the embodiment of all certainty and goodness, remain.

Eustace Cleugh, Mary's cousin, whose financial support has maintained her at Xanadu and to whom she leaves the property in her will, appears only in Part One. An unattractive individual, Eustace is reminiscent of Elyot Standish and suggests, like Elyot, the spiritually dead. Mary wonders "whether Mr. Cleugh realized how dead his own words were, and if he was suffering for it. There were, after all, many things he and she had in common, if they could first overcome the strangeness of their separate existences, and crack the codes of human intercourse" (p. 24). The final phrase points to the pun (*clue*) concealed in Eustace's last name.

But what do Mary and Eustace have in common? Nothing, as appears obvious from his visit, but their humanity. Eustace does not believe "in the existence of anything outside the closed circle of himself" (p. 30), while Mary is the only one of the four

Riders who relates to God *solely* through nature. It is Mary's *animality* which so offends her father and initiates the events of the night of the false suicide. He finds her munching and scratching *intolerable*. The same word recurs in Part Two as Himmelfarb, in the first flush of adult experience, begins to feel that the animal behaviour of his father, "the ridiculous old satyr" (p. 118), is the more intolerable for its familiarity—that is, its similarity to his own behaviour. But animals are at least honest; and the animal Mary, unlike the youthful Himmelfarb, can understand and pity her cousin and her father:

> If Mary was less upset by Eustace Cleugh's behaviour, it was because she already expected less of the human animal, and in consequence was not surprised when he diverged from the course which other people intended he should take. The ugliness and weakness which his nature revealed at such moments were, she sensed, far closer to the truth. (P. 30.)

It is not the Urquhart-Smiths but Eustace, the "human animal," to whom Mary wills her Xanadu, her beloved world. Although the inheritance is demolished, and her physical body appears to have suffered a similar fate, she is still present in spirit. It is our last "clue" to the woman who was "at most an animal" (p. 502) and to her legatee.

As the serpent brings about man's exclusion from paradise, in the Edenic myth, so the arrival of Mrs. Jolley as housekeeper is the first link in the chain of events which culminates in the demolition of Xanadu: "Miss Hare's trial by Mrs. Jolley had begun" (p. 62). Since cruelty frequently assumes a comic mask, and Blue's sadistic treatment of the Jew masquerades as a joke or *jolly* prank,[12] it is fitting that it should be unmasked and exorcized by the technique of comic parody. Mrs. Jolley and Mrs. Flack are ludicrous characters, and the humour in dialogue and action is supported by a pattern of macabre witch-imagery as their plot thickens. There is also, however, something gruesome

---

[12] The word *joke* is used repeatedly in Chapter 13 in the "crucifixion" scene.

about the pair, with Mrs. Jolley appearing "half devilish, half girlish" (p. 87). The diabolical attitude, as C. S. Lewis notes in his Introduction to *Screwtape Proposes a Toast,* is "not fun, or not for long. . . . The world into which I had to project myself while I spoke through Screwtape was all dust, grit, thirst and itch. Every grace of beauty, freshness and geniality had to be excluded." This explains the fear which these two women, "her tormentors-in-chief" (p. 81), inspire in Miss Hare. She feels that these women have insinuated themselves into the very cracks in the stones, and fears for the safety of her property, until she comes to understand that some part of her is beyond their reach: " 'I shall not fear if it is taken away, because my experience will remain' " (p. 82).

Within the mandala formed by the branches of a flowering plum tree, "booming with bees and silence" (p. 100), Mordecai Himmelfarb tells Miss Hare the story of his life—or rather, his experience is relived and mutually endured at this time. The evil which she has sensed and actually observed in the housekeeper and her friend is now identified with the events of the holocaust in Europe. Both *Riders* and *The Solid Mandala* demand that we relate obvious dramatic evil, such as the Nazi treatment of the Jewish people, to the quietly insidious evil lurking in the acts of daily life.[13]

Chapter 6, the short chapter between the two long ones which contain the Jew's story, returns us to the events occurring in the basic fictional present in Sarsaparilla, in order to focus the meaning of all that Himmelfarb has experienced in Europe. In their talk, Miss Hare confesses that the notion of *sin* is foreign and unacceptable to her, despite the testimony of her servant Peg, for she knew that Peg was good. Similarly, she brushes off the possibility of redemption as mere "words," and in reply to the Jew's queries, " 'Then how do you account for evil? . . . And who will save us?' " (p. 162), she can only offer her faith in the natural

---

[13] The rational man in us is reluctant to do so; like Waldo, faced with the unpleasant reminder that whole families were cremated, we reply: " 'What's that to do with us? We don't put people in ovens here' " (*The Solid Mandala,* p. 165).

powers of cyclic rebirth, as grass grows again after fire. The Jew is clearly unconvinced.

Both Himmelfarb and Mary, however, have seen the Chariot. And Mary's reassurance that the Riders will be revealed in good time makes the Jew pronounce her to be "the hidden zaddik," one of the thirty-six holy men of Jewish tradition: " 'It is even told . . . how the creative light of God poured into the zaddikim. That *they* are the Chariot of God' " (p. 163). The beauty of the moment is interrupted by Mrs. Jolley's call, a reminder that "shoved them back" (p. 163) from the salvation which the natural beauty beneath the tree appeared to offer. Protected by the tent of the tree, suggestive of the ancient Israelite tabernacle in the wilderness, their minds are free to voyage into hell.

Himmelfarb's experience prior to Sarsaparilla is given in greater detail than that of the other main characters because it is central to the novel's vision and framework of values. As a Jew, he belongs to an ancient people whom centuries of history have accustomed to look inward—although Jews, as Miss Hare notes, are not the only ones who do this. The marked contrast between his parents sets religious faith within the context of the rational, "liberal," worldly spirit of the age (the *zeitgeist,* as it is termed in *The Solid Mandala*). Faith co-exists with the world, being *in* it but not *of* it. The boy develops out of the mother's silence and spiritual depths. His father Moshe, a worldly Jew of liberal tastes, yearns for "an outside world" (p. 108), beyond the closed circle of their faith. The reasonable man, in fashion as in faith, Moshe is only too ready to believe that the age of enlightenment and universal brotherhood has dawned in Western Europe, that the old dark days are done. Mr. Brown and Mr. Feinstein, in *The Solid Mandala,* are very similar.

Such men, like Moshe Himmelfarb and his friends, are "filled with every decent intention . . . reasonable, respectful, rather than religious men" (p. 103). Of the religious festivals, Moshe most enjoys Succoth or Thanksgiving, which makes the least spiritual demands upon him. The ultimate in reasonableness, to Moshe, is his conversion to Christianity, in order to take advantage of the material and social advantages and the security which the change appears to offer. Mordecai reacts to this apostasy with horror, as to a spiritual death. Moshe does not live to see the Nazi holocaust, but Mr. Feinstein is shattered by its acts and implications. Both novels use the classical age and the Renaissance to symbolize part of the *zeitgeist* of our own age. The Renaissance marked the end of the age of faith and the beginning of neo-classical values, including pride in man's self-sufficiency and in the powers of reason. White's novels reveal the inadequacy of the rational position which, like Moshe, expects and hopes "that the world should recognize a good man" (p. 116), but is frail and ineffectual when faced with active evil.

Himmelfarb's experience, like that of all White's protagonists, follows the fourfold pattern of spiritual development. In the innocence of childhood, he drinks from the same source which nourishes his mother's goodness. Spiritual and intellectual arrogance begin with adolescence. The ripening of self-love and the loss of religious faith is described by the cyclic imagery of the seasons: "Religion, like a winter overcoat, grew oppressive and superfluous as spring developed into summer, and the natural sources of warmth were gradually revealed" (p. 105). He enters the second stage, that of adult experience and the "rage to live" (p. 115). His visits to houses of prostitution resemble the adolescent experiences of the young Stephen, in Joyce's *Portrait of the Artist as a Young Man*. The second stage is marked by the assumption of the mask, Jung's *persona*; Himmelfarb is the respected intellectual to others, the man of animal passions and spiritual desolation to himself.

Many of the key events in the lives of each Rider are paralleled by psychically similar, though superficially different, events in the lives of the others, a parallelism which is often emphasized by the repetition of words. Thus Mordecai's "trial by charity" (p. 114), through exposure to the dreadful little dyer with repellent purple skin and greasy coat, parallels Miss Hare's "trial by Mrs. Jolley." Noticing his repugnance, his mother warns him that he has not yet experienced the hundredth part, just as the Cantor has warned that pride will be humbled.[14] The apostasy of Mor-

---

[14] The Cantor's conviction that Mordecai will bite the dust is both warning and prophecy; it is similar to the drunken salesman's remark, in *The Tree of Man*, about the hand of the Almighty.

decai's father touches him deeply and reinforces his spiritual withdrawal. But almost every soul, as the narrator observes, must endure a period of spiritual probation "before receiving orders" (p. 124).

Driven by longing, Himmelfarb recovers his faith with the dyer's relatives in Bienenstadt, within the circle of the Liebmann family's lovingkindness. At Himmelfarb's wedding to Reha Liebmann, the crippled dyer emerges from the past to lay on the groom, whose heart has been touched and changed, the mantle of the "expectations" of his race.[15] The wedding episode establishes the Jew as a dedicated and sacerdotal figure, conscious of some special destiny, and committed to a love which must discover how to reconcile the natural feeling he has towards his wife with what has hitherto been the disgust he has felt for the dyer.[16] Although Himmelfarb must continually wrestle with faith, as Jacob wrestled with the angel, this struggle is within the context of his wife's tangible goodness, "the full goodness of their married lives" (p. 137). They remain childless, like Israel the dyer, for "the seed can be sown . . . in many ways" (p. 129) and neither babies nor the work which is glorified in the kibbutz is the "panacea" (pp. 139, 202). Himmelfarb's way is now *inward,* the route taken by all White's questing characters; and for a time, like Voss, he must traverse "his own desert" (p. 143), for he is still a spiritual probationer, despite his recovery of faith.

It is during this time of his suspension of will that the Nazi persecution of the Jews sets in. The crisis highlights the inadequacy of reason by revealing the gulf between words and acts, between theory and involvement. Twentieth-century European civilization, with its reliance on reason, is exposed as only a mask, a Greco-German façade, like the house in which the Himmelfarbs were permitted to live for a time, before the pretence is over and the house becomes a hollow shell. The flames of the burning synagogue cause the ugly, squat old building to assume

---

[15] The episode suggests John the Baptist's public recognition of Jesus as the man who will justify their expectations; the emphasis in this scene on the bridegroom also recalls biblical imagery of Christ.

[16] Cf. Kierkegaard's emphasis, especially in *Works of Love,* on the paradox of Christian love as the *duty* to love one's neighbour. This is an *absurdity* to the natural man, for whom preferential love is always highest.

"a Gothic grace in its skyward striving" (p. 159); the image adds one more brick to White's Judaic-Christian edifice.

In the Jew's story the crucifixion or Passion archetype is used twice, in Germany and in Sarsaparilla. The European episode has several parallels with the historic crucifixion, although these are more in evidence in the factory yard at Barranugli. After his escape from the death camp his pierced forehead and hands, the description of his rest "in the bosom of his Lord" (p. 196), the dressing of his wounds by the peasant women, even the detail of the third day—all suggest Christ's Passion. Himmelfarb's Passion begins on the night of the destruction of the property of the Jews and the loss of his wife Reha. He considers his failure to be with her and his people at this time a betrayal, something for which he can never atone. This moment is for him the conjunction of time and eternity, as he tells the woman under the flowering plum tree, an eternal moment of failure which casts its shadow over all that follows.

The solitary confinement provided by the Stauffers' secret room is a time of rest and spiritual rebirth for the Jew, after his psychic death. He refrains from suicide because he is unable to see any point in "dying twice" (p. 165). The little, tomb-like room becomes a symbol of death and rebirth, a place to continue "his search for a solution to the problem of atonement" (p. 166). Perhaps, as Konrad Stauffer suggests, the pure are those who have tried and not succeeded, and atonement is possible " 'only where there has been failure' " (p. 171). Himmelfarb describes himself as the beetle of faith, who continues to claw while daily slipping back. Where Elyot Standish's room is a cocoon of deathly isolation, Himmelfarb's is an *egg,* inside which he has been allowed to grow in strength. His psychic death is completed on the night of bombing near Herrenwaldau, his last night of hiding and the end of his fear for his own person. Just as Miss Hare survives the fear engendered by the housekeeper and passes into a new stage of confidence, so Himmelfarb, consumed by "the quicklime of compassion" (p. 176), has finally reached the state of equanimity or disinterested love from which, as the dyer suggested, he may illumine the world.

Having given himself up for arrest, the Jew is immersed in the full horror of the holocaust with "the untouchables—the Jews" (p. 190). Individual anguish, such as that of the Lady from Czernowitz, co-exists with a unity of experience, the suffering of the mass soul of the Jewish people. As Eustace is the legatee of Xanadu, so Himmelfarb is the "legatary" of the dyer, who has bequeathed to him "the peculiar duty of loving his children" (p. 182), the elect of suffering whom Himmelfarb now embraces. After his miraculous delivery from the death camp at Friedensdorf, and his blind wanderings without spectacles, his sight and something of his own identity are restored on reaching Istanbul. In Israel he encounters arrogance of two kinds: the intellectual arrogance of the physicist in Jerusalem is matched by the physical arrogance of his healthy relatives on the kibbutz who find fulfilment in the activity of farm work and children.

Himmelfarb rejects these solutions as false or, at least, impermanent. As he continues to seek the place that God intends for him, Australia suggests itself, "possibly because it was farthest, perhaps also bitterest" (p. 203). The image of a pillar of fire, rising before the Jew as he enters this new and bitter land, identifies him with the Jewish people leaving Egypt after centuries of slavery to begin the journey through the desert to the Promised Land. The Jewish archetype of bondage in Egypt, identified in the seder meal with the bitter herbs, is suggested by the descriptions of the Jewish death-camp workers as *slaves* and of the Australian experience as *bitter*. Thus the Jew's experience is based on two archetypes of suffering, that of the Jewish people in Egypt and the desert, and that of the crucifixion of Jesus of Nazareth. The identification of the seder meal and the Christian eucharist in Part Six is prepared for and continuously reinforced by imagery throughout the novel.

Ruth Godbold, introduced through her care for Miss Hare when the latter is seriously ill, remains "the most positive evidence of good" (p. 66) to the animal woman. Laundress, nurse, mother, neighbour, and servant to all who are in need, this third Rider illustrates the truth of Himmelfarb's comment to Miss Hare that the simple acts of daily life may be the best protection against evil. These acts are Mrs. Godbold's protective shield, in the same way as the Jew is protected by his daily ritual of prayer, and Miss Hare by her little rites with the creatures of Xanadu.[17] Like the other Riders, Ruth is engaged in a quest, a search "for that most elusive needle of salvation" (p. 237). Only too aware of evil as a fact, not a theory, she is determined to try to bear the brunt of it herself, to deflect the blow and prevent it from falling on others. Each of the Riders experiences a feeling of failure. Ruth is tormented by her mistress's refusal to see the truth *for herself*,[18] and, even more poignantly, by Tom's alienation from the Christian faith. Her refusal to turn away from suffering for his sake, even to protect herself from his blows, fills her husband with horror and disgust. The temporary shed in which the God-bolds live and in which Ruth carries out her "life sentence" (p. 68) of loving labour is dominated by the great copper washtub with its steam and constant fire. The description of the shed, like that of Holunderthal during the bombing,[19] suggests the Apocalypse, and prepares us for the major apocalyptic imagery in Part Seven, that of the demolition and reconstruction of Xanadu.

The wholeness of Ruth's feeling for Tom Godbold is illustrated by the physical consummation of their love before marriage. Unlike Lawrence's Miriam, in *Sons and Lovers,* Ruth's love is not only spiritual but involves her entire being, body and soul. This is signified in her maiden name, Joyner, while her married name denotes her evangelistic fervour and her daily witness to her faith. Her "errand of love" (p. 294) in following Tom to Khalils'[20] is patterned on the archetypal descent to hell in search of lost souls, for Khalils', as even the youngest Godbold

---

[17] The shield, as a figure of God's protecting care, is a favourite with the religious poets of Israel (Psalms *passim*). St. Paul uses the "shield of faith" in his great military allegory (Eph. 6: 16).

[18] Mrs. Chalmers-Robertson refuses to emerge from her own distraction to receive. Her effort to extract a statement of her maid's belief is not the desire to hear, "only to know," in order "to rob and to humiliate" (pp. 285-286).

[19] It surprises a citizen that the apparently staid town should prove "inflammable" (p. 180). The image, like that of the house with "Greco-German facade," suggests the fiery passions and disorder which underlie the surface rationalism and imposed pattern of law and order. Cf. Max Frisch, *The Firebug.*

[20] The *relentless* quality of her following after Tom, " 'to hell if need be' " (p. 306), suggests Francis Thompson's portrait of Christ as "The Hound of Heaven," in his *Poems* (1893).

children understand, is "perhaps the very depths of the pit" (p. 290).

This is one of White's great comic scenes, its mood both funny and fearsome, like something from the Theatre of the Absurd. Forms sway and swell in the fearful fug of the bawd's kitchen, where Janis and Mr. Hoggett, an impatient customer, are conducting a discussion on death, a suitable topic considering the locale. Even the cat is "after" love, " 'like anybody else' " (p. 296). Ruth's thoughts of her own home, its clean ironing-table and atmosphere of light and honesty, form a striking contrast to her present surroundings, just as Sanderson's station is contrasted with Boyle's, in *Voss*. The abo enters on what he calls a mission of love, but is rejected by the bawds, whose principles of decency suggest they draw the line at "blacks." Mrs. Godbold, however, recognizes in the abo's voice the certainty and authority she has heard only once before, when she experienced ecstasy upon hearing Bach's music in the cathedral. The abo and the laundress inhabit an island in hell's kitchen, where her wiping the blood from his mouth is both an act of devotion and her work of art.

At Khalils', Ruth's understanding, suffering, and compassion move into a new stage: "She no longer blamed her husband, altogether. She blamed herself for understanding" (p. 296). Tormented by her inability to help Tom, she feels, like Arthur in *The Solid Mandala*, that she herself is "reduced by half" (p. 306). Several years later she is called to identify her husband's body. The experience completes her psychic death, similar to that suffered by the Jew in the little room at Herrenwaldau:

> Mrs. Godbold's self was by now dead, so she could not cry for the part of her which lay in the keeping of the husband she had just left. She cried, rather, for the condition of men, for all those she had loved. . . . She cried, finally, for the people beside her in the street. (P. 307.)

At the traffic crossing, Ruth reaches the state described by the dyer as equanimity, where love is no longer preferential and personal but is both passionate and impartial.[21]

Alf Dubbo, the half-caste, is known to each of the other Riders. He has been recognized by Miss Hare, in a brief encounter on the road below Xanadu, as a fellow illuminate. Ruth Godbold has wiped blood from his mouth as he lay on the floor of Khalils' kitchen, although they will not meet again, except in thought and dream. Between abo and Jew a certain warmth has been silently established in the Brighta bicycle lamp factory, a warmth which is intensified by their mutual interest in the prophets.

As the Four Living Creatures of Ezekiel's vision are joined to one another by wings, White's four protagonists are joined by silence and dedication. Their faith is expressed in acts, not words: "Nor would the boy, it appeared, attempt to express himself, except by those riddles in paint which his teacher so deplored" (p. 344). Just as Waldo and Arthur Brown compose one man, on one of *The Solid Mandala*'s multiple levels of meaning, so one perfect man of intuition, intellect, practical action, and artistic talent is suggested by the quaternity of Four Living Creatures, joined by love and their common identification with the Godhead, source of the fiery Chariot itself. Manfred Mackenzie describes the Four as "the sides of the soul of a giant Everyman, which is seen here as a divine quaternity."[22] Ezekiel's Creatures are in the likeness of a man—of one man, that is, not of *men*. In Alf's final painting of the Chariot, the Four Living Creatures are depicted as the massive, inviolable laundress; the Jew, crowned with suffering; the animal woman of Xanadu; and the painter himself, his head a whirling spectrum: "As they sat facing one another in the chariot-sociable, the souls of his Four Living Creatures were illuminating their bodies, in various colours. Their hands, which he painted open, had surrendered their sufferings, but not yet received beatitude" (p. 494).

---

[21] The foreman considers Himmelfarb foolish for not having a particular friend or mate, and is horrified at the Jew's suggestion that his mate is "Anybody" and "Providence" (p. 331).

[22] Manfred Mackenzie, "Patrick White's Later Novels: A Generic Reading," *Southern Review* I, 3 (1965), 17.

As Mrs. Godbold's acts of devotion are her works of art, so Alf's paintings become his acts of devotion and his special contribution to the sum of truth. They serve as both a means towards achieving the understanding for which he longs, and an expression of that understanding in a way which makes its communication possible. As the rector puts it, the boy's gift may have been given to him as a means of expressing his innermost convictions.

Like White's other key figures, Alf passes through four archetypal stages of experience. His early vow to Mrs. Pask, to paint Jesus Christ, has been conceived in a moment of deceit—an inadequate basis, as he discovers, for art, which flowers out of personal understanding and conviction. As a child, he paints the *Crimson Ramblers,* "a kind of mandala painting of Meroë-Innocence."[23] *My Life,* painted in the first flush of adult experience at the age of thirteen, includes all that he has ever known, much of which Mrs. Pask calls mad and dirty, but which Alf claims is all really beautiful if only he could develop his ability to express it. Dubbo's quest, following the inner route of all White's heroes, takes him to the city, a suitably savage background for exploring "his personal hinterland" (p. 366). His secret sickness and his secret gift he considers the negative and positive poles of his being, the one destructive, the other creative and regenerating.[24] As a youth he has suspected that his immature vision will be completed eventually by revelation. Maturing, he finds this revelation to be not purely transcendental but dependent upon "his struggle with daily becoming, and experience of suffering" (p. 368). Out of the suffering of this period and "the dull hell of disintegration" (p. 376) comes his painting of the fiery furnace of Daniel's vision. His paintings are still his only proof of an absolute, and his act of faith. Hence his destruction of his paintings, after being betrayed by Hannah and Humphrey Mortimer, constitutes a kind of psychic death, like that of the Jew at Herrenwaldau or of Ruth Godbold at the traffic crossing.

[23] Mackenzie, "Patrick White's Later Novels," p. 16. Mackenzie selects four paintings: *Crimson Ramblers, My Life, The Fiery Furnace,* and *The Chariot,* as illustrating the four archetypal stages.

[24] Much of D. H. Lawrence's writing is based on his view of life as polarized. In Lawrence *both* poles are seen as necessary and desirable.

The effect of Himmelfarb's "crucifixion" upon the reader is channeled through the abo, with whom the author intends us to identify. Alf, weaponless and afraid, watches in silence that which he does not dare to oppose. When the Jew has been hoisted above the crowd, Dubbo knows "that he would never, never act, that he would dream, and suffer, and express some of that suffering in paint—but was, in the end, powerless" (p. 441). By his silence at the time of the "crucifixion," and by his subsequent denial to the bus conductor of any acquaintance with the Jew, Alf betrays his friend in the manner of Peter's denial of Christ after his arrest in the garden of Gethsemane. Alf feels, with horror, that it was his nature to betray; he repeats the phrase to himself several times. This is Alf's great failure, the mystery of failure experienced by each of the Riders: "He had not borne witness. But did not love the less" (p. 466). Through the window of Godbolds' shed, Alf sees the women caring for the dying Himmelfarb. This is his vision of the Deposition, seen as the supreme act of love.

Some days later, the abo reaches the point of compulsion or commitment. He paints the Deposition, with Ruth Godbold as the "First Mary" (p. 489), both Mother of God and Magna Mater, the "immemorial woman" whose breasts run with milk. The madwoman of Xanadu is the Second Mary, the Second Servant of their Lord, and the Christ is the tattered Jew from Sarsaparilla. Finally, in the paradisal state in which everything is a source of wonder and love, he paints his last picture, the Chariot which has haunted him for so long but which he has never before fully understood. In White's novels we frequently find the other arts—music, drama, dance, painting—incorporated within the art-form of the novel as metaphor. Thus Alf's paintings contain the meaning of the entire novel, just as Arthur's mandala-dance conveys the essence of *The Solid Mandala*.

The Riders and their demonic antagonists are shown as two cohesive groups or societies, closely related both to other characters of similar intentions and to cosmic powers beyond themselves. An intricate pattern of imagery supports the links which are established on narrative and psychological levels. This grouping belongs to the novel's basic conception and its underlying metaphysics. In White's vision, individual actions are not isolated phenomena but facets of two great spiritual forces in the universe. His characters are shown as having freely chosen to associate themselves with one or the other. The apocalyptic image by which this is expressed most frequently in *Riders* is that of a *chain* (ladder, rope) or, rather, of two opposing chains. The chain affords a particularly suitable image because its basic connotations are twofold: the prisoner's chains, bonds, fetters contrast with golden chains of ornament and honour common to many civilizations and epochs; and, by a natural development of these two contexts, enslavement or captivity is contrasted with true freedom. A concordance reveals that the chain image is commonly used throughout the Bible and with the same two connotations of good and evil, freedom and captivity that we find in *Riders*. These two patterns correspond to archetypal patterns of imagery as apocalyptic or demonic, desirable or objectionable.[25] White's vision, however, is not ultimately dualistic, and the chain also suggests the unity or continuity in which the individual links are contained, the same unity which underlies the mandala image found in all White's novels. The chain image, like that of the Four Living Creatures of Ezekiel joined by wings and created in "the likeness of man," is an apocalyptic metaphor for man's oneness with other men, in and through his oneness with God.

An Either/Or, in Kierkegaard's famous phrase, underlies the novel, in that each character forms part either of the *community* of goodness, freely associated in love, or of the *collusion* of evil, co-operating in fraud.[26] Himmelfarb assures Miss Hare that at some future time it will be revealed what link each provides in

[25] See Northrop Frye, *Anatomy of Criticism: Four Essays* (reprint ed., New York: Atheneum, 1965), pp. 141, 147.
[26] John McLaren, "The Image of Reality in our Writing," *Overland*, Nos. 27-28 (Winter/Spring 1963), 45, ignores White's contrast between the two types of association, community and collusion: "In conversation, the characters neither discuss nor conflict, they deliberately pare at each other from their individual fortresses of isolation. The exception to this is when, like Mrs. Jolley and Mrs. Flack, they unite in a communion of evil to slice at the virtuous. It is noteworthy that their communion is far more realistically conveyed than its mystical counterpart between the four charioteers."

the chain of events. Mrs. Flack's relationship with Mrs. Jolley is a demonic parody of true friendship: "*Her friend. The word was quite alarming, if also magical. . . .* This could have been the perfect communion of souls if, at the same time, it had not suggested perfect collusion" (pp. 74-75). All bad things, as Miss Hare informs Mrs. Jolley in their final confrontation, have a family resemblance, and lovingkindness "might save, if it were not obliterated first by conspiracy of evil minds" (p. 320).

The fetter image is implicit in our last view of Mrs. Jolley as prisoner of Mrs. Flack; the two women, left to sharpen their knives upon one another, provide a mutual hell. Inversely, faith and love are the golden chain which links man to God. Rope and ladder images are used to describe the Jew at prayer: "He flung his rope into the dusk. . . . His ladder held firm. . . . So he added, breath by breath, to the rungs of faith" (p. 210). Similarly, Ruth's ecstatic bliss at hearing Bach's organ music in the cathedral raises "golden ladders . . . heavenly scaffolding" (p. 253) by which she mounts to God. Her preferred themes, as she sings at work, are death and judgment and the future life; and her favourite hymn celebrates the prisoner's throwing off his chains and receiving freedom from God.

The unity and continuity of White's art is evident not only in his use of images in patterns throughout one novel, and between novels, but also in the relation which these basic patterns have to one another. Thus the golden chain of being is identified with the mandala image of perfection and with Himmelfarb and the Godbold children on their mission of love: "So the golden chains continued to unwind, the golden circles to revolve, the dust of secrecy to settle" (p. 235). Wherever our attention is drawn to roundness, a circle, or the centre of a circle, the context suggests some aspect of divinity, primarily peace and love. In *Riders,* the Jewish faith is repeatedly imaged as a "closed circle" (pp. 108, 129), one lit up by the love of God. Other mandala figures include Miss Hare's great wicker hat which serves as her protective shield; the flowering plum beneath which Himmelfarb tells his story and which promises continuity; the round table at which his mother pens her letters of love; the geometric carpet at the centre of which the boy receives a blessing from the Galician rabbi; and the wedding rings of Himmelfarb's bride Reha and of Mrs. God-bold, on her errand of love to Khalils'.

As a symbol of love, the wedding ring is not in itself a novel image. White's images take their freshness and unique power not only from each particular context but also through his technique of grouping images into patterns, so that their effect is *cumulative* as well as individual. The four seasons are used as images of the four archetypal stages of experience. Thus Himmelfarb's child-hood innocence and effortless faith is identified with spring; his rage for life and discovery of sex, with summer; his psychic with-drawal and "death," with winter; and his spiritual rebirth, and actual death, with spring. The experience of the other Riders has similar cyclic associations, the pattern being unobtrusive and subtly varied, for the novel covers the passing of many years in the life of each character.

The first words of Part Six, "Passover and Easter," suggest the theme of this section and of the entire novel, the problem of re-demption. The events which converge on Blue's sadistic "joke," the "crucifixion" of the Jew, are accompanied by pairs of apoca-lyptic images or archetypes which convey the meaning of the paired feasts, Passover and Easter. Ultimately, the two become *one,* "the Season of Freedom" (p. 409). To a Jew, Pesach (Pass-over) signifies *freedom,* with the deliverance from Pharaoh's bondage in Egypt serving as the archetype for all freedom; and to a Christian, Easter signifies freedom from the bondage of guilt and sin through the Atonement of Christ. On the seder table, set by Himmelfarb in a mood of foreboding and a longing "to con-tribute, if only an isolated note" (p. 409), are the shankbone and egg, the flat matzoth or unleavened bread, the dish of bitter herbs, and the cup for wine.[27] The door stands open to welcome the Stranger to the feast.

[27] There are seven objects on the traditional arrangement of the seder tray: matzoth, baked egg, shankbone of a lamb, haroseth, karpas, hazereth, and bitter herb. The *three* absolutely essential items (from Num. 9: 11) are the Paschal lamb, the unleavened bread, and the bitter herb. Himmelfarb's table has these three, along with the egg (symbol of the Resurrection) and the cup for wine. The *two* items of the Christian eucharist, bread and wine, cor-

After Himmelfarb has returned from his useless journey to the Rosetrees, he is visited by Ruth Godbold, who offers him a lamb-shank as food for the holiday weekend; for her, the date has only *one* significance—Easter. Later, he sees "that the wretched shankbone which his neighbour had brought as an offering was almost the twin of the one he had laid that afternoon on his own Seder table" (p. 424). The next morning he eats splinters of meat "from each of the identical shankbones" (p. 431). The identification of Passover and Easter in Chapter 12 through the image of the Paschal lamb underlies the simplicity of Ruth's statement to Harry Rosetree after Himmelfarb's death, a statement which Harry repeats to his bewildered wife: *it is the same.* Formal religion, to Ruth, is no more than a coat which a man puts on, and sometimes feels he should change: " 'Only at the end, when everything is taken from them, it seems there was never any need. . . . That is how it strikes me, sir. Perhaps you will remember, on thinking it over, that is how Our Lord Himself wished us to see it' " (p. 480).

Himmelfarb's journey on the seder night to the Rosetree Home Beautiful in Paradise East is clearly an archetype of man's "perennial journey" (p. 417) through life, his quest of paradise. Journeys, as Himmelfarb has been taught, imply a promise; he has known this, but has not yet dared to accept the spiritual promise. The Rosetrees' intended journey to My Blue Mountain Home affords a parody of the archetypal journey of man's spiritual quest.

Just as the novel uses two archetypes of freedom—Passover and Easter—so it employs two archetypes of suffering: one, of the sufferings or "perennial Egypt" (p. 401) of the Jewish people, not only under Pharaoh but throughout their history; the

respond to the *three* of the seder meal, with wine (representing the blood of Christ's sacrifice) replacing both the lamb and the bitter herb, as the bitterness of Calvary is translated into joy. The apocalyptic symbol of the Paschal lamb is common to Passover and Easter, and both are concerned with bondage and freedom—the same contrast which underlies the chain imagery in *Riders.* Cf. Bro. P. P. P. Kantor, "Jews and Jewish Mysticism in Patrick White's 'Riders in the Chariot,' " *B'nai B'rith Bulletin*, XI (March 1963), 20: "Judaism, Jews and Jewishness are treated objectively and with a surprisingly comprehensive knowledge of the detail."

other, of the Passion of one Jew which culminated in Calvary. The descriptions of the bridge which carried Himmelfarb to and from Rosetrees' (pp. 412, 421) suggest the Israelite crossing of the waters of the Red Sea to begin the journey to the Promised Land. But on the return journey Himmelfarb's hope has died, and he moves through a surrealist city of oozing syrup, neon glares, "pools of vomit and the sailors' piss" (p. 421) which identifies Sydney with the doomed city of Sodom and the sorrow of the Babylonian exile and captivity.

At the same time that Himmelfarb is repeating the archetypal sufferings of Jewish history, he is moving through the events of Christ's Passion, both at Rosetrees' and in the factory scene which follows. Mrs. Rosetree's telephone reference to the stations of the cross; Rosie Rosetree's narcissistic desire for the stigmata; Harry's surprise at his own use of the word *flogged* to describe the Jew's exhaustion; and the parallel with Pilate[28] suggested by the vain attempts of both Harry and Shirl Rosetree to absolve themselves from guilt—all serve as preparation for the Calvary archetype which follows. Through the failure of the journey on the seder eve (p. 421), the "disaster" (p. 424) or "wreckage" (p. 431) of the seder table, and the use of the crucifixion as archetype of redemptive suffering, the novel suggests that Easter is the fulfilment of the freedom celebrated in the Passover; but that Easter is a hollow sham unless it incorporates the faith and suffering of Himmelfarb's experience. The terrible irony of Mrs. Flack and Mrs. Jolley invoking "an Easter that was their due, as regular communicants, and members of the Ladies' Guild" (p. 401) is repeated in the description of the gaily dressed crowds passed by Dubbo on his way to Godbolds' shed and the "customary efficiency" of the Easter celebration: "Outside the churches, everyone was smiling to find they had finished with it; they had done their duty, and might continue on their unimpeded way" (p. 476).

Blue's "joke" is prepared for by two archetypal incidents

[28] Mrs. Rosetree stands "in an attitude of formal guilt. From the very beginning, the tips of her fingers could have been dripping blood" (p. 414). Harry is the tortured non-spectator of the disgraceful spectacle in the factory yard, "inadequately protected by the knowledge that he had done his best" (p. 437).

which, like Passover and Easter, are finally identified, so that the meaning of both is contained in one. Past the Brighta factory, while Harry Rosetree's distress is becoming unbearable, roll two processions, circus and funeral, with one of the clowns enacting a public hanging on the platform of a lorry. The narrator suggests that since the suffering of some live man is lacking, the crowd is temporarily appeased by this puppet or effigy of a man. The description of the lolling clown anticipates the description of "the Jew of lolling head" in the events which follow. But the circus and funeral are "interlocked processions," and in the effigy of the clown the widow recognized "the depth, and duration, and truth of grief, which she had failed to grasp in connection with that exacting male her now dead husband" (p. 435). Each of the Riders has been shown, more than once, to be a *comic* figure in the eyes of the world, although each experiences the depths of suffering. In the interlocked processions of life and death, seen by White as the Divine Comedy where death is not an end but a beginning, the answer to the mystery of failure is centred in the lolling figure on the "divine tree" (p. 440). The demonic parody of this aspect of White's vision is found in "the convention which demanded that cruelty, at least among mates, must be kept at the level of a joke" (p. 440), and the fact that "there is almost no tragedy which cannot be given a red nose" (p. 438).

Harry Rosetree is an apostate Jew, one who has found it prudent to change his "coat," as Mrs. Godbold terms religion. His story, like that of Himmelfarb's father Moshe, affords a tragic subplot within the great comic framework, although apparently not even a dead body in the bathroom can make "tragedy, vice, retribution" (p. 475) anything but incredible in Paradise East. His writing on the steam of the bathroom mirror adds the last facet to the multiple meanings in Mordecai Himmelfarb's name. "MORD" suggests both death and bitterness, which is what Himmelfarb's suffering means to Harry Rosetree.[29] The experience

---

[29] *Mors,* Latin and *mort,* French, 'death'; *mordant,* French, 'bitter,' 'caustic,' also the fixative in a dye solution, a meaning which may relate to Himmelfarb's being the "legatary" of the dyer's suffering "children." Some of White's names reward the ingenuity commonly expended upon Joyce's *Finnegans Wake.*

of the four Riders, however, shows that suffering can be transmuted into joy. In the crucifixion archetype, Harry is both Pilate and Judas Iscariot, and, like Judas, he chooses to end a situation which has become unbearable by hanging himself. But perhaps Harry belongs to the same mystery of failure which brings the dying Himmelfarb into touch with his father Moshe, for Harry has also failed to acquire the ruthless materialism which his wife has cultivated so successfully.

Part Seven, with its mood of apocalypse—the revelation of divine judgment and deliverance, of repentance and return—further illustrates the fusion of Jewish and Christian tradition and imagery which is found throughout the novel. The underlying theme of Rosh Hashanah, the Jewish New Year, is repentance and return. Jewish tradition uses the apocalyptic metaphor of a Divine Judge writing the deeds of men into an eternal book of records, the Book of Life. Both Judaism and Christianity posit a God of justice and an evening of the scales which keeps the world in spiritual balance.

In the imagery of this novel, Miss Hare's Xanadu is identified with both the natural world and the human body. In Part Five, as Mrs. Jolley's "suspicious" relationship with Mrs. Flack matures, a great fissure opens in the foundations of Xanadu, portent of some future crumbling. The light which enters through the fissure, however, is "victorious" (p. 312). At the very hour that the Jew is hoisted on his tree, the crack widens: "Miss Hare saw the marble shudder" (p. 441).[30] In Part Seven her property appears as the stage-set for a play of divine retribution, its history celebrated in the young labourer's improvised dance of death, its mystery a broken comb from which the honey has run. The fallen Xanadu is linked with the events at the factory at Barranugli[31] in Part Six, and with the entire community at Sarsaparilla, which has taken for granted "its right to pass judgment on the human soul" (p. 224) but which discovers, like Miss Mudge, that it "might be responsible for some man, even all men" (p. 446). In

---

[30] Cf. the Gospel record of the earthquake and the rending of the temple veil which accompanied the crucifixion: Matt. 27: 51; Mark 15: 38; Luke 23: 45.
[31] *Barranugli* 'bare-and-ugly,' 'barren-ugly.'

White's apocalypse, Mrs. Jolley and Mrs. Flack provide their own hell, and the Bon-bon, the Crab-Shell and the Volcano are left craning hopefully after grace from the depths of their "obscure purgatory" (p. 525).

Much of Xanadu, however, is still a natural wilderness, welcoming the lovers with open arms. Whereas Himmelfarb's journey to Rosetrees' has been a failure, Mrs. Godbold's "proper journey" (p. 527) to Xanadu is surrounded by joyous and victorious imagery. Her children and grandchildren are arrows aimed at the darkness and she is herself the infinite quiver. A new settlement at Xanadu has replaced the old disintegrating house. There Mrs. Godbold "would build. Or restore" (p. 530). Her spirit of love dominates the ending of the novel. Like Reha Himmelfarb, she restores to those around her the sense of continuity with all that is solid and good: "all certainty was here, and goodness must return, like grass" (p. 506). Like grass—or like sarsaparilla, for the name of White's mythic community and the setting for this great comedy is also the name of a common flower which the Godbold children wear as they clown and sing.

If the doors of perception were cleansed, everything would appear to man as it is, infinite.
WILLIAM BLAKE, THE MARRIAGE OF HEAVEN AND HELL

"For you must know, beloved, that each one of us is beyond all question responsible for all men and all things on earth, not only because of the general transgressions of the world, but each one of us individually for all men and every single man on this earth."
DOSTOYEVSKY, THE BROTHERS KARAMAZOV

chapter **10** The solid mandala

The Solid Mandala explores another world, the world which its first two epigraphs describe as being "in this one," "wholly within." It is a world perceived as vividly by twentieth-century artists such as Eluard[1] and White as by a mystic of the Middle Ages. Starting from the facts of death and suffering, two facts which the *zeitgeist* prefers to ignore, the novel examines the meaning of life, permanence, and freedom. These, indeed, are the typical concerns of White's novels. In *The Solid Mandala* this great theme is developed through probing man's twin consciousness or the apparent duality of his nature. The twin brothers, Arthur and Waldo Brown, embody man's flesh and spirit, reason and will, and, more importantly, the interdependence and essential unity of these attributes. As the children scream at play, " 'One a one makes two,' " but " 'One a one a one' " (p. 192).

---

[1] The novel's first epigraph is from Paul Eluard, pen name of Eugène Grindel (1895-1955), one of the founders of surrealism. Eluard became the poet of the couple, of loving communion with *the other*, as well as with the universe of nature. He was deeply moved by the Spanish Civil War, and his later poetry extends this communion to the whole fraternity of mankind.

One remains one, while appearing to be two; yet " 'Two a two is never one,' " for man's true unity and perfect state is reached not in this life but only after the death of one of his two "selves," the one which refuses to love anyone or anything but itself. Everyone, as Crankshaw the librarian suggests to a sceptical Waldo, has the "potentialities" (p. 168) for this true humanity.

One of the basic structural principles in the novel is the quaternary, used as an apocalyptic image of man's humanity, but a humanity intimately related to divinity. The development of this image in mystical tradition may relate to the Hermetic or alchemical concept that man is composed of four elements or qualities (wet, dry, warm, cold), and to the experience of four colours (gold, red, blue, green) which has frequently been recorded by religious mystics widely separated in time and place.[2] The square or rectangle suggests *four,* and is a common shape for altars, rooms, houses. There are four Christian evangelists. Irenaeus argues that there must be four canonical Gospels because there are four cherubim, four winds, four cardinal points of the compass or quarters of the earth.

In many ways the human body suggests *two*: two eyes, two hands, two feet, and so on. In White's fiction, two becomes four either through narcissism (which "doubles" the self in the mirror image of selfish preoccupation) *or* through love, by joining hands with the beloved. The former is Waldo's image of his "twin" or *alter ego,* while the latter is Arthur's way to wholeness. In *Riders* the comment in Merle's letter to her mother, " 'Every mirror has its double,' " draws our attention to another demonic parody of

[2] See C. G. Jung, *Psychology and Religion: West and East: Collected Works* XI, ed. G. Alder and trans, R. F. C. Hull (New York: Bollingen Series, 1963), p. 37: "the number four plays an important role in these dreams, always alluding to an idea akin to the Pythagorean tetraktys. The *quaternarium* or quaternity has a long history. It appears not only in Christian iconology and mystery speculation but plays perhaps a still greater role in Gnostic philosophy." In the notes to this passage, Jung writes that Plato derives the human body from four, that Pythagoras called the soul a square, and that "four" in Christian iconography appears chiefly in the form of the four evangelists and their symbols. See also p. 56: "The idea of those old philosophers was that God manifested himself first in the creation of the four elements. They were symbolized by the four partitions of the circle." Cf. "But the quaternity as produced by the modern psyche points directly not only to the God within, but to the identity of God and man. . . . The voice of Nature is clearly audible in all experiences of the quaternity" (p. 61).

the true reflection of love, this one afforded by Mrs. Jolley and Mrs. Flack. Their relationship parodies the concept implicit in Arthur's thoughts and acts of the true double as the beloved. Laura's letter to Voss employs a similar image: " 'can two such faulty beings endure to face each other, almost as in a looking-glass?' " (*Voss*, p. 181). Laura senses that their mutual frailty, even "mutual hatefulness," may be overcome by love: "The weaker is stronger, O Voooooss" (p. 183).

The mandala and the quaternary are the two predominating images of the novel. These forms and their variants have been extensively explored by Carl Jung, through his studies of dreams, of European and Eastern iconography, and of the writings of mystics. The mandala, as an image of divine perfection and harmony, is of particular importance in Jung's theory of the archetypes of the collective unconscious. But while there is evidence within White's novels that he is familiar with Jung's work, it does not follow that his mystical and visionary material is necessarily derived from the writings and observations of Jung.[3] Contextual evidence also indicates that White has a direct acquaintance with many of the mystical and alchemical writings and much of religious iconography known to Jung, as well as with the work of many artists whose experiences have led them to formulate a vision of life not unlike White's own. Jung considers that the mandalic visions of modern man, unlike those of past ages, do not contain a deity at the centre,[4] but we should not assume that White is necessarily using the mandala in the same way it

[3] A. P. Riemer, "Visions of the Mandala in 'The Tree of Man,' " *Southerly* XXVII (1967), 3, contends that both title and "explicit concerns" of *The Solid Mandala* "declare unambiguously his use of a body of mystical and visionary material *derived from* the writings and observations of Carl Jung" (italics mine). Judith Wright, "Novelists and Poets—the Decade in Australia," *Current Affairs Bulletin* XXXIX, 3, 26 December 1966, 36, speaks of the influence of Jung on White as "too obvious to be overlooked."

[4] See Jung, *Psychology and Religion*, p. 82: "There is no deity in the [modern] mandala. . . . The place of the deity seems to be taken by the wholeness of man." Riemer, "Visions of the Mandala," assumes that White's use of the mandala follows the modern tendency remarked by Jung. But see John Warwick Montgomery, "Cross, Constellation, and Crucible: Lutheran Astrology and Alchemy in the Age of the Reformation," *Transactions of the Royal Society of Canada* I, series 4, June 1963, 266, where Jung's views are criticized. See also Jung, *Psychology and Religion*, p. 72, where Jung describes the mandalic dream-vision of another patient as meaning "the *union of the soul with God*."

has occurred to Jung's twentieth-century patients. While man himself seems to be at the centre of White's mandala images, their circumference connotes some aspect of transcendence or divine love. And in Arthur's four-cornered mandala-dance the two basic images of square and circle, man and God, come together and *coalesce*.[5]

Arthur's dance, executed within the mandala formed by the bay of blackberries, is equated with life itself. The mandala-dance, like the apocalyptic paintings in *Riders,* summarizes the meaning of the entire novel in a way that no direct statement could do. The first corner of this square mandala belongs to Arthur himself: "He danced the gods dying on a field of crimson velvet. . . . Even in the absence of gods, his life, or dance, was always prayerful" (p. 256). The second corner unites Dulcie with Arthur and Saporta; their mutual love creates a three-cornered relationship, imaged by the triangle and the Star of David which is, as Arthur realizes, another mandala. In Mrs. Poulter's corner, the images are suggestive of the Magna Mater or Earth Mother at harvest time, while Arthur is himself the child that she has never carried. The fourth corner belongs to his brother. Here, the images are of desert deadness, withering, and discontinuity,[6] like the fragments of Waldo's literary compositions. Arthur is unable to dance his brother out of himself, and equally unable to save.

At this point, then, Arthur's dance, and hence his life, appears as a failure. The imagery identifies the four corners of the dance with the four seasons, and the four ages of man: infancy, adult love, maturity, and death. These multiple patterns converge in the fourth corner where Waldo is identified with life's winter and with death—*a dead end,* apparently, like the Terminus Road

---

[5] Cf. Louis Untermeyer, "Einstein," *A Treasury of Jewish Humour,* ed. Nathan Ausubel (New York: Paperback Library, 1968), p. 106: "But ah, with a fourth-dimensional grin/ He squared a circle that took us in." "Einstein" is a parody of Edwin Markham's "Outwitted," which depicts divine love as an inclusive circle. This corresponds to White's usage. See also Jung, *Psychology and Religion,* p. 55.

[6] In *Riders in the Chariot* a similar feeling is conveyed by the description of Harry Rosetree's return from Godbolds' shed after Himmelfarb's death; the images suggest deathly splinters, things ugly, nervous, torn, and disparate.

where the brothers reside. In the mandala-dance this apparent failure is resolved by an archetype of the crucifixion, which Arthur understands to be the centre of *both* square and circle: "Till in the centre of their mandala he danced the passion of all their lives, the blood running out of the backs of his hands, water out of the hole in his ribs. His mouth was a silent hole, because no sound was needed to explain" (p. 257). Thus the conclusion to the mandala-dance does put man at the centre of the mandala, but a man whom image and archetype identify with divinity. After Arthur's enactment of the Passion, and his "little quivering footnote on forgiveness" (p. 258),[7] he falls into an exhausted sleep, which completes the analogue with Christ's death and entombment. When he recovers, he gives Mrs. Poulter the gold mandala.

Arthur's other artistic creations, drama and poetry, also express the tragic aspect of the novel's core. Arthur sees that *life* is the drama performed in the darkened theatre where the audience is one with the actors and the spectators sit waiting to see "how their own blood would run" (pp. 280-281). At the end of Part Three his shocking cow-tragedy, "the tragedy of all interminably bleeding breeding cows" (p. 222), is evoked by the verb *stampeding,* and by Arthur's own tortured cries, so that Arthur is identified with the bellowing cow; both have been deprived of a life which has been united with their own until then. The tragedy, described as both ridiculous and frightening, forces its audience to share the agony, "but that, surely, was what tragedy is for" (p. 222). Arthur's poem, "all Marys in the end bleed," has been written after his glimpse of Waldo in their mother's dress. Arthur shares all Waldo's frustrations, and his poem celebrates "their common pain" (p. 284).

Arthur accuses himself of failing to love Waldo sufficiently, otherwise he would be able to help him, "not to be how you are" (p. 198). He is distressed that he cannot "save" (p. 257), and that he cannot lessen Waldo's ignorance: "Waldo could only relieve himself" (p. 242). Arthur's failure in this respect is part

[7] Cf. Christ's last words from the cross: "Father, forgive them, for they know not what they do" (Luke 23: 34).

of the tragic aspect of life expressed in his poem, his drama, and the fourth corner of his mandala-dance. The pattern is summed up in the thoughts of the dying Himmelfarb: *the mystery of failure*.

Attention is drawn to Arthur's dramatic function or fictional role just before Waldo's death: "Arthur Brown, the getter of pain" (p. 284). Arthur has intuited this role much earlier, as the first corner of his mandala-dance shows. As an individual, Arthur loves those he knows and is ready to suffer in order to help them. Archetypally, Arthur is associated with the dying god whose own suffering is a cause of suffering in others, the latter a therapeutic suffering leading to repentance and redemption. The dance conveys the archetype, while the discussion in the kitchen about love between Waldo and Arthur, after the climactic scene in the library, shows it in the plainest terms of ordinary life. Arthur blames himself for not loving sufficiently, and admits to hating himself at times: "Then Waldo wanted to cry for this poor dope Arthur. Perhaps this was Arthur's function, though: to drive him in the direction of tears" (p. 197). In Socratic terms, Arthur is the divine gadfly whose function is to drive Waldo in the direction of tears—that is, towards the understanding and love which seem to be beyond Waldo's capability. Socrates saw himself as a goad driving man towards the truth.

The image of Arthur as the getter of pain, however, is closer to Kierkegaard's conception of *bearing witness*. Kierkegaard insists that the maieutic form of witnessing to the truth of Christianity is incomplete, since it is rooted in human intelligence, and a merely logical system does not encompass existential or subjective truth.[8] Where the truth is considered to be objective, it *is* possible for the agent to have a maieutic relation to the learner. Kierkegaard describes the ultimate truth as *subjectivity*, lying not in the object of apprehension or the *what* of thought but in the subject's relation to what he believes. White's insistence on the importance of suffering, from his first novel to his most recent, seems rooted in an existential metaphysics such as Kierkegaard's.

[8] *The Journals of Kierkegaard 1834-1854,* a selection, ed. and trans. Alexander Dru (London and Glasgow: Collins, Fontana, 1958), pp. 145-146.

White's fondness for three-cornered relationships is apparent from his first novel, but the geometry of *The Solid Mandala* is far more intricate than that of *Happy Valley*. Two of its trinitarian groups consist of Arthur and his two "wives," and Dulcie and *her* two loves. The latter triad (Dulcie, Arthur, and Leonard Saporta) form the triangular second corner of Arthur's dance. In White's symbolic use of number, *three* and *four* are closely connected. Thus Leonard, Arthur, and Dulcie are united with Dulcie's mother, whose character and attitudes strongly resemble those of her daughter: "There was now no need, he saw, to offer the mandala, but he would, because he still wanted to, because they were all four, he and Dulcie, Mrs. Feinstein and Leonard Saporta, so solidly united" (p. 245). Arthur's deep love for Waldo and for his two "wives" unites these four persons. Quaternary images occur in several of White's earlier novels, but first become prominent in *Riders,* where the four protagonists are imaged as Ezekiel's Four Living Creatures.[9] Dulcie and Leonard's son and daughter make a quaternary of the Saporta family. The Brown family is another foursome, a quaternary which becomes three in the allegoric interpretation whereby Arthur and Waldo are together one individual.

There are four parts in the novel, four epigraphs, four corners to Arthur's dance, and four marbles. Arthur's four "solid mandalas," destined to belong to the three people whom he loves most deeply and to himself, provide another link between square and circle. These geometric shapes are White's apocalyptic images for man and God, with man at the centre, *knotted* in all the problems of his humanity, subject to time, pain, and death, but surrounded by the mandalic protective circle, an image suggestive of the encircling arms of love. Arthur reads from Mrs. Musto's encyclopedia: " '*The Mandala is a symbol of totality. It is believed to be the "dwelling of the god." Its protective circle is*

[9] Cf. John Crowe Ransom, "Blake Triumphant," *New York Review of Books* XIII, No. 7, 23 October 1969, 5: "In his *Four Zoas*—so called after the Four Beasts in the Book of Revelations—he identifies the four persons or powers of the mind. . . . Blake has anticipated precisely the quaternity of the Swiss psychologist Jung." We should not lose sight of the fact that while Jung is responsible for having made many people *aware* of quaternary symbolism, the phenomenon itself is a very ancient one, as Jung emphasizes.

a pattern of order super—imposed on—psychic—chaos. Some-times its geometric form is seen as a vision (either waking or in a dream) or—. . . . Or danced' " (p. 229). This vision of the fusion or interpenetration of matter and spirit which lies behind the conjunction of square and circle is the other world of the novel's epigraphs which is not outside but inside, "wholly within" the visible world. The vision which is given artistic expression in White's novels corresponds to the Christian doctrine of immanence and transcendence, which stems from belief in the Incarnation of the divine in human form. The concept of divinity as *filling all things* agrees with White's choice of the adjective *solid* to accompany his mandala image.[10]

As in White's earlier novels, one of the recurrent motifs is the inadequacy of reason to explain the central concerns of life or death. Arthur is repeatedly *dragging back* Waldo behind the line where knowledge could not help, an area which includes the simple fact of death (pp. 39, 41, 196). *Totality,* as George Brown reluctantly admits, is one of those words so simple in themselves as to defy explanation. The dictionary yields only a tautology: "Then Arthur realized Dad would never know, any more than Waldo" (p. 232). It is Arthur, the keeper of the mandalas, who must guess its meaning through the senses of his body and the intuitions of his mind and spirit. Time, as the rationalist Mr. Feinstein points out to Waldo, " 'becomes unbearable if you don't approach it rationally' " (p. 98). The image is central to the irony which surrounds the presentation of Waldo's feelings and thoughts, for White's novels suggest that there *is* something "unbearable," to use Amy Parker's word, about man's life in time, something for which reason has no answer. Waldo continues to hope that "time, naked but finally rational, might solve his problem" (p. 99), but White's reader should be considerably less sanguine.

To the same ironic context belong the references to Christian Scientists who " 'by *logic,* wouldn't you say?' " (p. 107) cannot die, but who cannot avoid the unfortunate position of having

[10] Cf. Ephes. 4: 10.

their principles contradicted by their death.[11] The descriptions of Waldo's father, compressed by the "narrow cage" (p. 47) in the bank, and of Waldo himself, caged between stacks of books in the library, suggest that these two intellectuals are caught in the same trap and that both have refused to allow themselves "any avenues of escape from that intellectual ruthlessness" (p. 112).[12] They have failed to find the freedom of the spirit which belongs to the true permanence sought by White's heroes. If their life has its compensations these are seen as being no more than "an orgasm in dry places" (p. 114). Waldo's demonic version of freedom is isolation, spiritual celibacy (pp. 72, 109).

Unlike most of White's main figures, the Brothers Brown[13] do not progress or proceed through the four archetypal stages of experience, from innocence to spiritual rebirth. Cyclical images are part of certain descriptions, such as Arthur's mandala-dance; and secondary characters such as Dulcie and her mother advance along the inward route of the spiritual quest,[14] the road taken by

[11] " 'Mrs. Allwright took up Christian Science. She'd do anything not to wake up and find she was dead' " (p. 107). Similarly Waldo, in old age, is described as being "still young enough not to believe in his own death" (p. 110). In *Riders in the Chariot*, Ginny Chalmers-Robinson turns to Christian Science, but confesses to her maid Ruth that it is something of a disappointment.

[12] "Neither light nor air played much part in the sinecure his patroness had bought him. . . . the cages were jammed" (p. 113). "After he retired, Dad would sometimes recall . . . his escape by way of Intellectual Enlightenment . . . but in the telling, he would grow darker rather than enlightened . . . clogged with the recurring suspicion that he might be chained still" (p. 137).

[13] White's frequent descriptions of the Brown brothers as the Brothers Brown is obviously intended to emphasize a relation between *The Solid Mandala* and Dostoyevsky's *The Brothers Karamazov*. Dostoyevsky's reference to "the force of the Karamazov baseness" *The Brothers Karamazov* I, trans. David Magarshack (Harmondsworth, Middlesex: Penguin, 1958), p. 309 points to his use of the brothers as an archetype of fallen humanity. Ivan Karamazov *wills* his father's death, and plans for it, just as Waldo does with Arthur. Both novels have an ironic reversal of these plans.

[14] Dulcie and Mrs. Feinstein have obviously been altered by their European experience. They describe themselves as being "a lot older than they were" (p. 125), whereas "poor Arthur was almost unchanged and, as things were, probably wouldn't alter much" (p. 124). Part Two emphasizes the same point, as Arthur notices that Dulcie and her mother are older and *different*: "It continually amazed Arthur Brown that other people were growing older" (p. 238). In Part Four, unlike the first three parts, there are faint suggestions of Arthur's spiritual advance or growth, although even here these may be ambiguous, as in the following: "All his family gone, he was threatened with

Oliver Halliday, Theodora Goodman, Stan Parker, Voss, and the four Riders. The brothers, however, display in childhood the characteristics which mark them as adults. They do not change through the many years covered by the novel, and thus the allegoric level of meaning which belongs to each brother and to their interdependence is sustained.

The cyclical movement, then, is less prominent than in most of White's novels, but the dialectical movement is very strong. Waldo alternates between desire and repugnance, experiencing these feelings both in relation to himself *and* to other people, especially his brother. The resulting tension is the key to the dual point of view, compassionate and ironic, through which Waldo is presented to us. I do not think that Waldo is intended to be a *totally* unsympathetic figure.[15] Indeed, in the different treatment of Elyot Standish and of Waldo Brown we find a clue to the development of White's vision over the twenty-five year period which separates *The Living and the Dead* from *The Solid Mandala*. It is most important that we should remember Arthur's own insistence on his love and need for his brother Waldo. To read *The Solid Mandala* merely as a revised version of Eden and Elyot Standish, or the spiritually living and the spiritually dead, is surely to miss its main point, man's interdependence.

Watching Arthur, Waldo is "half guilty, half loving" (p. 30). The tension between desire and loathing underlies several of the novel's motifs which centre in Waldo's narcissism and fear. Waldo is fond of contemplating himself in a mirror, even to the

permanent manhood. *Or protected by his permanency*" (p. 300, italics mine). Waldo's death necessarily alters the allegoric position of Arthur as part of *one* man. In becoming a whole individual, he also becomes less rational, less competent generally. In *Voss*, we find a similar change in the way Laura is treated by the author after Voss's death.

15 Thelma Herring, "Self and Shadow: The Quest for Totality in 'The Solid Mandala,'" *Southerly* XXVI (1966), 185, finds that Waldo "alone is denied the author's compassion." Barry Argyle, *Patrick White*, Writers and Critics Series (Edinburgh and London: Oliver and Boyd, 1967), p. 64, notes that Waldo's realization that human relationships are confusingly marbled is "a habit and sentiment" we associate with White himself. Argyle finds it confusing that these sentiments should be attributed to Waldo, where "we despise them because there is nothing in Waldo to persuade us to do otherwise: but this is to learn to despise an aspect of White's work which elsewhere we have found valuable." The latter response is too simplistic, too black-and-white for understanding Waldo or any of White's characters.

extent of pressing his mouth against the glass. This image is a demonic parody of the eucharistic image which is used after the discussion of love between Waldo and Arthur in their kitchen, where Waldo has begun to suspect that Arthur's "function" in relation to himself is to drive him towards tears. Arthur soothes Waldo, who is engulfed in intolerable longing, as they lie in bed with faces melting together: "All the bread and milk in the world flowed out of Arthur's mouth onto Waldo's lips" (p. 198). Waldo's nostalgia for his own absent reflection in Dulcie's children, his desire to talk and to write only about himself, his intention that his reading and learning be only "for his PRIVATE pleasure" (p. 112) form a consistent pattern which is part of the terrible scene between the brothers in the public library. Arthur gasps: " 'Because we are—didn't you say yourself, Waldo?— abnormal people and selfish narcissyists' " (p. 274).

Despite his self-love, Waldo does occasionally "drag himself out of the mirror's embrace" (p. 26) in order to embrace his brother. By so doing, the novel shows, he is embracing both his own best self and the archetypal brother, every other man. His longing for his brother and for love, however, is something which he most frequently despises and refuses to accept. Waldo's narcissism also expresses itself in his fondness for playing a part, his "*Rigoletto*-tenor tones" (p. 66) which seduce no one but himself. The extent of this hypocrisy is revealed in his dream of what he would do if Arthur died: "Of course, in spite of his intellectual tastes and creative gift, it was the hotels he was craving for. Always had been" (p. 109). In this demonic parody of true bliss, characterized by bars, wealthy tourists, flash cars, and "the pox," Waldo anticipates enjoying not physical pleasures but the monstrous swelling of his own ego.

In *Riders* Alf Dubbo arrives at the agonizing conclusion that it was his nature to betray. The allegorical level of meaning in *The Solid Mandala* makes it impossible that Waldo should be granted any such self-knowledge. Betrayal is one of the continuing motifs which underlie the apparently random succession of incidents which are relived during the course of the brothers' walk. Waldo betrays Dulcie Feinstein in his conversation with his co-worker, Walter Pugh, and the betrayal is acknowledged by his flesh, if not by his mind: "Betrayal brought the gooseflesh out on Waldo. Irresistibly" (p. 115). At home he attempts to cover one betrayal with another, by repudiating the entire Feinstein family. As the narrator points out, his rejection of the Feinsteins is linked with his rejection of his brother and father and is connected "with some far deeper, even less desirable, misery" (p. 118) which is, in fact, the rejection *of himself*. His denial of Cissie Baker in the library prefigures his denial of his brother in the same place. Although Waldo has been in the habit of calling her Cissie, he addresses her there as Mrs. Baker. He does this just at her moment of need, in her distress over her brother's death. Similarly, as he orders Arthur to leave the library, Waldo addresses him as *Sir* indicating that "his brother, his flesh, his breath, was a total stranger" (p. 275).

The *fear* which characterizes the life of Waldo and his father brings the latter to burn his copy of *The Brothers Karamazov*. This fear is focussed in Waldo's repudiation of his brother in the library. On the superficial level, Waldo's fear is that others will associate him with Arthur's "hysteria." He wishes to disclaim even acquaintance, let alone the ties of blood, with this disreputable old man. At a deeper level Waldo's fear stems from what " 'this Dostoevski is partly going on about' " (p. 190), the need to find someone to worship and to love. It also stems from his fear of death, a fear which forms a recurrent motif. As Arthur bursts into tears, Waldo expects to find faces waiting to accuse *him,* not Arthur. When Arthur seeks to reassure his brother that because they have each other they need never be afraid, Waldo removes his hands from Arthur's reach. Waldo's belief that his hands are "his property" involves a denial of relationship. His use of the formal "Sir" follows the removal of his hands.

Arthur is associated with angelic qualities, both avenging and beneficent. His name may have been suggested by Spenser's *Faerie Queene,* where Prince Arthur is the perfect Christian knight, engaged in the quest for salvation under the allegoric guise of the chivalric quest.[16] In the encounter between the

---

[16] See Thelma Herring, *"The Solid Mandala*: Two Notes," *Southerly* XXVIII (1968), 216-217. See also Herring, "Self and Shadow," p. 180.

brothers and Johnny Haynes, Arthur becomes the avenging angel to the school bullies. Fire shoots from his flaming hair: "Waldo Brown shuddered to remember his deliverance by what had appeared to be the flaming angel" (p. 39). When the brothers go to tea at Mount Pleasant, Arthur is welcomed by Mr. Feinstein as " 'blowing like a flame, or spirit of enlightenment, through a Jewish household' " (p. 100). As in *Riders,* White's vision tends to fuse Judaism and Christianity. This is effected through both imagery and narrative. The common denominator is love and faith, with the resulting hybrid imaged in the double name borne by Dulcie Saporta's son, Aaron-Arthur. The Feinstein sabbath gathering is represented as a family feast, both social and religious, and one no longer restricted to Jews. White uses Arthur's extreme simplicity or "gibbering" just as he uses drunkenness, delirium, dream, and the commonest clichés of local idiom. All become vehicles for double entendre and apocalyptic utterance.

Both brothers are attracted to Dulcie Feinstein. Arthur's true love contrasts with Waldo's imagined love, which is one of the forms taken by Waldo's egoism. Love, as Arthur and Dulcie know, has a different shape and meaning from *amour*; these "long-legged lovers" (p. 237) are under the spell of *caritas,* not *eros.* Arthur's first love is "plain and sane" (p. 89), "so very practical" (p. 132). Talking to Dulcie at Mrs. Musto's reminds Waldo of the simple happiness he has experienced at the smell of Arthur's baking bread. Dulcie's honesty and childlike candour contrast with Waldo's continual deception. Despite his scoffing, Arthur suspects that Dulcie may be unhappy, for he intuits that the efforts of the girl and her mother to conform to Mr. Feinstein's idea of progress have left them inhabiting a spiritual wasteland. Dulcie and Waldo, as Arthur and Mrs. Musto realize, are " 'a *couple* of lost souls' " (p. 230). When Arthur gives Dulcie the blue mandala he is prompted by the fear that, if she is not intended to marry Saporta, "then without his help she would have no means of relieving her continued drought, of filling her dreadful emptiness" (p. 244).

Dulcie's cup, however, *is* destined to be filled by Saporta, and filled to overflowing. When the death of his brother has shut out Arthur from happiness, he secretly observes the Saporta family at dinner. They appear to be completely fulfilled. Dulcie is as physically unattractive as Theodora Goodman or the four Riders, and like Theodora she suffers the humiliation of a moustache. Inside the external form of an ugly old woman, Dulcie's beauty is "still aglow" (p. 302). Nevertheless it is Arthur who is instrumental in Dulcie's recovery of religious faith, just as he is instrumental in the aged Mr. Feinstein's surrender to love and to God.[17] After receiving the blue mandala, Dulcie tells Arthur that she knows herself to be " 'hideously weak' " (p. 246), and it is he who has given her the strength to face the truth about herself.

Mrs. Poulter is linked to Dulcie by a pattern of ship imagery. Waldo is reminded of a ship's prow by Dulcie's buck teeth, and the Feinstein house has a ship's bell which Arthur loves to ring. Mrs. Poulter's house is repeatedly described as boat-shaped (pp. 137, 176, 250). Thus Arthur's two "wives" are connected by an imagistic pattern as well as by qualities of mind and spirit. The mandala formed by the *bay* of grass in which Mrs. Poulter's houseboat is moored is associated with her lovingkindness. Dulcie and Mrs. Poulter are plain, sane, and very practical, although both women accept matter as the expression of spirit. Their point of view, to which we are frequently returned throughout the novel, helps us to realize what is lacking in the attitudes of Waldo and his parents, Mr. Feinstein, and some of the other characters. An existentialist concept of truth as subjective, or dependent upon the nature of the relation between the subject and the object of his perception, underlies Dulcie's (and Mrs. Poulter's) attitude towards life.

A houseboat suggests a haven or refuge, like the arks which protected Moses and Noah. Indeed, any ship on the high seas is a place of safety in the midst of danger. Biblical imagery identifies Christian hope with a ship's anchor.[18] As the very first words of the novel tell us, Mrs. Poulter is concerned with life, and with

---

[17] Cf. *Happy Valley,* where Oliver Halliday discovers that his vocation lies in being an instrument of divine mercy to suffering men.

[18] See Heb. 6: 19: "Which hope we have as an anchor of the soul, both sure and steadfast, and entering into that which is within the veil." The latter phrase is echoed in the first two epigraphs of *The Solid Mandala.*

making a sacrament of common life. From the beginning, as the narrator notes, she gives the impression of wanting to perform some charitable act. Eucharistic images are associated with both Mrs. Poulter and Arthur. Her little kindnesses in taking food to her neighbours become the subject of George Brown's irony, as he laughingly objects to her making a sacrament of food: " ' "Take, eat" is what she would *like* to say,' said Dad, laughing for his own joke at the expense of the churches and Mrs. Poulter" (pp. 151-152).

Mrs. Poulter's passionate love for her husband Bill, like Ruth Godbold's feeling for Tom in *Riders,* is both spiritual and physical. Her feeling for Bill unites Christian charity with erotic love, just as her love for Arthur unites charity and maternal love. Arthur becomes the child she has never had, the child parodied by Waldo's plastic doll. Nobody, as Mrs. Poulter cries out to Arthur in anguish when he discovers her dressing the doll, " 'ever wants half of what they're given!' " (p. 279). Her statement is streaming with implications, like the image of the Chariot of God which Himmelfarb discovers in the old manuscript. The unwanted half of Mrs. Poulter's life is her barrenness. Her emptiness, however, is finally filled completely by Arthur's great need after Waldo's death. Their unity in love is imaged by their two faces becoming one reflection at the centre of Arthur's last mandala. Arthur, identified with man's physical body *and* with his spirit which is capable of love, is Waldo's unwanted half, "Waldo's club foot" (p. 41). And Waldo's deadness, his terrible isolation, fear, and incapacity to love, make up the unwanted half of Arthur's life and are the source of his suffering.

Dostoyevsky's handling of the "good fool" in *The Idiot* illustrates some of the difficulties of the theme and affords many analogies with *The Solid Mandala.* Dostoyevsky's novel was written abroad. During his travels he had seen at Basel the Hans Holbein painting of Christ being taken down from the cross. It made a tremendous impression on him at the time, and haunted him subsequently. He describes the picture in *The Idiot,* returning again and again to this theme. Dostoyevsky's use of the Deposition may have influenced White's treatment, in *Riders,* of the women and the dying Himmelfarb. The scene is witnessed by Alf Dubbo and has profound effects on his life and art.

When he was beginning his work on *The Idiot* Dostoyevsky wrote to Maykov: " 'The idea is the representation of a perfect man. Nothing in my opinion can be more difficult, especially nowadays.' "[19] The psychological and spiritual depths of his theme involved Dostoyevsky in countless drafts and reworkings of his novel. The earliest versions present the perfect man in the process of evolving and not, as in the final version, in his perfected state. In White's daring conception, Arthur and his "twin in the sun" together make one man, *potentially* capable of perfection. Waldo is man's intellect and will, obviously corrupt in the present state. After Waldo's death Arthur calls him " 'more than half of me,' " but Mrs. Poulter objects: " 'Oh no,' Mrs. Poulter said. 'No more than a small quarter' " (p. 303). Arthur represents both man's physical body and his spirit, capable of worship and of compassionate love.

Waldo and Arthur also function as very real individuals. On this level, Arthur's love for his brother is an apocalyptic image of man's love for the archetypal brother, every other human being. Man's divided state, which is identified with the number two or with the first two corners of a square, is *squared* through love. The wholeness achieved through love is identified with the quaternary and the square which, in turn, is closely associated with or contained within the mandala. Despite his mental deficiencies, Arthur also embodies true wisdom, similar to the *gnosis* in which the intellect co-operates with and is enlightened by the spirit. Arthur declares his own love to be far from perfect, and blames himself for being inadequate. After Waldo's death, his rational abilities show a marked deterioration, for in losing his brother he has, on the allegoric level, lost his intellect.

The notes for Dostoyevsky's first version of the novel describe the idiot as a man of powerful passions with a burning need for love: " 'Chief characteristic of the idiot: self-mastery from pride (not from morality) and a frenzied desire to solve his own prob-

[19] Fyodor Dostoyevsky, *The Idiot*, trans. David Magarshack (Harmondsworth, Middlesex: Penguin, 1955), translator's Introduction, p. 9.

lems—so far only attempts: in this way he might have committed monstrous crimes, but love saves him—he is filled with profoundest compassion and forgives mistakes . . . attains high moral perfection through his development and heroic self-renunciation.' "[20] In the fifth version, Dostoyevsky notes that the main theme of the novel is the struggle of love with hatred (compare Waldo and Arthur). In this version, the idiot appears for the first time as a "real" idiot. The idiot of Dostoyevsky's sixth version is depicted as a man who is morbidly proud and vain yet impassioned for truth. This dichotomy may have offered White a clue towards the Brothers Brown and Waldo's narcissism. Dostoyevsky notes: " 'A Christian and at the same time he does not believe in God: dichotomy of a deep character. N.B. tongue in mirror.' "[21] The notes for this version also refer to the strange and childish friendship between the idiot and Olga Umetsky (compare Arthur's friendship with Dulcie).

By the last versions of *The Idiot,* Dostoyevsky had decided to make his hero a real idiot, one who had suffered from mental deficiency since childhood. The plans for the last version note that " 'the idiot is a prince!' " and that there are three kinds of love depicted in the novel: love based on passion, on vanity, and the Christian love embodied in the idiot prince. Whereas Dostoyevsky had no intention of making his hero comic, he hoped to make him sympathetically attractive to the reader through his innocence and meekness. White, however, has managed to make Arthur both comic and heroic. Dostoyevsky's final version identifies the idiot prince with Christ, and has what the author describes as an "unexpected ending," a bedroom murder of a young woman. The idiot is *not* the murderer, in the Russian novel.

David Magarshack, translator for *The Idiot,* is convinced that the novel successfully portrays the ideal Christian, and that in placing him in a real world, unlike Bunyan's pilgrim, Dostoyevsky provides a crushing criticism of the Russian aristocracy of his time. At the end of Dostoyevsky's seventh chapter in Part IV, the prince appeals to the aristocrats to be servants in order to

[20] Ibid., p. 12.
[21] Ibid., p. 16.

become masters. He includes himself with his audience; all are
absurd, frivolous, full of bad habits, yet "promising material."
This theme clearly underlies *The Solid Mandala* as well as *The
Idiot*. Arthur's appeal to Waldo in the library parallels the idiot's
appeal to the Russian aristocrats. Like the prince, Arthur includes himself in the charge that they are "abnormal" and entirely selfish. *The Solid Mandala,* like *The Idiot,* involves a social
and spiritual commentary, one which is both contemporary and
universal. White's criticism of the *zeitgeist* of our own age includes the rationalist attitudes of Mr. Brown and Mr. Feinstein,
the perversions of Waldo, the general horror which blares from
Mrs. Poulter's radio and television screen, and the neuroses of
her husband and her neighbour, Mrs. Dun.[22]

It is interesting to compare Faulkner's *The Sound and the
Fury,* structurally and thematically, with White's *Mandala*. Both
novels have four parts which are viewed from four different per-
spectives. Both handle time impressionistically rather than
chronologically, and manage to give the effect of telling us everything that passes during the course of many years while actually
concentrating on a few central events. In Faulkner's novel these
central events or emotional clusters include Caddy's pregnancy,
Benjy's castration, and Quentin's suicide; in White's, the after-
noons at the Feinsteins', the Encounter with the Saportas in the
street, and the confrontation in the library. Benjy's rational deficiency does not permit him to interpret events for the reader,
or to distort them in order to justify his own actions. Hence by
putting Benjy's section first and an ostensibly objective section
last, Faulkner creates the effect of an objective frame around the

[22] The tendency of our age to confuse rationalism and higher education with
understanding is implicit in a comment such as the following on Stan and
Amy Parker in *The Tree of Man*: "They are on the edge of making dis-
coveries about themselves and other people which are sometimes incredible in
the light of their almost complete lack of education and reading." Nancy A. J.
Potter, "Patrick White's Minor Saints," *Review of English Literature* V, October 1964, 14.
    One of White's funniest puns is concealed in Mrs. Dun's name, and re-
vealed in Mrs. Poulter's confused thoughts after her discovery of Waldo's
death: "She would never of dared call Mrs. Dun Edna" (p. 297). *Dun* is a
slurred form of 'don't,' and *Edna,* a near-anagram of 'need'; certainly Mrs.
Dun is someone who would not be greatly missed.

two subjective sections narrated by Quentin and Jason. White's first and fourth parts have a similar effect.

Objective and subjective are only valid in a comparative sense, since the total effect combines the author's viewpoint with that of the fictional characters. In *The Solid Mandala,* Waldo's section includes the actions, not the thoughts, of Arthur, Dulcie, and Mrs. Poulter. Their attitudes, expressed in sane and practical acts, are important touchstones which alert the reader to the ironic framework in which Waldo's reactions are contained. The following section retraces most of the events covered in Part Two, this time from Arthur's point of view. The last part alternates between the viewpoints of Mrs. Poulter and an omniscient narrator, with breaks in the text to indicate a change in point of view.

Faulkner stated at the Nagano Seminar (1955) that he conceived of his idiot as "truly innocent" or amoral: " 'I mean "innocence" in the sense that God had stricken him blind at birth, that is, mindless at birth, there was nothing he could ever do about it.' "[23] Benjy is contrasted with Jason, whom Faulkner described as representing " 'complete evil. He's the most vicious character in my opinion I ever thought of.' "[24] White's Waldo is not vicious or aggressively evil like Jason, but repellent and pathetic through his inability to love: "Waldo had always hated people, but always rather, well, as a joke. . . . The life, the sleep they had shared, must have been jingling brassily all those years with the hatred which only finally killed" (p. 299).

Faulkner's novel lacks the allegoric dimension of *The Solid Mandala,* where the two brothers form one man. And White's Arthur, for the novel's first three parts, is far more rational than Benjy, hence capable of being morally responsible for his actions. Arthur degenerates to Benjy's amoral level in Part Four, after Waldo's death. Just as our last sight of Miss Hare, in *Riders,* is of a woman who is "at most an animal, at least a leaf," so Arthur is here described as "at most an animal, at least a thing" (p. 299).

[23] William Faulkner, cited in Michael Millgate, "The Sound and the Fury," *Faulkner: A Collection of Critical Essays,* ed. Robert Penn Warren (Englewood Cliffs, N.J.: Prentice-Hall, 1966), pp. 96-97.
[24] Ibid., p. 97.

His collapse confirms the allegoric level of meaning, where Waldo is the rational intellect and the will, half of Arthur, as he tells Mrs. Poulter. The description of Arthur as a child "too tender to be born" (p. 305) recalls the image of Mary Hare as one of the unborn, hence pure and sinless. It is this *sinless* Arthur whom Mrs. Poulter accepts "as token of everlasting life" (p. 305).

Both novels are basically affirmative and optimistic about mankind. As Faulkner put it in his Stockholm Address (1950): "I decline to accept the end of man. . . . I believe that man will not merely endure: he will prevail."[25] *The Solid Mandala* contains the suffering and tragedy of life within a larger comic framework. The tragic corner of Arthur's dance, the corner belonging to Waldo's spite, to winter and to death, is only one corner in four. After the "death" experienced here, Arthur finally emerges refreshed. And this corner, like the other three, is contained within the protective circle of the mandala. After Waldo's death Mrs. Poulter states her belief in men and in Arthur (p. 307) and thinks: "nothing can touch Arthur nothing can touch me not the part of us that matters" (p. 309).

Dostoyevsky was trying to portray the perfect man. Arthur is not perfect, although we tend to forget this since Waldo is so unattractive and Arthur so loving. Two men of faith, Christian and Jew, are the novel's whole or undivided men who seem to have kept the "solid shape" of their original mould: "In Arthur's life there were the convinced, the unalterable ones, such as Mr. Allwright and Leonard Saporta, as opposed to those other fluctuating figures, of Dulcie, Waldo, his parents, even Mrs. Poulter, all of whom flickered as frightfully as himself. . . . Arthur was grateful for knowing they would never divide, like the others, in front of his eyes, into the two faces, one of which he might not have recognized if it hadn't been his own" (p. 240). In their simplicity and the perfection of their faith these men seem to exist beyond the average man's experience of the twin consciousness, beyond

---

[25] F. J. Hoffman and Olga W. Vickery, eds., *William Faulkner: Three Decades of Criticism* (New York and Burlingame: Harcourt, Brace and World, 1963), p. 348.

doubt and temptation. They are necessarily minor characters, like Mothersole in *The Vivisector* and the Sandersons in *Voss,* since their very goodness restricts the dramatic possibilities of their fictional role. They resemble Kierkegaard's Knight of Faith, who is able in the common acts of daily life "to transform the leap of life into a walk, absolutely to express the sublime and the pedestrian."[26]

A circular movement may be discerned in the historic progression of artistic technique. The stylized sophistication of modern art sometimes resembles the extreme simplicity of primitive art, just as modern ironic fiction often includes a return to primitive myth. We find this in the novels of Kafka, Joyce, and White. Thus the apparent simplicity of technique in *The Solid Mandala,* especially in "Mrs. Poulter and the Zeitgeist," affords an extremely sophisticated anagogic perspective, where things flow into other things without losing their own identity. The dying soldiers in the butchery of war on Mrs. Poulter's television are one with the squealing, bleeding pigs being butchered for consumption, and with the "bleeding Marys" of Arthur's poem. The chain reaction does not stop there, for the curly pig loved by Mrs. Poulter is also linked to her lost child, and the child to Arthur.

There is an inverse pattern of things insensitive and impassible. The rubbery plastic doll belongs to this pattern. Part of its horror is that it *refuses* to decay when buried beside the creek.[27] The rubbery doll is associated with Waldo's "old soft perished rubber" (p. 295). His sterility, which has been depicted in part through the Tiresias myth, is emphasized by this image and its associations. Waldo is unloving in life and seems somehow less than human, like the doll, even in death.

Prior to her dreadful discovery in Part Four, Mrs. Poulter is shown accepting and affirming life, like Joyce's Molly Bloom. Her love, whether for her husband or for Arthur, fuses physical

[26] Søren Kierkegaard, *Fear and Trembling,* in *A Kierkegaard Anthology,* ed. Robert Bretall (Princeton, New Jersey: Princeton University Press, 1947), p. 121.
[27] Cf.: "The bodies of the boys denied the myth of putrefaction" (*The Aunt's Story,* p. 7). On one level, this suggests that the decay of the flesh after death is not the ultimate reality. Ironic variations in the word "myth" call attention to the mystery of the relation between body and spirit.

love (erotic or maternal) to spiritual *caritas*. Through Mr. Brown's amusement the narrator has drawn our attention to her sacramental attitude towards life. Her discovery of Waldo's body is for her the Armageddon of which she has read and heard. All the evil and suffering of the world become real for the first time in this, her private apocalypse. As she runs from it, her watermelon cardigan flickers through the rainy green. The colours of red and green are used as apocalyptic images of suffering and hope. The same two colours and the spiral pattern belong to the third mandala which Arthur associates with himself. These colours dominate the last chapter of *Tree,* and recur frequently at critical points in White's later fiction.

Mrs. Poulter's apparent repudiation of her religion, the fact that Waldo's death means to her that "her God was brought crashing down" (p. 304) and "her Lord and master Jesus had destroyed Himself that same day" (p. 305), must be seen within the total context of the part which contains it and of the entire novel. At the end of *The Tree of Man,* Stan Parker rejects the young Christian evangelist for his superficiality and pride. Yet the vision behind both *The Tree of Man* and *The Solid Mandala* is not only Christian but deeply orthodox, in a mystical rather than a dogmatic mode. White's vision, unlike the numerous Christian heresies which hold that Christ's body was either a phantom or of celestial substance, affirms the full humanity of Christ and the substantial reality of his human body. The heresies follow from the belief that matter is essentially evil. Like the writings of Pierre Teilhard de Chardin, White's novels affirm the goodness of matter, and the fusion of matter and spirit or nature and grace. They affirm the immanence of the transcendent God in his creation.

Throughout her life, Mrs. Poulter has believed in "her Lord Jesus. Who was a man" (p. 292). Nevertheless, prior to her private Armageddon, Christ has been to her more divine than human. After this apocalypse the remote Christ who has been relegated to dusty canvases through the art of many centuries "released His hands from the nails. And fell down, in a thwack of canvas, a cloud of dust" (p. 296). Christ is brought "crashing down" to earth. His full humanity is affirmed and, inversely, man's divinity, but *only through* him. Instead of the safety of conventional religion,[28] Mrs. Poulter is "given" Arthur, the man-child, to believe in and love, "as token of everlasting life" (pp. 304-305). Yet Arthur has repeatedly found, prior to Waldo's death, that his love was insufficient to save his brother. And at the centre of their common mandala he had danced the crucifixion as "the passion of all their lives" (p. 257) and the answer to the mystery of failure. In Part Four the child-man Arthur, whom Mrs. Poulter accepts as the centre of her religious life, has become *sinless* and hence a mythic analogue of the Messiah. Thus the total pattern formed by image and event suggests that our union with God and with our fellow men is effected through the Incarnation and the crucifixion.

As Mrs. Poulter kneels beside Arthur to comfort him, the sergeant is reminded of "a boyhood smell of cold, almost deserted churches, and old people rising, transparent and hopeful, chafing the blood back into their flesh after the sacrament" (p. 307). His thoughts remind us of the novel's fourth epigraph, in which Dostoyevsky relates age to poverty and prayer. In Arthur, Mrs. Poulter embraces "all the men she had never loved, the children she had never had" (p. 304). She embraces all men in need of love, the dyer's seed for whom Himmelfarb inherits responsibility in *Riders*. Her barrenness is ended as the ritual circle of her arms presents us with the novel's final mandala, with Arthur as its solid core.

---

[28] Arthur tells Mrs. Poulter: " 'You're safe. You've got your religion to believe in' " (p. 304). Cf. Jung, *Psychology and Religion*, p. 43. Jung suggests that an indisputable Church authority and emphasis on the evangelical message may be used to protect people *against* religious experience.

'Dreck! Dreck! The Germans express it best. Well, I will
learn to live with such Dreck as I am: to find a reason and
purpose in this Dreck.'

PATRICK WHITE, THE VIVISECTOR

chapter **11** Ggoddd, the divine vivisector

The Vivisector marks a change, not in vision, but in emphasis,
tone, mood. The physical world of matter is still the "divine
milieu" of de Chardin's phrase, the medium in which man's
destiny is worked out. But now matter is predominantly *Dreck*:
ordure and filth of every kind. Instead of cabbages, fresh bread,
the clean grain of wood, and the blue shadow of milk, we are
more frequently forced to focus upon excrement, rot, and putrefaction. The novel smells—or rather, the human beings depicted
there are a malodorous lot indeed. This interest in putrescence is
by no means new in White's work. Part of Stan Parker's final
illumination in *The Tree of Man* is conveyed by his belief that
his jewel-like spittle *is* God. Similarly, Voss ends with Willie
Pringle's conviction that the blow-fly on its bed of offal is but a
variation of the rainbow. The idea of an unending process of
genesis and decay, which is suggested by Samuel Beckett's conjunction of eggs and excrement and emphasized in Joyce's last
two great novels, underlies White's habitual emphasis on flux
and his mystical view of matter. But in none of White's earlier

novels do we find such an obsessive preoccupation with snot, spit, spilled semen, dung, vomit, dandruff, blackheads, foul breath, grease, sweat, farts, rats, flies—in a word, with things rancid and rotting and putrid.

In *The Vivisector,* we are still in a world of tables and chairs, objects whose simple honesty most nearly approach a numinous state. Hurtle Duffield, the artist-protagonist, does a series of paintings of simple furniture. He remembers the kitchen table of the old Duffield home in Cox Street: "Mightn't the Whole have been formally contained from the beginning in this square-legged, scrubbed-down, honest-to-God, but lacerated table?" (p. 337). In his depressed mood, just before his seizure, the butcher's chopping block, which resembles a work of art, is Hurtle's one comfort. But sound tables and chairs, even "lacerated" ones, loom as oases in a desert of *Dreck,* for White is throwing at his reader the same problem which is torturing Hurtle's Greek mistress, Hero: man is *Dreck,* and if reason and purpose exist, they must be wrung out of such *Dreck* as we are. When Hurtle, in age and sickness, approaches the final illumination of his indigo or "indi-ggoddd" vision, his own tired and broken body is "exhausted, ugly, human furniture" (p. 554), furniture scarred by years of living and sometimes by the lightning strokes of coronaries or the understanding of the infinite.

Like Dostoyevsky, White is identifying the filth which necessarily accompanies man's bodily life and his eventual putrescence in death with man's inner spiritual state. This is the "odour of corruption"[1] which rises from Zossima's corpse and Dostoyevsky's living characters just as it does from White's characters in *The Vivisector.* As Hero says, just before describing herself as *Dreck:* " 'I think we have lost our faith in God because we cannot respect men. They are so disgusting' " (p. 355). Rot prevails,

---

[1] Fyodor Dostoyevsky, *The Brothers Karamazov* I, trans. David Magarshack (Harmondsworth, Middlesex: Penguin, 1958), p. 383 ff. The pious are upset by the odour coming from the corpse of the saintly Zossima. The pious peasants' belief in the incorruptibility of the bodies of the righteous forms an interesting parallel with the upper-class Australian determination to evade the *Dreck* aspects of human existence. The eyes of Boo's friends, "trained to ignore everything that might seem odd or repulsive" (*The Vivisector,* p. 130), are the opposite of the artist's Mad Eye of truth.

and this complicates the search for God. *The Vivisector,* as clearly as any of White's previous works, is a quest novel. Hurtle Duffield is stumbling along the same tortuous route taken by Oliver Halliday, Theodora Goodman, Stan Parker, Voss, the four Riders, and Arthur Brown: the quest of permanence, or the long desert trek towards the Promised Land. *Dreck* is two-sided, moreover, like many of White's images, for man's bodily existence is seen to be his glory as well as his doom.

The novel's first epigraph, from the English artist Ben Nicholson, identifies painting with religious experience, and posits the understanding and realization of infinity as man's common goal. The quest, then, is common to all men, but greatly intensified in the artist. Hurtle Duffield dares to hope that his art "might eventually suggest—why not?—the soul itself: for which the most sceptical carcasses of human flesh longed in secret" (p. 519). Man's search for beauty is at the same time a search for God and for man's own soul.

The Solid Mandala gives us two worlds, the other world being "wholly within" the one perceived by our senses. *The Vivisector* also gives us two worlds, the Courtneys' and the Duffields', which are gradually seen to be analogues of eternity and mortality. In the latter half of his life, the two faces of Hurtle's Sydney house continue this beauty-versus-*Dreck* pattern, the Flint Street façade suggesting aristocratic elegance while the Chubb Street side is a slum. There are two façades or two aspects but only one house and one inhabitant. Hurtle finally sees his own life as "looking for a god—a *God*—in every heap of rusty tins amongst the worm-eaten furniture out the window in the dunny of brown blowies and unfinished inscriptions" (p. 515). Like Stan Parker, Hurtle seeks the unity in which these apparent contradictions are resolved.

The Courtney world is also, of course, the object of biting satire, and on this literal level of meaning its inhabitants and their acquaintances are condemned for superficiality and sentimentality. Numerous images, however, identify Sunningdale with an idealized world of beauty and light, so that the environment which enraptures the awed child-artist is identified with the paradisal aspirations of the human quest. The Courtney house to which the laundress takes her young son is "his other world: of silence and beauty" (p. 24). Its chandelier, which forms a running motif, is not only beauty itself but also the artist's Mad Eye and his power to express his vision of truth and beauty. The chandelier, whose light burns within the artist himself, is one of the anagogic and mandalic metaphors of *The Vivisector*. Its rainbow-coloured glass fruit, impervious to rot and decay, forms part of a pattern of desirable images associated with truth and beauty, which contrasts with the demonic images centred in *Dreck*, suffering, and the colour black. At Sunningdale, as Rhoda and Hurtle remember in their old age, the light was always golden, always suggestive of morning. Sunningdale, that is, occupies the same mythic position in *The Vivisector* as New Abyssinia occupies in *The Aunt's Story*. Outside the silence and beauty of its "meticulous womb men were fighting, killing, to live to fuck to live" (p. 147).

Hurtle's dual personality (as idealized artist and moral leper), his two surnames with their associated puns,[2] the "two languages" he masters at an early age, are all part of an elaborately developed pattern whose paradoxes converge in two artists, Hurtle Duffield and "ggoddd" (p. 567). The novel's fourth epigraph, from Rimbaud, describes the poet-artist as "the great Invalid, the great Criminal, the great Accursed One—and the Supreme Knower," who reaches the unknown. In his search for beauty and truth the artist is an addict, an inebriate and a masochist. Nevertheless, the seeker is on the right route, the desert route of suffering leading to the Promised Land.[3]

[2] *Courtney*: "Court-nee" (p. 567) conceals 'born at court' and 'born short' (i.e. too short, dwarfish, which becomes a metaphor for affliction in all its forms); the student's pronunciation of her name is altered in the mind of the dying artist to "Cauter" (i.e. cautery, cauterize, painful searing which results in healing, suggesting redemptive suffering). Duffield: *du*-field, of the field, composed of earth, clay, dust, carries the biblical and traditional literary associations of this metaphor of man.

[3] In the last two chapters of *The Vivisector* there are numerous images of waters being held back by Jehovah, of enemy chariots, Egyptian army, desert crossings, etc. (pp. 555, 524, 529, 552, 553). This novel employs the same pattern of images from the biblical Genesis-apocalypse and Exodus-millennium myths that is used in White's earlier novels. *The Vivisector* varies the pattern by the classical myth of the Elysian Fields (p. 555) and by the mythic Sunningdale, domain of the sun-god or the God of Light.

The artist, whether human or divine, is the vivisector, or destroyer-*cum*-creator. The dwarfish Rhoda, Hurtle's hunchback sister, knows herself to be "born vivisected" (p. 407), and fears that if she comes to live with her brother, Hurtle's art will strap her to the table again, like the model of the little dog which had so horrified Maman in London: " 'I might be vivisected afresh, in the name of truth—or art' " (p. 406). The artist's vision resembles that of the child, as Rhoda tells Hurtle, " 'too large and too hectic' " (p. 429). It is a distortion which is necessary to get an effect and which is still a more accurate reflection of truth than the mirror image of verisimilitude. This distortion may appear as cruelty, which is the aspect of Hurtle's treatment of Rhoda, in *Pythoness at Tripod,* that strikes Olivia Davenport when she first sees a version of this series of paintings (p. 265). The novel's third epigraph, from St. Augustine, points up man's hatred of being forced to look upon the naked truth of his own heart. And it is the artist's Mad Eye or third sense which uncovers this unwelcome and shaming truth.

Man's afflictions, depicted as the distortions of God in his dual role of vivisector and artist (pp. 279, 361), are more difficult to comprehend and to justify than the distortions of the human artist. The bitterness of the vivisector image, with its connotations of sadism, is found in Hurtle's comment to Mrs. Volkov, Kathy's mother, on " 'God's kindness? Which let her off with a *little* stroke!' " (p. 452), and his thought of Rhoda's deformed body as "a body only malice could have created" (p. 564). Man's suffering proves the existence of God the Vivisector. The problem posed by Hurtle to himself is: can he also believe in "God the Merciful" (p. 448), and in one God whose Being includes these two sides or aspects.

The image of God as divine vivisector is reinforced by several other major metaphors. Hurtle's painting of *Lantana Lovers Under Moonfire* depicts a vindictive moon as "shitting" on the unconscious lovers. The demonic moon is identified with the light of the "Divine Destroyer" (pp. 306, 307) and described by Olivia as "waves of enlightened evil proliferating from above," while the body of a solitary masturbator suggests a damned soul. Olivia explains to Hero that the lovers in the painting are not innocent, and hence not entirely undeserving of the attack. The context suggests that Olivia's conviction that no one is innocent, "not even a baby" (p. 305), is shared by the author.

Even more striking is the image of mankind as God's bagful of cats (p. 320). The cats, condemned to drown, struggle desperately inside the bag tied and held by a cruel God: "Many cats with parti-coloured skins were fighting their sentence inside the bag ever more heavily clinging its smell of sugar soon drowned" (p. 322). The doomed cats, introduced into the narrative when Hurtle discovers that Hero's husband Cosmas has ordered the gardener to drown their cats, are identified with the lovers, Hurtle and Hero, and with Hurtle himself as a child sold by his father. Hurtle's painting depicts the writhing despair of the condemned animals, some of whom "look skinned, or human" (p. 323). Later, these and numerous other cat-images merge with Rhoda's adult mission, her attempt to feed and to minister to a multitude of starving cats. As in White's earlier novels the effect of the interrelated web of images is cumulative. Vivisection and drowning are two forms which the crucifixion archetype takes in this novel.

Rhoda's affliction becomes a radical metaphor for all the sufferings of mankind. Almost everybody, as she points out to her brother, " 'carries a hump, not always visible, and not always of the same shape' " (p. 429). Hurtle's own suffering and "deformities" (p. 433) are thus joined to Rhoda's, for the human artist, *qua* human, is victim as well as vivisector, and, *qua* artist, is freak and madman whom the "sane buggers" fear and shun.

Similarly, Rhoda's ministration to the needy cats widens into an archetype of protective maternal behaviour, so that Rhoda, saviour of cats, is also Earth Mother. As Mrs. Volkov puts it in her anguished letter to Hurtle, "Miss Courtney is of the earth she is *strong* and would carry us all on her back—or so I would say—to the end" (p. 563). Rhoda, the suffering freak, thus emerges as a Hercules-*cum*-Christ figure, carrying a broken world.[4]

---

[4] The conjunction of these archetypes—of Christ, mystically involved in all human suffering, and the mythic Hercules or Atlas, bearing the world on his shoulders—is beautifully suggested in a sculpture by the Japanese artist Keizo

The characters in the novel tend to one of two extremes, one beautiful and brilliant, the other ugly and deformed. As Rhoda points out to Hurtle, both extremes are equally disturbing to the complacency of the average person. Frequently, the characters make a rapid *trompe l'oeil* shift from one extreme to the other. Hero Pavloussis is introduced as a pure soul or "spiritual bride."[5] Her purity promptly undergoes a transformation to putrescence, as Hurtle gains a mistress and loses his "stillborn" idea of the pure soul. Similarly, Kathy Volkov, Hurtle's longed-for spiritual child, purposely plumbs the depths of depravity in order to nourish the artist within herself. Later she resumes angelic garb, as the dying Hurtle's psychopomp. The archetypal artist embodies both extremes in one. White is using these exaggerations of beauty and ugliness just as his artist-protagonist does in the novel, as distortions through which the truth can be shown, its brilliance "increased by distance" (p. 87).

Nance Lightfoot, the Sydney prostitute who is Hurtle's mistress at the start of his independent adult life after the war, is a wonderfully incongruous yet fully believable creation, coarse and tender, brutal and compassionate. Hurtle's relationship with her dominates the long fourth chapter, just as his relationship with the Greek woman Hero and with the young musician Kathy Volkov dominate Chapters 6 and 8 respectively. The "Nance" chapter poses the question of how far art is dependent on sexuality, and offers a matchless demonstration of sexuality as a source of humour in art. As Nance says: " 'Wonderful—the way —they—worked—*out*—the *joinery*!' " (p. 167).

Nance Bloody Lightfoot, a descendent of Doll Tearsheet and Mistress Quickly, is far more complex than Shakespeare's bawdy women, for she is heroine and tragedian as well as comic relief. Her relationship with Hurtle, who is simultaneously attracted and repelled by Nance, is poignant, tender, sad, ridiculous, and up-

---

Kosaka. This sculpture, entitled *Christ Holding a Broken World,* depicts a man with a jaggedly rent globe upon his back. It was displayed in the Christian pavilion at Osaka, 1970.

[5] In Greek legend, Hero was a priestess of Venus who set a torch in a tower each night to guide her love Leander as he swam to visit her. Leander's fabulous feat, swimming the mile-long channel of the Hellespont, was a test of skill and endurance and a proof of passionate devotion which could typify the artist as well as the lover.

roariously funny. Nance is surely one of the crudest characters ever found in literature. Her language would have been unprintable in Joyce's day. Molly Bloom, by comparison, is the essence of refinement. Nance, gnawing a chicken leg, reminds Hurtle of Goya's *Saturn*. Her plump, coarsened form is seen with a poet's eye, while at the same time always remaining the solid body of a prostitute: "In her enthusiasm and hurry a roselight had begun to pour out of the straining camisole; her natural, moist mouth had worked off the cheaper veneer; the whites of her eyes, rolling and struggling in her fight for freedom from her clothes, were brilliantly enamelled with naked light" (p. 166). Her marbled flesh, smelling of scent and brandy, is also the "acrid flesh of all fruit ever" (p. 166). Nance is a completely unsentimentalized version of the archetypal whore with a heart of gold. It is White's vision of unity, of the ultimate oneness of *Dreck* and light, which makes possible the creation of such a character.

Much that Nance says and does is funny, but the humour is multi-faceted, the mood variable, and the undertone sometimes tragic. Nance and Hurtle share laughter, as in their "Siamese" joke at the landlady's expense: " 'a cow's arse is decenter' " (p. 165). The landlady, her jaw sprouting orange stubble, has retired from "the trade" after developing varicose veins. Nance's neighbour, equally colourful, knocks on the door at dawn because she wants to cook a pudding and finds herself " 'fucked for fat' " (p. 167). Nance explains her own choice of profession by her aptitude for the work: " 'Because I do ut good,' she shouted. 'It's my *art*—ha-ha!' She got, or fell, off the bed. 'And brings the gravy in' " (p. 178). She contemplates going into the sandwich business as financial backer to "poor bloody One-lung Rafferty," but later decides that " 'all-night snacks are off. . . . The sandwich dodge wouldn't work, one look at Mick's mug and they would start to quote the Pure Food Act' " (p. 179). When she expects to be employed all night with the members of a football team, she promises to think of Hurtle between the scrums. Her artist-lover sees her plump form, seated beneath a giant fig, as the first original work of sculpture seen in a Sydney park.

Nance's attitude towards Hurtle's "nutty paintuns" provides a comic context for airing some of White's own ideas on art. Without recognizing herself as the model for the painting of a spread-eagle female form coaxing fire from a grate, Nance knows that it is not exactly pretty and learns that it is not supposed to be. She is afraid of some of Hurtle's paintings, such as the giant rocks under a "thinking" sun. Her own idea of a suitable subject for art is half way between nineteenth-century sentiment and twentieth-century burlesque: herself, seated on the rocks, naked save for pearls and ostrich fan. Nance's self-consciousness about her inability to understand Hurtle's work, and the resultant barrier to their closeness and communication, adds a poignant note to their relationship. The artist is disturbed by her accusation that he is not a human being but " 'a kind of perv—perving on people—even on bloody rocks!' " (p. 203), just as Alf Dubbo, in *Riders,* feels guilty about his inability to act except through painting.

The prostitute's story of her life forces Hurtle to face his own failure and disgusting depths. Parts of Nance's story, especially her memories of puberty, her joyous pride in her own developing body and its resemblance to the sea things, remind us of Molly Bloom's soliloquy at the end of *Ulysses.* But Nance's story is a tragic version of Molly's affirmation. Her first full sexual experience is with her father. Her mind fuses this lesson with her father's instruction in fishing and with the cruel necessity of the hook in the fish's mouth. Still she longs to meet a strange man who could teach her something she might not otherwise have understood (" 'Not about sex. Well, about sex as well' ") so that she would " 'see things as they're supposed to be' " (p. 223). Nance believed that she had met this apocalyptic stranger in Hurtle. Her story builds to the terrible irony of her hare-lipped mother's conviction that their daughter was " 'born whole' " and would lead a happy life, and to Hurtle's horrified realization that his participation in Nance's life has been a kind of vivisection of her. Until now, he has never loved her, never really shared in her life, but only used her for his art. He drinks, with the bad brandy, the burning truth of this ignominious understanding of his failure. His subsequent smearing of the self-portrait with his own excrement is his attempt to destroy "all that he repudiated in himself"

(p. 226), and the excrement is identified with his egotism and failure to love. In the depths which they have now both reached, the lovers are *one* with Nance's suffering and unattractive parents.[6] Hurtle's discovery that Nance has fallen, or jumped, over the cliff is his first experience of the full stop of suffering.

Earlier, Hurtle has envisaged his overwhelming need to paint as a desire "to shoot at an enormous naked canvas a whole radiant chandelier waiting in his mind and balls" (p. 187). The idea that art flowers out of the genitals as much as from the mind inevitably reminds us of D. H. Lawrence's credo. Moreover, White's identification of the colour grey with rational thought exactly parallels Lawrence's use of this colour in his short story "Sun."[7] In White's work, however, we see sexuality as part of man's physical life—a very real and important part, but only a part. The importance given in *The Vivisector* to the sexless Rhoda points up this difference between the two artists. Lawrence does not make heroes out of cripples—witness Clifford Chatterley.

The minor characters in this epic novel, White's longest to date, are both individually vivid and thematically significant. Through honest May Noble, the Courtneys' cook, White introduces a new art to his canon—the art of cooking. Hurtle acknowledges May as his fellow artist, and his effort to produce truly original, not derivative, art is paralleled by her pride in her creation of lobster, cream cheese, and brandy (p. 161). The letter of Caldicott, the pathetic little art dealer who makes a tentative pass at Hurtle, reminds us that any sensitive person is an artist in his personal relationships.

Cecil Cutbush, the homosexual grocer encountered by Hurtle after Nance's death, is another tragi-comic character. The short fifth chapter which covers this meeting on a piece of wasteland

---

[6] Making love to Nance, Hurtle is described as kissing "her harelip, her disgusting john" (p. 226); cf. Nance's description of *her parents*: " 'I hated the look of 'is dirty-lookun old man's john. . . . Mother was always lovun, but disappointed. She had a hare-lip they'd sewed up badly' " (p. 223).

[7] In *The Vivisector,* grey is the colour favoured by the spinster governess (p. 77), and the colour which describes her thoughts (p. 169). Cf. D. H. Lawrence, "Sun," *The Complete Short Stories* (New York: Viking, 1966), where grey is the colour consistently associated with the half-dead intellectual, Maurice (pp. 538, 539).

known locally as "The Gash" concentrates on the problem of human suffering. Nance has died agonizingly, and so has Caldicott, in an off-stage passage of time. It is in this chapter that we find the first references to God as the divine vivisector and to human suffering as vivisection. The artist asks the grocer if he believes in God or the divine vivisector, and offers his own tentative faith: " 'Yes, I believe in Him. . . . Otherwise, how would men come by their cruelty—and their brilliance?' " (p. 236). Several of White's most persistent themes, such as fate, and the illusory nature of appearances, are prominent in this chapter. The stranger tells the grocer that " 'human beings aren't allowed to choose what they shall love: woman, man, cat—or God' " (p. 237). And the moonlight falls on a world which "looked as plain and consistent as your hand—but wasn't, it seemed" (p. 236).

A fortune in sugar supports the sweetly comfortable existence of Olivia Davenport, alias Boo Hollingrake. Although different from most of White's characters, she has affinities with Madeleine, in *The Tree of Man*. By means of Boo, White takes his protagonist into the world of wealth. For Hurtle Duffield, it serves as a relief from accidie; for White, it affords an opportunity for satirizing Boo's friends: the fritterers, the tortoises, and the foreigners. Boo herself, with her mystique of worldliness, is "full of the affectations and inflections of the class to which he had been given the opportunity of belonging" (p. 267). Boo's intelligence, combined with her sensitive appreciation of Hurtle's work, makes her the best critic of his paintings. And despite Hurtle's insistence that what art says cannot be said in any other way, White makes effective use of Boo's comments on Hurtle's work. There is a sexual quality in Boo's appreciation of the paintings, and she takes vicarious sexual pleasure in his affair with her friend, but her relationship with Hurtle remains on the intellectual level. He recognizes in Boo "a core he desired to possess, and which she was apparently determined he shouldn't" (p. 271). His later omission of Boo from the triumvirate of women who have been really significant in his life reflects her refusal to share the personal core, either sexually or psychically.

Hurtle's second mistress is Hero Pavloussis, procured for him by Boo's careful calculations. Previously, as he realizes, he has loved only painting, his pursuit of truth. He is attracted to Hero as the pure soul for whom he longs. Hero tells Hurtle the story of her life, from the catastrophe at Smyrna in which her aristocratic family lost everything but their lives, to her meeting with the peasant-millionaire Cosmas Pavloussis. The first impression of Hero's purity is purposely emphasized so as to dramatize the irony in her relations with both her husband and Hurtle, and in Hurtle's hope for innocent or pure relationships. He is to find this hope, with Hero as with Kathy Volkov, a "stillborn idea" (p. 322), "a miscarried child" (p. 314). Here is one form of White's failure motif and also one aspect of the theme which underlies the emphasis on *Dreck,* the identification of inner human corruption with physical putrescence: "nothing develops as conceived: the pure soul, for example; the innocent child, already deformed, or putrefying, in the womb" (p. 317). Hero is described as demanding the ultimate in depravity from Hurtle, and their passion is described as lust and obscenities. Years later, Hurtle describes Hero to a stranger as the most depraved woman he has ever met, a woman driven by her own sense of unworthiness.

The stage has been set for Hero's dramatic revelation of the tragic irony of her relationship with her husband: having married Cosmas for his money, she discovers her strong sensual attraction to the sturdy peasant body. But Cosmas is shocked, horrified, and even made impotent towards his wife by a puritan reaction to his wife's sexual behaviour. A pattern of imagery connects the black and swarthy Cosmas, who orders the drowning of the cats, with the black-browed divine vivisector.[8] Yet Cosmas is also a good man, tragically unable to help his wife in her desperate search for sanctification. At death she acknowledges the failure of her attempt to exorcize her devils through her relationship with the artist, and Hurtle knows that he has never really loved her.

Hero sees men as the bagful of cats held by a cruel God. The lovers' gestures are the struggles of drowning lover-cats, whose agony and despair is depicted in Hurtle's *Infinity of Cats.* The

---

[8] In this connection, Cosmas' name puns upon *cosmos.* The black Vivisector God, as cruel and domineering as an oriental satrap, is also "the doomed god . . . as tragic as the cats he had condemned" (p. 326).

titles of Hurtle's paintings, as with those of Alf Dubbo in *Riders,* serve to focus attention upon themes. Hero resents Hurtle's series of cat-paintings, seeing them as a perverse misrepresentation of her husband.

A pattern of selling or prostituting oneself runs through this novel. Hurtle has been sold at the age of six. Hero has married Cosmas for money. The mother of the Pavloussis' aboriginal foster child is paid to take back the child onto the reserve. The child's glance seems to imply that Hurtle was "prostituting himself like anybody else" (p. 323). Is the artist a free soul, or a prostitute? Both Nance and Hero have accused Hurtle of egotism and perversion in *using* people for his art.

At one point, Hurtle and Hero lie together "no longer sexually. . . . They were holding in their arms mild dyspepsia, incurable disease, old age, death, worst of all—scepticism" (p. 325). Loss of faith is man's severest trial. Hurtle tries to assure Hero that what appears ugly and morbid, in life and art, has not yet grown to be beautiful, but will in time. Meanwhile, the ugly truth has a beauty not found in pink and dimpled prettiness. Hero, unable to recognize this embryonic beauty in Hurtle's painting of their love, attempts suicide. She fails even in this, just as she feels she has failed in living, and she asks Hurtle to pray for her.

Having passed through a kind of psychic hell and death, Hero and Hurtle embark on a pilgrimage to Perialos, the Greek island where Hero had found a temporary spiritual peace soon after her marriage. The trip is described as their "union through atonement," and Hero is Hurtle's "hushed bride and fellow neophyte" (p. 347).[9] There is, then, a circular movement in their relationship, despite the failure of Hurtle's original idea of the pure soul. The island pilgrimage sharpens the paradox which underlies the whole novel, the glory and horror of man's *Dreck* condition. The section abounds in apocalyptic images of glory and in religious terminology, yet Hero's sentimental ideas of piety are consistently satirized and the smell of *Dreck* is all-pervasive.

---

[9] Cf. "in his role of stand-in groom he took the bride's hand" (p. 344). The inference that Hurtle is stand-in for a spiritual bridegroom recalls the mystical identification, in *Riders in the Chariot,* of Himmelfarb and Adam Kadmon. In Jewish and Christian mysticism the spiritual bridegroom's marriage signifies man's union with God.

Everything in the Perialos pilgrimage points to the earthly, human equality of man's existence, and drives towards Hero's epiphany, centred in her recognition of man as *Dreck*. The little funeral procession, where a disgusted Hero is invited to kiss the corpse, is "not only a matter of life" (p. 347). Here are circus and funeral, the two processions of life and death which precede the stringing-up of the Jew in *Riders,* now condensed into one. After the procession their way to the Convent of the Assumption is marked by excrement, both human and animal. The abbess is concerned with money and the material needs of her orphan charges. The girls look like sturdy animals, and some are pregnant or have bastard children. Craving a conventional piety in ascetic garb, Hero's sensibilities are outraged, but Hurtle gives a strange turn to her reference to scepticism: " 'Can God be sceptical of us?' he suggested" (p. 353).

Hero's mood of conventional piety surges again as they climb towards the cell and chapel of the hermit Theodosios. The mountain top is the traditional setting for the point of epiphany. At the top they find corruption: cold candle droppings, rotten musty wood, and a mound of human excrement beside the altar. The antiphony formed by light and the sound of birds' wings fails to soothe Hero, since one shaft of light falls on the offending mound: "She was drunk, but with disillusion and helplessness" (p. 355). The absent hermit is envisaged as filthy, lousy, stinking. Worse, she now realizes that her own condition and that of all other human beings is essentially the same.

Hurtle shares Hero's concerns but not her disillusion. Unfortunately, he finds himself incapable of expressing *in words* his intuition of hope. The hermit's chapel is called St. John of the Apocalypse, as the saint was reputed to have passed through Perialos and to have performed miracles there. The images of Hurtle's own apocalypse are both original and traditional. Colour symbolism is prominent in all White's novels. In *The Vivisector,* blue and gold, the colours of the sky and sun, are associated with celestial glory, just as they are in Renaissance art, where blue symbolizes truth, heaven, and heavenly love. Blue is the traditional colour of the Virgin Mary, and Renaissance paintings frequently show both Christ and Mary in mantles of blue. On Perialos, Hurtle sees "the scaly sea, like a huge live fish, rejoicing in its evening play" (p. 355); next morning, he remembers the coiling blue sea-creature but is unable to convey to Hero its message of hope. The sea creature is recalled once more after his encounter with Mothersole on a ferry. The blue sea is both fish and serpent while remaining the sea itself, "coiling and uncoiling . . . in its ritual celebration of renewal" (p. 370). The fish, as an apocalyptic image of divine life, is important in *The Tree of Man*. The identification of the serpent (traditionally demonic, in Western literature) with the fish demonstrates what Northrop Frye calls "demonic modulation," or the deliberate reversal of the customary moral association of archetypes.

Throughout *The Vivisector* a pattern of images connects the colour blue with Hurtle's spiritual aspirations and prepares for the emphasis in the last two chapters on indigo blue. Olivia, when she comes to tell Hurtle of Hero's false suicide, is revolted by the milky opalescent blue on cold cooked sausages. Hurtle, however, mindful of bluish ice on frozen milk and bluish human skin, is sensitive to the "bloom on blue" (p. 331) or the beauty in *Dreck*. Later, the bluish sausages are linked with golden and multi-coloured objects, "all all of these and more fused in one— not to be avoided—vision of GOD" (p. 336).

Indigo has affinities with violet and purple, the colour of kings, and the structure of the word is more suited to punning than is *blue*. Indigo dominates the novel's ending. Hurtle's "vision of indigo," the colour of the sky, is "the last and first secret," the "code word" he has used at the time of his seizure (pp. 504, 511, 518). He identifies his suffering and despair with the colour black, and attempts to paint out this death in a black painting, touched with a glowing white core of hope. Finally, with the last remnants of his strength and life, Hurtle begins an indigo painting. He mixes the "blessed" blue, the "never-yet-attainable," the "vertiginous" blue, which is not so much a colour as "a long-standing secret relationship" (p. 566)—with God.[10]

On Perialos, Hurtle's intuition of hope is further strengthened

[10] The connotations of *vertiginous,* one of the final modifiers of blue, are clearly mandalic; the novel's last letters, "end-less obvi indi-ggoddd," pun upon death as *end* and life as *endless,* and the final grouping contains 'obvious,' 'indicate,' 'vindicate,' 'indigo,' 'God.'

by the little golden hen which pecks round their feet. Her warm feathers are described as being of the same inspiration as the scales of the great sea creature, and she remains "consecrated to this earth even while scurrying through *illuminated dust*" (p. 358, italics mine). The last phrase, like the description of the dunny as a shrine of light or the puns in Hurtle's names, reminds us of the human condition as a paradoxical union of *Dreck* and spirit, indissolubly joined in the divine *milieu* of the world and the flesh. The maternal hen image recurs several times with similar connotations. Kathy's concert performance is a calling of her brood, "the golden chicken-notes" (p. 485).

The Pavloussis' aboriginal child is driven away by a chauffeur cryptically named Sotiri, "Saviour," whose company she disdains. This touch combines with the mythic child of joy and purity developed in the latter half of the novel, and with the imagery of the Promised Land and the other apocalyptic images, to form a pattern which contrasts with the demonic version of selling or prostituting oneself. The apocalyptic or desirable pattern suggests divine sonship by adoption or man's reconciliation with God.

The Vivisector's first reference to a child of joy and purity, an analogue of the New Adam or unfallen man, is through the quintessential Mothersole. Like Stan Parker, Mothersole's hope and consolation lies in his grandson. Mothersole's talk raises Hurtle's own hope of rebirth, through the "unborn child" (p. 370) carried within himself, "this child of joy he was preparing to bring forth" (p. 372). In the golden-haired Kathy Volkov, aged twelve, Hurtle sees his spiritual child of infinite possibilities. Kathy, however, tells the artist that she is not a child, and soon proves her point. Although Hurtle meets Rhoda, after twenty years apart, and this "sister of his conscience" (p. 399) moves into his Flint Street house, Kathy nevertheless becomes Hurtle's mistress. Kathy later attributes her musical creativity to this relationship, calling Hurtle " 'the father of anything praiseworthy that will ever come out of me' " (p. 494).

The spiritually aborted child, like the pilgrimage to Perialos, forcibly confronts us with the novel's paradoxes of *Dreck* and

beauty, rottenness and purity: "Sometimes Kathy's breasts developed with the purity and logic of flowers, sometimes they had
the wholesome stodginess of suet dumplings, but a wholesome-
ness which threatened to explode. He could see how rotten they
might become, like persimmons lying in long damp grass" (p.
410). Both artists are nourished by the beauty and joy as well as
the horror of their relationship, and art itself rejuvenates and
purifies. Kathy and Hurtle are not lovers but "dedicated collabo-
rators," and she is finally exorcized by artistic success. This does
not prevent the lonely Hurtle from fearing that art is a miserable
refuge, or protect him from a conviction of his own artistic and
personal failure (pp. 433, 474). Yet Katherine Volkov, his
flawed masterpiece, remains the work "in which the artist most
nearly conveyed his desires and faith, however frustrated and
imperfect these might be" (p. 471).

Rhoda Courtney, the artist's hunchback sister by adoption, is
the divine fool of this novel. In the first chapter of *The Vivisector*
there are brief and scattered references to the artist's soft and
hopeless brother Will, whose helpless dependency makes Hurtle
very aware that he is *his brother*. The fool, however, is not Will,
who soon drops from sight and is never mentioned again, but
the freakish Rhoda, a misshapen dwarf, defective in body rather
than in mind. Her childlike body seems asexual, a characteristic
of White's fools, although the divine vivisector has left his victim
Rhoda with the desire and longing for the sexual role which has
been denied her. There are numerous references to Rhoda as
clown and jester. The medieval fool was not infrequently a dwarf
or hunchback or suffered, like Rhoda, from both these afflictions.

Rhoda is good, but without the absolute simplicity of White's
earlier fools. She suffers from religious scepticism, although her
faith in nothing shifts at times into a faith in everything, and
when Hurtle accuses her of being a sceptic, she replies that she is
and she is not. The changes in her relationship with Hurtle take
on the shape of an hourglass or figure eight. At first, Hurtle's
strength contrasts with Rhoda's weakness, and he plays artist-
vivisector to her role as vivisected victim. An older, wiser, and
weaker Hurtle is united with Rhoda, giving us two freaks or dere-

licts who are shunned by conventional "Christian" folk. Finally, their roles reversed, the hunchbacked woman is the *strong* one who, in Mrs. Volkov's description, would carry mankind on her back " 'to the end' " (p. 563).

Rhoda's personal suffering or vivisection, and her role as mother to "all spawned and spawning cats" (p. 442), takes us further into Mrs. Volkov's striking image. The cats, as quarrelsome and ungrateful as human beings, have already been identified with men by Hero Pavloussis.[11] Maman's planchette has prophesied that Rhoda's future role would be "woman." The grotesque child-woman, "unrelentingly" chopping up horsemeat for cats and dragging her blood-stained cart through the streets to distribute it, is a strange maternal figure, mother to the world, like Arthur and Mrs. Poulter. Here, as in *The Solid Mandala,* we find a mystique of masculine and feminine qualities. White depicts the sacrificial love and submissive nature of the spiritual elect as maternal or feminine. He also reveals the strength of their weakness. The suggestion that Kathy is the child of Rhoda and Hurtle (p. 457) belongs to this mystical sexual pattern.

After Kathy leaves to study music, Rhoda is Hurtle's remaining prop. There is a paradoxical emphasis on his growing need of her and her repulsiveness. Rhoda recognizes that both she and her cats are aesthetically offensive. Yet Hurtle considers that his sister is not so much a relation as "a growth he had learned to live with" (p. 471). The image of one's sister or brother as part of oneself, often an unwelcome part, recalls the intimacy of Waldo and Arthur in *The Solid Mandala.* Rhoda's repulsiveness, combined with the redemptive archetype of Mrs. Volkov's postscript, reminds us of the grotesque aspects of the four Riders and White's other elect, all of whom are as undesirable in external appearance as the suffering servant of Isaiah's prophecy. Rhoda typifies for Hurtle the inevitable, unsought relationship between man and his archetypal brother, every other human being: "He hated Rhoda, the reflection of his complacency: when Rhoda,

---

[11] Cf. George Ferguson, *Signs and Symbols in Christian Art* (New York: Oxford University Press, n.d.), p. 8: "The cat, because of its habits, was taken as a symbol of laziness and lust in the religious art of the Renaissance. There is also the legend about the 'cat of the Madonna' . . . which tells that at the birth of Christ a cat gave birth to a litter of kittens in the same stable."

the reality, not Kathy Volkov, the figment, was what he had been given to love" (p. 466). Hurtle sees his gift of a fur coat as a guilty substitute for the affection he has withheld. And in his dream it is part of his agony that he is unable to put out his hand to Rhoda. He finds it difficult to exorcize his resentment at this existential trap: "Cursed with a dwarf. She, cursed with *him*. When there were comfortable upholstered normal people walking throwing bread to ducks in parks" (p. 506). Hurtle's feeling is solemn but White's expression of it takes comic form.

Rhoda's name puns on beauty and *Dreck*, whose paradoxical unity is explored in the novel. She is the apocalyptic rose (the Greek root of her name) who is also a rodent (Rhod-ent). Hurtle frequently sees her as a pink-eyed mouse, even a rat, and the type of fur which she insists upon is squirrel. The rodent (rat, mouse, squirrel) pattern belongs to the demonic or undesirable images centred in *Dreck,* since rodents are generally destructive, and associated with conditions of dirt. Rhoda's favourite colour is rose, although Mrs. Volkov's home-sewn rose creations only emphasize her comic ugliness. In his confused, ill state, Hurtle calls his sister *Rose*. The rose, in Western literature, is traditionally associated with the Virgin Mary and the flowering wood of the cross. In her mackintosh cape, Rhoda also appears as a tent hastily erected in wet and darkness, an image which suggests both the Israelite journey and her maternal, sheltering aspects. Little girl, rose clown, grotesque hunchback, and mother to all spawned and spawning cats: Rhoda emerges as one of White's truly great fools.

The Vivisector traces the artist's life from the time he is six to his old age and death. At the beginning, much of the humour stems from the child's-eye view of the world, and at the end, from the punning technique which is justified at the literal level by the defective working of the artist's mind after a stroke. The child, already resigned to being considered unusual or mad because of his drawings, is more tolerant of human nature than are the adults around him: "of the people he knew, one half called the other half hopeless" (p. 26). His awed appreciation of beauty, including the beauty of his foster mother, never dulls the sharpness of his eye. Mrs. Courtney's pursed mouth reminds the child of "a pullet's arse the moment before it drops the egg" (p. 69). The swelling, purple fruit of the banana tree reminds him "of his own paler one. Then of Pa's wrinkled-looking, ugly old cock" (p. 15). Similarly, the fingers of the new baby brother, nursing on Mumma's breast, appear as caterpillars trying for a hold on a pale fruit. The vision of the oneness of all material objects is thus expressed in comic form through the eyes of a child.

In earlier novels White uses drunkenness and delirium as vehicles to support his apocalyptic imagery. In the last two chapters of *The Vivisector*, after Hurtle's stroke, the distortions of language aptly illustrate the protagonist's own theory that art distorts in order to reveal. White's puns, like those of Joyce in *Finnegans Wake,* involve more than one language and historical and literary allusions. Joyce, as Marshall McLuhan has said, uses the pun to release the enormous stored perceptions of language.[12] Language itself becomes the matter to be manipulated into art. Language originates with the total perceptions of the race, and the artist's literary forms seek to release its stored powers.

The pun has a double advantage. It permits a tremendous concentration of meaning, while at the same time the very concentration of the form is a source of wit and humour. As Hurtle, "stroked" by God, wrestles with fears and doubts, the mimesis of an afflicted mind holds answering clues. The quest theme dominates the last two chapters, where Hurtle's seizure and semirecovery are repeatedly imaged as a death of his personal will and a rebirth through grace. The twin motifs of life and death are prominent in both chapters, but the references to death steadily decrease as the protagonist nears physical death, while the puns and images focus upon resurrection and life: golden, "indi ggoddd" life. " 'Few . . . near . . . real. . . . My own funereal!' " (p. 505) picks up a favourite motif, the illusory nature of appearances. Hurtle resists those who urge him to exercise, with the comment: " 'Snot my meteor' " (p. 510; i.e. snot or *Dreck,* it's not my *métier, meteor*). The next two sentences refer to the meteor's fiery curve, and associate it with the quest for an apocalyptic city whose streets are "rivers of life" (p. 511). Hur-

---

[12] Marshall McLuhan, "The Concept of Space in Art," Address to the International Association of Critics of Art, Ottawa, 23 August 1970.

tle's first name, which we have recognized earlier as a pun upon pain (hurt), is now linked with his quest, and man himself becomes a meteor *hurtling* through the cosmos seeking his eternal "HOME" (p. 511).

Rhoda, mother to all cats, is "prepurring" to nurse her brother into a state of dependence, but the artist's precious independence is preserved by Don Lethbridge, the art student who offers his help to Hurtle after his stroke. "Don the Painter-Heartstudent-Harkangel" (p. 567) is a delightful character whose self-effacing gentleness turns to sternness when an interviewer seeks to intrude on his own and Hurtle's integrity. In Hurtle's mental parenthesis, Lethbridge becomes "the other word for goodness" (p. 516). Tall, thin, and given to wearing a black sweater and jeans, Don evokes the lean Quixote, the legendary Spanish idealist: "The Don was no Sancho" (p. 509). Hurtle connects the lad with the best in himself, recognizing the "vulnerable indestructibility" of a kindred spirit. It is not easy to *scupper* ("scuppaidge") his vision, the twin of Hurtle's own. The puns and images concealed within the stumbling efforts of Hurtle's mind and tongue after his stroke create a striking threefold pattern which identifies the art student with archangel, servant of God, and Virgin Mary.

Another comic technique is the use of truncated party gossip, snippets of conversation overheard in the State Gallery at the crowded Retrospective Exhibition of Duffield's work. The technique, first used effectively by Ronald Firbank in *Valmouth,* was taken over and developed by Evelyn Waugh in *Vile Bodies* and *Brideshead Revisited.*[13] The viewers of Duffield's work are human sheep bleating their distress, who tend to throw off their sheepskins and reveal metal tongues and armoured claws as they vent their spleen at Hurtle's paintings. Surely aesthetic criticism has never been funnier, and the autobiographical connection with White's own work adds to the fun:

'They buy him overseas.'
'Oh yes, ill-advised Americans. The press never stops

---

[13] See Evelyn Waugh, *Brideshead Revisited* (Boston: Little, Brown, 1945), p. 293 ff.

telling us. But I can't believe in the great myth. I haven't
the faith expected of me.'
  'No, Elspeth. Faith isn't expected of university graduates.'
  'This is the biggest con man Australia has produced.'
(Pp. 530-531.)

  'Look at those saltcellars he's given her! The saltcellars
alone are genius.' . . .
  'The paintings are sick.' (P. 533.)

Hurtle thinks of them as detachable straw-remarks. The second
batch of remarks concentrate on his God paintings:

  'I wonder who ever thought it up. God is dead, anyway.
Anyway—thank God—in Australia.'
  'Only hypothetically, Marcus.'
  'I'm on your side, Sir Jack—at least, I think I am. . . .
I do hope the God paintings exist. The whole idea's rather
beaut.' (P. 540.)

This technique is not found in White's earlier novels, just as puns
have never played such a major role before *The Vivisector,* and
Dreck has never dominated the mood. As Hurtle Duffield notes,
an artist's style is subject to change if he is alive and growing.
White's vision remains essentially constant, but his conception of
that vision steadily extends its range.

  The Vivisector is a Rabelaisian celebration of physical life.
In White's earlier work the note of rollicking, boisterous, vulgar
humour is not infrequent: witness the hell's kitchen scene with
Alf Dubbo and the bawds in *Riders,* and the archetypal party
attended by Wally Collins and Kate Standish in *The Living and
the Dead.* But the emphasis in *The Vivisector,* where White refuses to allow his reader to forget that "much more depended on
the bowels than the intellect was prepared to admit" (p. 361), is
new. At Olivia's elegant dinner party the atmosphere owes less to
the centrepiece of roses and a crystal bird poised in flight than to
the Italian lady responsible for the prawn cutlets who has locked
herself in "the convenience."

The celebration of life is paradoxical, tinged with a Swiftian bitterness towards man as repellent Yahoo. *Dreck* is identified with "unconfessed putrefying sins" (p. 514) and Hurtle knows himself to be "so much scrabbled garbage waiting to be tossed into the pit" (p. 520). As in the earlier novels, the structure supports a twofold movement: a cyclic promise of renewal and re-birth, and a dialectical tension between *Dreck* and light, between man as a fallen Adam and the eternal potential of the human spirit. But in the synthesis towards which all White's work drives, the repellent *Dreck* is finally seen to be one with the sap of life, as "all the stickiness" of the flesh support the longed-for spiritual rider: "honey, sap, semen, sweat melting into sweat; the velvets of roseflesh threatened by teeth" (p. 554).

The optimism of White's comedy is contained in the apocalyptic images of light and colour, of ever-renewing sea creature and maternal golden hen, and in the affirmation of Hurtle's paintings. More important even than these, the optimism lies in the comic form itself. Man's behaviour may be putrid, but no moralist would depict it with such outrageous joy. White's vision is neither sentimental nor idealistic, and Maman's tender concern for vivi-sected animals and her charitable projects in general are satirized as a form of self-indulgence. The suffering of White's characters is shown to be a shared pain, and the sufferers are united both in affliction and in hope. Christiana McBeath's "horribly illuminat-ing" image of man as conscript in a limping army, sharing inevi-table agonies and a common eternal goal, belongs to all White's work.[14] Comedy's movement is towards inclusion, with charac-ters who first appear as undesirable becoming more attractive as the piece proceeds and finally taking their place in the human family, the Divine Comedy's cast. In *The Vivisector,* Mr. and Mrs. Cutbush, Mrs. Volkov, and Rhoda (undesirable as a child)

---

[14] Prior to her letter near the novel's end, Kathy's mother is known as Mrs. Volkov. The revelation of her own name, with its cryptic implications, adds to the other epiphanies in her letter: *Christiana,* fem. of 'Christian'; *Mac,* Gaelic for 'son'; *Beath,* punning on Latin *beatificus* (in etymologies, formed on *beatus*) 'making blessed, imparting supreme happiness.' She suggests that in the shared human pain, the artist suffers more than those who are " 'mere human diseased' " (p. 563).

are so treated, and only the dirty-minded critic Shuard remains excluded.

White shows us not only the unity of mankind but the unity of the natural world and of man with that world. Genitals and breasts become fruit; cloud masses are intestines; leaves have the stench of men; and rotting objects provide the setting for man's undesirable acts. The "warm wet love" which begins in the womb is one with the "white drool of hens" (p. 65). *The Vivisector* gives us life "at its most flickery, with the smell of death around it" (p. 154). Both man and his world are simultaneously "shit and light" (p. 64) or "illuminated dust," just as *Dreck* is the natural place of germination and new life (p. 356). The images of *The Vivisector* play constantly upon this paradoxical pattern.

Like *Finnegans Wake, The Vivisector* depicts "a funeral without a corpse" (p. 551). This description of Hurtle's escape from the Gallery vultures applies to the entire movement of the last two chapters. The change in mood is reflected in the clear colours of the last, lyrical phase of Hurtle's painting. The presence of laughter, one of man's most *human* qualities, is in itself an affirmation. There is a redeeming quality in joy, and White's comedies, like the plays of Christopher Fry, afford "an escape not from truth but from despair."[15]

---

[15] Christopher Fry, cited in Kenneth Hurren, "In Search of an Equation of Light," *Daily Telegraph Magazine,* no. 298, 3 July 1970, p. 32.
See Patricia A. Morley, "Doppleganger's Dilemma: Artist and Man in 'The Vivisector,' " *Queen's Quarterly* LXXVIII, 3 (1971), 407-420, for a further discussion of *Dreck* and of *The Vivisector* as comedy.

Faith . . . is the paradox of life and existence.

SØREN KIERKEGAARD, FEAR AND TREMBLING. A DIALECTICAL LYRIC

So we'll live,
And pray, and sing, and tell old tales, and laugh . . .
And take upon's the mystery of things,
As if we were God's spies.

SHAKESPEARE, KING LEAR

chapter 12 The mystery of unity

Each of White's novels has been examined and discussed sepa-
rately, with a view to bringing out its essential unity as a work of
art. Just as literature, however, is not simply a piled aggregate of
discrete works but forms an ideal order with continuing traditions and conventions which underlie the individual works, so
White's fiction expresses an underlying unity of vision. It is a
point of view which enables us to look at what Aquinas called
"the landscape of the universe," one from which the whole of
being and existing things is illumined. As R. F. Brissenden notes:
"Like Dostoievski's Russia or Faulkner's Yoknapatawpha
County, White's Australia reflects and incorporates its non-fic-
tional counterpart. . . . But the world he has brought into existence is animated by its own inner vitality."[1] White begins by
facing and accepting what Holstius tells Theodora Goodman are
the two irreconcilable halves: joy and sorrow, flesh and marble,
illusion and reality, life and death. He sees beneath this dualism to

---

[1] R. F. Brissenden, *Patrick White*, Writers and their Work Series no. 190, ed.
G. Bullough (London: Longmans, Green, 1966), p. 9.

what in his first novel is referred to as "a mystery of unity about the world, that ignores itself, finding its expression in cleavage and pain" (*Happy Valley*, p. 166). The treatment in his novels of suffering and of things ugly and repellent reminds us that beauty in art does not mean the merely pretty or attractive.

Patterns of imagery are established in each book,[2] and certain images are common to more than one novel. Moreover, the images tend to converge so as to create a vast anagogic perspective. His images of gardens, trees, rock, bread, roses, cabbages, chains, fire, and so on are bound to all the others "by a delicate web of interrelated significance," as Austin Farrer says of the images in St. John's Apocalypse.[3] Many of White's images, like those of the Apocalypse, have been drawn from the Old Testament, and many are common to the tradition of European literature as well as to the writings of religious mystics, which are often poetic in form. The mandala image, although frequently cited as an oriental image of perfection, has its place in the Christian mystical tradition, as in Dionysius' use of the circle as an image of the outgoing of all being from God, followed by its return.[4] The mandala is also prominent in Christian art, in the radiant halo of light surrounding the heads of divine personages. God is described as sitting upon the *circle* of the earth, and walking in the *circuit* of the heavens (Isa. 40: 22; Job 22: 14).

Like the music of the Greek 'cellist in *The Aunt's Story,* White's novels develop "the integrity of his first tentative, now more constant, theme" (p. 105). He is an artist who simply unfolds, like Blake; not a revolutionary whose ideas are constantly changing. We find this integrity of poetic vision in the work of many writers, as, for example, that of D. H. Lawrence. Any one

[2] Cf. Sylvia Gzell, "Themes and Imagery in *Voss* and *Riders in the Chariot*," *Australian Literary Studies* I (1964), 180.

[3] Austin Farrer, *A Rebirth of Images: The Making of St. John's Apocalypse* (Boston: Beacon Press, 1963), p. 18. Manfred Mackenzie points to the Revelation of St. John as "the poetic model for what happens in the kind of book White writes" ("Apocalypse in Patrick White's 'The Tree of Man,'" p. 413). Similarly, Northrop Frye calls the biblical Apocalypse the "grammar of apocalyptic imagery" for Western literature: *Anatomy of Criticism: Four Essays* (reprint ed., New York: Atheneum, 1965), p. 141.

[4] See David Knowles, *The English Mystical Tradition* (New York: Harper Torchbooks, 1965), p. 29.

of the novels of such a single-minded author helps towards a deeper understanding of his other works. Some identification with the underlying vision, at least temporarily, would seem to be a necessary requirement for understanding and enjoying these works.[5] Judging by much of the criticism of White's novels, it appears that this is a difficult task for many critics today. As Geoffrey Dutton points out: "White's work has always been a trap for critics, both in Australia and overseas, for there are few who can cope both with the complexity of his response to Australia and the nature of his understanding of European civilization."[6]

Throughout eight novels and over a span of more than thirty years, White's vision appears to falter only once, in parts of his second novel, *The Living and the Dead*. In places this novel seems to share the poetic point of view common to the other seven. It contains, for example, a mandala image which is associated with goodness and continuity. Perfection, as Voss sees it, "is always circular, enclosed" (*Voss*, p. 194). The mandala image

---

[5] Either an inability to share White's view of man and the universe, or a failure to understand the technique through which this vision is presented, must account for much of the adverse criticism of White's novels by Australian critics. Peter Wood, "Moral Complexity in Patrick White's Novels," *Meanjin* XXI (1962), 27, complains of an absence "of issues that we can take seriously at an adult level." John McLaren, "Patrick White's Use of Imagery," *Australian Literary Studies* II (June 1966), betrays an obvious preference for what he calls the "psychologically credible" rather than the "metaphysical," but his own charges that White's novels are vague ("they suffer from ambiguity and pretentiousness," p. 217) and that they fail in the "metaphysical dimension" (p. 218) are vague in the extreme. John Thompson, "Australia's White Policy," *Australian Letters* I, 3 (1958), finds that much of the criticism of White's first five novels by Australian as distinct from overseas critics may be summed up as "prejudice, ignorance, pomposity and venom" (p. 42). John Rorke, "Patrick White and the Critics," *Southerly* XX (1959), renders a similar verdict: "The reception given to *The Tree of Man* and *Voss*, with a very few exceptions, measures the demoralization of Australian literary criticism. It had participated for so long in the traditional novelists' kind of ritualistic thinking about Australia that to contemplate a radical vision of it and its people was presumably unbearable. . . . It was because it was both radical and compellingly good *in artistic terms* that serious attention was denied the works" (p. 69). Ronald McCuaig, "Contemporary Australian Literature," *The Literary Review* VII (Winter 1963-64), 170, speaks of Geoffrey Dutton as having "helped to force the appreciation of Patrick White's novels against the by no means small Australian critical opposition."

[6] Geoffrey Dutton, *Patrick White*, Australian Writers and Their Work, ed. Dutton (Melbourne: Oxford University Press, rev. 1963), p. 12.

found in all White's novels supports the concept of a Design or Providence in the universe which underlies apparently random acts or chance occurrences. Elyot's childhood experience at Ard's Bay (p. 98), a peaceful circular basin of water, gives him a feeling of security and solidity, and recurs in memory some half-dozen times, always with the connotation of ultimate significance: "Because there is a kind of connexion between all positive moments. These also are interchangeable" (p. 128). He remembers the bay on his journey to Julia's home in Clerkenwell, where the cramped houses seem to contain more life than his own comfortable quarters and bespeak "a mystery of juxtaposition" (p. 190) or the interrelatedness of all things. This same bay dominates Elyot's consciousness as he says goodbye to Eden at the railway station. Although the bay seems to hang between the brother and sister, it does not unite them: "You went down alone" (p. 332).

This novel also demonstrates White's mastery of the comic, as in the scenes where Mrs. Standish is playing a part, playing at sympathy and concern for the men in her lives as she vainly attempts to lose herself or to escape from the abject dictatorship of the body. With Wally Collins, she thinks: "My lover is a saxophonist. It was both terrifying and comic" (p. 263). White's comedy is itself frequently both terrifying and comic.[7] Such scenes are not only humorous but are perfectly integrated with the novel's presentation of the spiritually living and the living dead.

There is, however, something unsatisfactory in the contrast posed between the "positive life" of the "positive people" (p. 16), or the "positive acts and convictions" (p. 293) of Joe and Eden, and the negative pseudo-actions of those who are spiritually dead. Something of Connie's attitude of wishful thinking, her

---

[7] See Dutton, *Patrick White*, p. 33: "Amongst White's other accomplishments, he has a sense of the comic denied to most Australian writers, whose furthest range of reference is the night Dad put his foot in the rabbit-trap. White is capable of rough-and-tumble comedy, as with the O'Dowds in *The Tree of Man*; the traditionally ironic comedy of Jane Austen, as in the society episodes in *Voss*; a Restoration wit of epigram; and most important of all, an understanding of the shockingly complicated relations between tragedy and comedy, illusion and reality."

agonized desire for the dead to become able to see, seems involved in Eden's refusal to accept "the blood, the torn face of
Guernica" (p. 293). The reader can see the narrator's dissoci-
ation from the attitudes of Mrs. Standish concerning the artificial
division between the spiritual and the substantial. This difference
is shown by juxtaposing the attitude of Mrs. Standish and that of
Julia Fallon, which has the narrator's approval, and by marked
irony, such as we find in the opening paragraph of Part Two,
where Mrs. Standish's tone of voice is described as being the
consequence of many years spent ignoring the "material second-
best" (p. 167).

The narrator, however, seems to be personally involved in the
attitudes of Eden and Joe, in Joe's faith in faith and Eden's faith
in passion. And whereas the narrator rejects the sentimentality
of wishful thinking illustrated by Connie Tiarks' sympathy for
the Spanish people, and suggests that true concern is better
expressed by physical activism, the novel also points to the inadequacies of the latter alternative as a final solution,[8] so that something of the uncertainty of Joe and Eden as to the right course of
action seems inherent in the basic conception of the novel itself.

After Joe's death, Julia remembers his conviction that "it will
be a world to live in" (p. 325), a conviction which expresses his
faith in the coming of a better world. Joe's use of the future tense
contrasts the present and the future, *being* and *becoming*. We
find a similar contrast in the kind of ideology which is ready to
sacrifice the present on the altar of the promise of better things to
come. Marxist-Leninists have used such an ideology to justify
not only present deprivation and hardship but also present atroci-
ties. White's fiction generally is marked by the fusion rather than
the contrast of being and becoming, and the world that is fit to
live in is shown, despite pain and evil, to be a present reality as
well as a constant flux which is moving in accordance with some
great Design.

The rest of White's fiction clearly posits a third alternative of

---

[8] Referring to Eden's outburst against "ideological labels," Dutton writes: "It
is a proof of White's honesty as an artist that such an outburst solves nothing,
and Joe's passion still firmly expresses itself in politics, with the final irony
that Eden follows his death to go to Spain herself" (p. 18).

spiritual activism, one which is linked with acceptance of the substances of the natural world as inherently good, and which is neither quietism nor dependent upon outward physical activity. Whereas White's vision is not *idealistic* in the sense in which this word is opposed to *realistic*, the "selfless aspiration" of the young Eden Standish is. Experience teaches her that such willed selflessness is hypocritical, and ultimately futile: "you were your own focus, you were your own mind, your own body" (p. 156). White's vision, unlike Eden's youthful one, is not the milk of idealism but the strong meat of a realism which accepts the pain and suffering so evident in men's lives, accepts human inadequacy and failure but sees that this need not be man's final end. The conception of an "intenser form of living," which is merely suggested in the last chapter of *The Living and the Dead* as the alternative to the protest of self-destruction, is fully realized in White's other novels.

The need to accept apparent failure and defeat belongs both to White's great theme and to his technique of paradox and inversion. As man's insanity is depicted by Melville as "heaven's sense," so the defeats of White's heroes are shown to be victories from another perspective. All that is required is a change in point of view, and these shifts between what Holstius calls the reality of illusion and the illusion of reality are constantly being effected by White's technique. The dying Himmelfarb thinks that "the mystery of failure might be pierced only by those of extreme simplicity of soul, or else by one who was about to doff the outgrown garment of the body" (*Riders,* p. 460). Palfreyman fails, in this ironic and temporal sense, as do Voss and Harry. Alf Dubbo and Mr. Gage die and their paintings, after causing some ribaldry, disappear. Dubbo's body, after being dead for some days, has the appearance of a papier-mâché joke. Mr. Gage has always been a weak man, and marriage has only made him appear weaker. The "blasphemous Christ" of his painting depicts "a poor sort of a scrawny fettler-Christ, a plucked fowl of a man that had not suffered to the last dregs of indignity, but would endure more, down to gashing with a broken bottle, the meanest of all weapons, till left to suppurate under the brown flies, beside the railway lines" (p. 289). Thus we are reminded of what Voss, in private indignation, terms "the Christ-picture," the archetype of redemptive suffering and supreme "failure" which recurs in some form in nearly every one of White's novels. The desolate cry from the cross, "My God, my God, why hast thou forsaken me?", indicates that Christ was also subject to the conviction of failure.

To the roster of White's fictional "failures" we may add Theodora Goodman, Doll Quigley, and Arthur Brown, who end in mental hospitals. Hurtle Duffield condemns himself for failing to love his afflicted sister and his mistresses; he hardly dares to believe in his own success as an artist, and sees himself as the black stroke in an indigo landscape. Stan Parker, reduced by the indignities attendant upon physical aging, is regarded as a child or fool by his daughter Thelma; undaunted, Stan contemplates "his inadequacy, which also can be, in a sense, a prize" (*Tree*, p. 433). Ruth Godbold fails to rescue her husband Tom. Laura Trevelyan fails to surrender Mercy, but believes that God will accept failure "in the light of intentions" (*Voss*, p. 390). As Himmelfarb leaves the factory yard, "in which it had not been accorded to him to expiate the sins of the world" (*Riders*, p. 449), he feels a sense of failure, since he has no idea of the effect which his suffering has upon those who witness it. We are reminded of Konrad Stauffer's question at Herrenwaldau: " 'I wonder whether the pure aren't those who have tried, but not succeeded. Do you think, Himmelfarb, atonement is possible perhaps only where there has been failure?' " (*Riders*, p. 171). The failure of Konrad and Ingeborg Stauffer contrasts strikingly with the success of Jürgen Stauffer in his military career.

White's first hero, Oliver Halliday, makes the discovery that, without faith, pain only made one bitter or ashamed—a principle we see illustrated later in the experience of Harry Rosetree in *Riders*, or Waldo Brown, whose corner in Arthur's mandala-dance is full of unrelated fragments and dead things. White's heroes, from Oliver Halliday to Arthur Brown, "getter of pain," have the kind of faith that transforms failure into triumph; by accepting suffering, they transmute it into joy. Thus Dulcie can

laugh "for the riddle solved" (*Mandala,* p. 246) when she tells
Arthur that by helping her to face the unpleasant truth about herself he has been instrumental in her present happiness. We have
noted that the basic movement in the novels is twofold: cyclical
and dialectical. While sustaining the dialectical tension of the
conflict between the forces of good and evil, creation and destruction, White's hero moves forward so as to reach or approach
the fourth stage analogous to the "heaven" of religion. It is within
the perspective afforded by the spiritual quest that temporal failure appears ironic and impermanent.

There is another myth common to White's novels which draws
jointly upon the natural hope afforded by all new birth and the
supernatural hope of a Messiah to be born into the natural order.
This "child of promise" myth is evoked in varying degrees in all
but *The Living and the Dead,* which is in general the least mythic
of White's novels. In *Happy Valley* the experiences and hopes of
Rodney Halliday and Margaret Quong reflect those of Oliver and
Alys, and Rodney anticipates Sydney as a golden apocalyptic city
pealing with bells. Katina, Theodora's niece Lou, and the mountain boy Zack evoke the "child of promise" myth in White's
third novel. Stan Parker's grandson, inheritor of the red glass
which reveals the world as a crimson mystery, puts out the green
shoots of the endless tree of man. The child Mercy, a " 'green
girl' " (*Voss,* p. 431), is firmly bound by her love to her mother
Laura, from whom she has received "a respectful love for the
forms of all simple objects, the secrets of which she was trying
perpetually to understand" (p. 433). Mrs. Godbold's children
and grandchildren are her arrows aimed at the forms of darkness.
In *The Solid Mandala,* the promised child is the son of Dulcie
and Leonard Saporta, "their Aaron-Arthur" (p. 302), who holds
the wine while his father blesses it. Arthur, watching the family
feast and listening to the songs and prayers, blessings and
laughter, is shut out from this vision of bliss by the death of his
brother.

In *The Vivisector* the myth is evoked by Don Lethbridge, a
strong and gentle youth who attends to Hurtle's physical needs
after his stroke. Don, like Mary Hare in *Riders,* is associated with

the "unborn" (p. 557). His name becomes "the other word for goodness" (p. 516) in Hurtle's stroked mind, and the artist thinks of Don as his desired godson or adopted son. A threefold pattern of apocalyptic images connect Don with archangel, divine servant, and the Virgin Mary. "Archangel Lethbridge the art student and footwasher" is described as the simple saint, the faithful disciple, and the unsavoury disciple shining with "Luv." There is a marked emphasis upon the washing of feet (pp. 508, 515, 545); like the Sandersons' behaviour in *Voss* (p. 122), Don's humble service in this is an imitation of Christ, who washed his disciples' feet and commanded them to do the same to one another. Don is given both masculine and feminine characteristics and associations and is identified with both Adam and the Virgin in an imagistic pattern which continues the mystique of masculine and feminine aspects of divinity developed in White's earlier novels. *Lethbridge* also puns upon classical Greek myth, where Lethe is the river of Hades whose waters cause oblivion; the archangel-servitor's name thus suggests a bridge over death into life.

The mythic child is always a minor character, something more and less than the human protagonists who are engaged in the spiritual quest, for the child suggests the first and fourth stages simultaneously. For the normal human being no retreat to the primal ignorance or Edenic paradise is possible. In *Tree,* Thelma fails to realize that there is another route to recovered innocence, one which is achieved by going forward rather than backward: "Thelma Forsdyke knelt, worshipping a state of first innocence, which was the only redemption from sin, and because she could not recover this, any more than resume the body of Thelly Parker, sin would have to stay" (p. 431). The fourth stage to which White's heroes aspire is built upon the foundations of experience, so that time is fulfilled, not denied. Man's spirit develops in time, grappling with evil, enduring suffering and the dark night of the soul. By accepting this human experience which Thelma attempts to evade, Stan Parker is released not *from* but *into* reality.

White's novels express "the great simplicities in simple, luminous words for people to see" (*Tree,* p. 225), as Stan longs to do but feels he cannot. The total portrait of Stan's life succeeds where Stan's own words may fail.[9] White writes of the simplicities—or immensities—of love and hate, life and death, and their ultimate meaning. In his divine simpletons or fools and his celebration of things simple, *simple* is used wth its medieval connotations of *pure, bare, nothing added,* and as suggesting *unity* or the number one. *One* suggests uniqueness, self-sufficiency, indivisibility, and is identified in the Bible and in mystical writings with the divine unity.[10] In Stan Parker's final illumination, just before his death, he sees that *One* is the answer to all sums. Simplicity of mind and character is shown as being essential to the *gnosis* or understanding in which intellect and spirit co-operate under divine guidance.

While writing *The Aunt's Story,* White saw a big exhibition of Paul Klee's art. Geoffrey Dutton is confident that parts of Klee's credo ("In the highest circle an ultimate mystery lurks behind the mystery, and the wretched light of the intellect is of no avail") are profoundly relevant to White's own work.[11] Himmelfarb's " 'The intellect has failed us' " and the repellent characteristics of the pseudo-intellectual Waldo Brown should not blind us to the fact that the four Riders and all White's heroes and heroines are in search of true understanding or *epignosis*. It is in this sense that *rational* is used in the description of Himmelfarb as being undressed "gently and rationally" (p. 461) by Mrs. Godbold after his ordeal.

Human simplicities are linked in White's novels with those of substances, cabbage or rose, milk or bread, whose shapes are described as "good and touching, beginning and end, in fact, per-

---

[9] See Vincent Buckley, "Patrick White and his Epic," *Australian Literary Criticism*, ed. Grahame Johnson (Melbourne: Oxford University Press, 1962): "The tree of man: in short, unspectacular and unobtrusive, half of whose life is a spreading and deepening of roots, not an explosion and diffusion of heroic gestures. It survives . . . because it has a real relationship with the earth. . . . The rootedness, the naturalness of this life is the thing to observe. . . . There are flood, bushfire, and drought, certainly; but they are there as organic parts of Stan Parker's spiritual life" (p. 188). Originally published in *Twentieth Century* XII, (Autumn 1958), pp. 239-252.

[10] See Eph. 4: 5, "One Lord, one faith, one baptism"; Deut. 6: 4, "Jahweh is one."

[11] Dutton, *Patrick White,* p. 9.

fection" (*Tree,* p. 481). With reference to the most striking quality in White's work, Robert McDougall writes: "He is an intensely realistic allegorist and mystic. . . . Mr. White builds his spiritual world solidly out of the bricks and mortar of the material world, the world of 'real' appearances."[12] Underlying all his writing is a poetic vision which sees the entire natural world as a manifestation of divinity.

This poetic vision is almost identical with the traditional Christ-mysticism which provides a harmonized conception of the created universe through the union of the macrocosm (the universe external to man) and the microcosm (man himself, intimately reflecting God's external world).[13] I say *almost* because art, unlike theology, does not make a rational and conceptual identification between the universal Word of poetry and the man Christ. The anagogic perspective in art is conveyed through image and archetype and belongs specifically to no single religion.[14] Since the crucifixion, however, is used in almost every one of White's novels as the archetype of "failure" and redemptive suffering, and since both imagery and narrative identify this archetype with the suffering of White's fictional characters, it would seem that White's own vision is closely linked with the Christian mystical tradition of the divine immanence as the body of Christ present throughout the universe today. To this same context belongs the emphasis in White's novels upon compassionate love and the

[12] Robert L. McDougall, *Australia Felix: Joseph Furphy and Patrick White,* Commonwealth Literary Fund Lecture (Canberra: Australian National University Press, 1966), p. 13.

[13] See John Warwick Montgomery, "Cross, Constellation and Crucible: Lutheran Astrology and Alchemy in the Age of the Reformation," *Transactions of the Royal Society of Canada* I, series 4 (June 1963), 261 and *passim.* Montgomery demonstrates the importance of this belief in Luther's sermons and Bible commentaries. Many Reformation alchemists identified the "vitality" infused throughout nature with the real presence of God in Christ, and the alchemical quest of the Philosopher's Stone was a quest to restore wholeness to the macrocosm even as Christ had restored wholeness to man, the microcosm. Hence the conventional apocalyptic symbolism which presents the fiery bodies of heaven as inside the universal divine and human body. Cf. Northrop Frye, *Anatomy of Criticism: Four Essays* (reprint ed., New York: Atheneum, 1965), p. 146. White uses alchemical symbolism in the images of the Syrian's silver shawl in *The Aunt's Story,* and of the base metal in *Voss* (pp. 25, 375).

[14] See Frye, *Anatomy of Criticism,* pp. 121, 122, where this point is elaborated with references to Joyce, Hopkins, Eliot, Rilke, Valéry and Dylan Thomas.

unity of mankind, the identity of all men with each other as well as with God in an epithalamium rather than a unitive mysticism. His archetypes include the stranger, the scapegoat or outcast, and the brother, this last being *every man in need of love.*

In the three historical stages of man's total religious experience as described by Gershom Scholem, the formal and institutionalized stage lies between man's primitive state and mysticism. Scholem sees mysticism as striving "to piece together the fragments broken by the religious cataclysm, to bring back the old unity which religion has destroyed, but on a new plane, where the world of mythology and that of revelation meet in the soul of man."[15] Through archetypes White draws on man's first stage of religious experience, the primitive sense of a numinous world reflected in the ancient myths, as a means of expressing the third stage of religious experience, the mystical knowledge of unity between man and God through which the gulf between the finite and the infinite is bridged and overcome.

In "Art and Sacrament" (1955) and other essays, the Welsh poet David Jones emphasizes the traditional or conventional aspect in all art, and its religious nature.[16] Certainly this is prominent in White's novels, all of which are apocalyptic in the sense of effecting a rending of the veil, a showing-forth of things eternal. The breakdown of cultural traditions in our age creates a problem for art as communication, one which David Jones believes to be unequalled since prehistoric times.[17] He speaks of

---

[15] Scholem, *Major Trends in Jewish Mysticism*, p. 8.

[16] David Jones, *Epoch and Artist*, ed. H. Grisewood (New York: Chilmark Press, 1959), *passim.*

[17] Cf. A. A. Phillips, " 'The Solid Mandala' Patrick White's New Novel," *Meanjin* XXV (1966), 31: "I shall begin . . . by venting an irritation. . . . Early in the novel a hint is dropped that it will develop the theme of some Greek myth. . . . something to do with the prophet Tiresias. . . . I resent such arcane complications. It seems to me that they are as discourteous as whispering in company." Tiresias' sterility is associated with Waldo in a spiritual sense, while Arthur, physically sterile, is in possession of Tiresias' wisdom. Not only are these associations made clear within the fiction, without recourse to encyclopedias, but the myth is actually summarized in the novel (p. 215) in Arthur's personal reaction to his father's readings from Greek myth. The reader who knows more of Tiresias, or who knows White's use of this myth in his other novels, or the title of Joyce's first novel which is parodied in Waldo's fragment (*Tiresias a Youngish Man*), will have an added enjoyment. Mr. Phillips' strange resentment of the reference illustrates the breakdown of cultural traditions of which David Jones writes.

"signs" or the "language of allegory" as "almost the whole language of the arts,"[18] and emphasizes the sacramental quality of our daily acts. To Jones, the signs of art signify some existing reality; and since he finds all reality to be good or sacred, the artistic sign implies the sacred. Our humanity, our bodily existence, commits us to sign and hence to art. By insisting on the tactile, art compels us to do an infantryman's job. Art is anamnesis, a *re-presenting* before God of something from the past so that it is alive and effective again in the present. The theory suggests Joyce's idea of *epiphany* or showing-forth of reality. And the emphasis upon the sacramental character of art and life closely corresponds to White's sense of the transcendent as immanent in this world. Robert McDougall and Manfred Mackenzie emphasize that White is primarily a religious writer.[19] David Jones reminds us of the religious nature of art itself. He considers history and myth to be the poet's raw material, just as the visual world is the raw material for the painter. White makes less use of historical analogies, but presents the world of today in its timeless and mythic aspect, revealing the extraordinary behind the ordinary, the mystery and poetry of daily life. His novels seem easier to understand at first sight than the poetry of Jones or Eliot, or a work such as *Finnegans Wake,* but with re-readings they reveal layer after layer of meaning. They have the limitless quality of true art.[20]

A striking feature of White's fiction is the spirit of joy that breathes through all the novels. Judaism has obviously influenced his poetic vision, especially in the novels of the sixties, where it

[18] Peter Orr, ed., *The Poet Speaks,* Preface by Frank Kermode (London: Routledge and Kegan Paul, 1966), p. 101.

[19] McDougall, *Australia Felix,* pp. 15-16; see also Manfred Mackenzie, "Apocalypse in Patrick White's 'The Tree of Man,' " p. 405.

Ruth Bernard, "The Development of the Theme of Suffering and Redemption in the Novels of Patrick White," unpublished M.A. thesis (University of Tasmania, 1965) also emphasizes that White is primarily a religious novelist, although she finds that "he is not a Christian writer in the orthodox sense" (p. 129). Unfortunately, she describes as "animism" and "pantheism" White's depiction of the immanence of a transcendent deity in the entire natural creation.

[20] This point is amplified by Edwin Muir, in *The Listener* (quoted in Dutton, *Patrick White,* pp. 19-20), where he compares the experience of reading *The Living and the Dead* with that of reading Joyce or Eliot. Whereas White's second novel appears to me to be the weakest of his first eight, I agree with Geoffrey Dutton that Muir's criticism can be applied to any of White's novels.

seems to have given him a deeper understanding of Christianity and to have intensified the spirit of joy. It is a curious phenomenon that we find the people who have suffered more, as a people,[21] than any other race throughout history possessed of a marvellous sense of humour, and their religion expressive of thankfulness and joy. The paradox of joy and suffering expressed in White's novels has also been the experience of the religious Jew. After the almost Calvinistic austerity of parts of *The Tree of Man*[22] and of *Voss,* with its portrayal of "death by torture in the country of the mind" as the suffering necessary for the successful quest-journey of every soul, Judaism seemed to help White recover the serenity of his original vision, the mystery of unity about the world which is glimpsed by Oliver Halliday.

His art proceeds from a totality, as Maritain says of poetry, of "sense, imagination, intellect, love, desire, instinct, blood and spirit together."[23] His comedies move between the two poles of comic emotion, sympathy and ridicule: ridicule, rooted in human intelligence, and sympathy or compassion, rooted in a religious attitude towards life. Kierkegaard believed that whereas it requires only moral courage to grieve, "it requires religious courage to rejoice."[24] White's vision stems from religious courage in Kierkegaard's sense and issues in joyous comedy. His art reflects the landscape of the universe, the large triumphal scheme of his poetic vision.

---

[21] Jacques Maritain describes the spiritual essence of anti-Semitism in *A Maritain Reader,* edited with an introduction by Donald and Idella Gallagher, Image Books (Garden City, New York: Doubleday, 1966), p. 310. Originally published in *A Christian Looks at the Jewish Question* (New York: Longmans, Green, 1939), pp. 23-43. The contrast between grace and what Maritain describes as "the hope of animal life" is stressed in *Voss,* both in the imagery of oil and water and in the description of certain acts and feelings as natural or animal-like.

[22] At the evangelistic meeting to which Elsie takes her husband, Ray's suspicion that some have been "born with" (*Tree,* p. 395) the secret language of faith suggests the Calvinistic doctrine of the predestination of the elect and the damned.

[23] Jacques Maritain, *Creative Intuition in Art and Poetry* (Cleveland and New York: Meridian, World Publishing, 1955), p. 80.

[24] *The Journals of Kierkegaard 1834-1854,* a selection, ed. and trans. Alexander Dru (London and Glasgow: Collins, Fontana, 1958), p. 67.